ROADS...   MW01527536

Stephen Yanor

ROADSHOW: The Marketing of Corporate Finance

LAP LAMBERT Academic Publishing

Impressum / Imprint
Bibliografische Information der Deutschen Nationalbibliothek: Die Deutsche Nationalbibliothek verzeichnet diese Publikation in der Deutschen Nationalbibliografie; detaillierte bibliografische Daten sind im Internet über http://dnb.d-nb.de abrufbar.
Alle in diesem Buch genannten Marken und Produktnamen unterliegen warenzeichen-, marken- oder patentrechtlichem Schutz bzw. sind Warenzeichen oder eingetragene Warenzeichen der jeweiligen Inhaber. Die Wiedergabe von Marken, Produktnamen, Gebrauchsnamen, Handelsnamen, Warenbezeichnungen u.s.w. in diesem Werk berechtigt auch ohne besondere Kennzeichnung nicht zu der Annahme, dass solche Namen im Sinne der Warenzeichen- und Markenschutzgesetzgebung als frei zu betrachten wären und daher von jedermann benutzt werden dürften.

Bibliographic information published by the Deutsche Nationalbibliothek: The Deutsche Nationalbibliothek lists this publication in the Deutsche Nationalbibliografie; detailed bibliographic data are available in the Internet at http://dnb.d-nb.de.
Any brand names and product names mentioned in this book are subject to trademark, brand or patent protection and are trademarks or registered trademarks of their respective holders. The use of brand names, product names, common names, trade names, product descriptions etc. even without a particular marking in this work is in no way to be construed to mean that such names may be regarded as unrestricted in respect of trademark and brand protection legislation and could thus be used by anyone.

Coverbild / Cover image: www.ingimage.com

Verlag / Publisher:
LAP LAMBERT Academic Publishing
ist ein Imprint der / is a trademark of
OmniScriptum GmbH & Co. KG
Heinrich-Böcking-Str. 6-8, 66121 Saarbrücken, Deutschland / Germany
Email: info@lap-publishing.com

Herstellung: siehe letzte Seite /
Printed at: see last page
ISBN: 978-3-659-62640-1

Copyright © 2015 OmniScriptum GmbH & Co. KG
Alle Rechte vorbehalten. / All rights reserved. Saarbrücken 2015

Acknowledgments

I have had the privilege of working with many talented investment bankers, clients and colleagues, including Michael Greenwood, Brent Fullard, Tom Milroy, Omar Jaffrey, Michael Wise, Michel Mayer, Steve Schwarzmann, Mike Fraizer, Jean Peters, Alicia Charity, Judith Prior, Valerie Gerard, Annette Babich, Neil Parker, Simon Bruxner-Randall, Rob Jalil, Joel Freeman, Chris Mercredi, Jamie Webb, Ralph Wickens, Olympian Séan Greenwood and my friends Brian McInerney and Jon Elton. I am especially grateful to Jim Koziol and his first-rate team at PLS Staging. The outstanding work of Jay Ritter, Kenneth Posner and Nassim Taleb was particularly helpful to bringing this project to fruition.

Dedicated to Bunky.

Contents at a Glance

Contents

Introduction

"How'd the Roadshow go?"
"Tough deal."
"Shaky team?"
"Yup."

> *-- Overheard after a salesforce presentation at a New York investment bank sixteen hours before the launch of a major IPO.*

There are reasons why investors feel a heightened sense of expectation for some Initial Public Offerings (IPOs) but not others. It is the marketing of a transaction -- its Roadshow marketing -- that is largely responsible for creating the desire to own a new and unproven company, run by managers who are also new and unproven.

Marketing directly influences how much capital is raised and on what terms. Not only does it exploit the economic features of the equity transaction but other, subtler aspects related to investor psychology, sociology and "neuroeconomics", a new field. The Nobel prize winning economist Robert Shiller summed up the situation nicely when he said "decisions that matter for investment are intuitive rather than analytical".[1]

Complicating matters is the fact that each and every new listing suffers from the "liability of newness", as management has yet to demonstrate any ability whatsoever to cope in a public company environment.[2] Investors know that even the largest IPOs can end up lost at sea, treading water to stay afloat.

The Roadshow is a rite of passage designed to take much of the guesswork out of predicting future success. A rigorous and standardized process, a Roadshow's marketing effort provides an opportunity to highlights the firm's future opportunities and the expertise of its managers. It also ensures that every transaction has the possibility to form an impression with investors within strict boundaries of timing and disclosure. A successful Roadshow attracts new shareholders and solves difficult problems often seen in the first few months when a new stock starts to trade.

The marketing of a transaction reduces information asymmetry by providing investors with a solid opportunity to determine the value of a new company for themselves. It also gives them a chance to predict how likely it is that other investors will be interested.

Great marketing builds on previously established notions. It enables a good story to be told well. It weaves distinct threads of corporate narrative together, starting before a prospectus is filed. From the beginning of the campaign, the financial attributes of the firm, competitive advantages and strategic growth objectives must be evident. For legitimacy to take root, a considerable amount of time is required to craft and refine the message and execute the effort.

In an attempt to reduce the uncertainty inherent in new companies and management teams, investors and the financial media interpret the likely range of credibility an IPO possesses. Together, investors and the media determine how likely it is that a given firm will perform relative to benchmarks of established peers.[3] Research indicates that intermediaries such as financial analysts and the media influence the legitimacy of firms and also influence the expectations regarding future performance that take hold with a much wider audience.[4] Both of these conduits of information influence the other's allocation of attention to, and evaluation of, newly public firms.

With multiple transactions competing for the same capital, investors have less time to evaluate each transaction as thoroughly as they might otherwise. The consequence? Investors place more weight on qualitative information when deciding to buy shares.[5] Roadshow teams must remember the important role that subjectivity plays when the time comes to block off and coordinate calendars for Q&A coaching, presentation simulations and other IPO preparatory activities. Institutional investors are rigorous in their examination of management teams and are experts at piecing together data and behavioral patterns that may seem innocuous and unrelated.[6] An unprepared team will battle uphill.

Some investors need only to engage management in a private meeting to get an accurate reading about details related to risk, strategy and the future performance of a stock. Some investors may even go so far as to use techniques designed to agitate presenters so they can get a true "reading" relative to some personal baseline. Some purposely create uncomfortable conditions to witness how, for example, the CFO handles herself under a stressful line of questioning.

The first two days of the Roadshow campaign are especially important.

This is when the most influential investors get an early look at the firm's top executives and the IPO story. Experienced investors know there are ways to gather clues that others are unable to gather. With preferred access to management, the investor's asset management philosophy, trading style, holding period and ROI objectives provide a host of motivations to glean incremental information.

Critical opinions and perspectives are cemented early and become difficult to change. Just as a *New York Times* theater critic can make or break a production by what she publishes after attending opening night, a single investor can punish an IPO after attending a one-on-one meeting the first day of the Roadshow. As unfair as this is, it is reality. Early information exerts a disproportionate force on the marketing of equity securities, relative to information produced in the future. This is caused by a well-documented effect known as "anchoring". Views from credible parties that are received early tend to set the initial benchmark in the minds of others, regardless of whether the judgment is fair or not.[7]

The role of marketing is to maximize valuation by using both private and public "signals" to disclose information strategically.[8] Viewed through this lens, the Roadshow is essentially a strenuous effort that reduces the information gap between the all-knowing management team and varying degrees of uninformed investors. Investment banks have unique knowledge of this information gap and earn fees by exploiting this advantage by allocating shares before opening day and loaning shares to short sellers through over-allotment purchase agreements.

This book discusses the most relevant topics facing a senior management team preparing for an IPO. A detailed explanation of how to convey a cogent narrative provides unseasoned issuers with practical advice so they may position themselves as a legitimate and attractive investment. Should institutional investors accept the viability of an IPO and deem its differentiation enough to justify the final offering price, retail investors are more likely to subscribe to the transaction, thereby accelerating the development of a shareholder base. How long any investor will remain a stockowner is another matter.

Raising hundreds of millions of dollars should not satisfy managers pursuing an IPO. Capital alone is not enough. A successful IPO must also generate lots of "liquidity", an important Wall Street term that means large volumes of the firm's stock are bought and sold every day.

A well-marketed IPO not only raises the target level of capital and earns a trading symbol, but also ensures that ample liquidity exists to protect the new stock from demand shocks during the first few quarters of trading. An early, unexpected move of the market to the downside might force new investors to sell new shares. The problem then becomes: who will buy the shares and at what price?

If you are embarking on this exciting journey for the first time remember two things: you cannot be over-prepared. Second, all investors are either skeptical or hyper-skeptical. Investors actively seek flaws and find them.

The Roadshow marketing machine runs best when substantial track has already been laid. A persistent media presence combined with thorough preparation is a proven method for most, as few firms have the pedigree to rely solely on management's past success.

In the pursuit of a trading symbol, it is wise to prepare for a rocky ride. Over-optimism is not particularly useful. Pricing the transaction and completing an IPO can feel like a turbulent flight in a small plane. For most transactions this is acceptable, as any experienced pilot knows that any landing is a good one. But larger transactions demand flawless touchdowns.

If you're piloting your own IPO, this book represents both the flight plan and cockpit manual. Follow along and your passengers may return. Just be extra cautious of the mountains in the distance.

Stephen L. Yanor
Vancouver, BC

Chapter One

The Roadshow: A Rite of Passage

The defining feature of every Initial Public Offering (IPO) is its "Roadshow". As the kernel of the transaction's marketing effort, the Roadshow is the primary marketing tool used to reduce the risk premium associated with new issuers of equity securities.

Every IPO that seeks to raise large amounts of capital always involves a Roadshow. Satisfying the definition of a rite of passage, the Roadshow ritual begins on Wall Street and ends with a well-earned reward consummated by a ceremonial bell ringing. With executive compensation soaring at record levels (Facebook CEO Mark Zuckerberg earned $2.2 Billion in 2012), the financial community wants to know that the managers at newly-listed firms are ready for the demands of public ownership. The Roadshow is Wall Street's version of a standardized test. Despite the fact that balance sheets may be equal, some firms score much higher than others.

The Roadshow takes the firm's top executives to dozens of cities -- domestically and abroad -- to meet prospective investors. Prior to the

Roadshow, the firm is private. After the Roadshow, the firm is publicly-owned. The corporate transformation from private to public ownership has occurred. This rite of passage is well defined and complex.

The Initial Public Offering dates back to 1792 when The Bank of New York completed Wall Street's first IPO. Two centuries later, Roadshows continue to be a mandatory requirement for companies "going public". Investors around the world demand to hear an IPO story first-hand from the company's top managers so they can judge the firm's business, risks, growth prospects and valuation for themselves.

In 2012, 94 firms went public raising $31.1 billion, a substantial improvement from a dismal 2008 when only 21 companies went public, raising $22.8 billion.[1]

The stakes have never been higher for firms pursuing an IPO. Mismanagement of any aspect of marketing can lead to dire or even fatal consequences.[2] First impressions are vital to risk-averse investors familiar with the signs of a winning deal. When so many alternatives already trade and a fresh pack of new issues is never far behind, investors know they can be choosy.

Figure 1: IPOs by Volume and Value -- 1980 to 2012 [3]

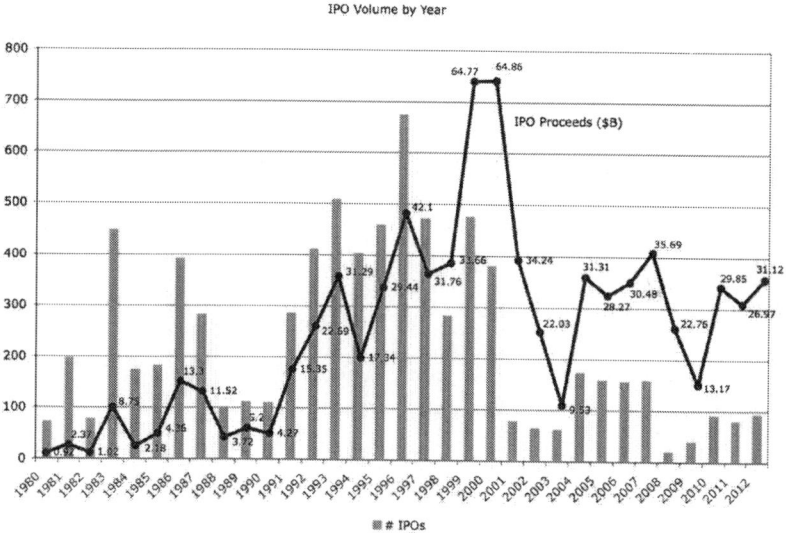

IPO Volume by Year

The process of taking a company public usually requires three to eighteen months but generally takes less than six months from the time the initial S-1 is filed. As the launch date of the Roadshow draws near, more of management's time is required until they are so consumed with IPO activities that they can no longer return calls from the office. When this happens the ritual has begun.

Wall Street and the financial media have an ongoing fascination with

Initial Public Offerings largely because of their unique ability to generate astonishing short-term returns.[4] But investors are also aware that IPOs can fail miserably after just a few short weeks of trading.[5] Only 15% of the five hundred largest companies that constituted the S&P 500 in 1957 were still around forty years later.[6] Investing in an IPO represents the riskiest class of equity investment for the investor who stands to lose the most: the retail investor.

For some reason, many IPO firms leave "money on the table". This is a well-known reference to the difference between the IPO price and the closing price of the shares at the end of the first day of trading. In 2013, the average underpricing for all IPOs was 17%.

Consider Veeva Systems, a provider of enterprise cloud software for the global life sciences industry. Veeva priced its IPO at $20 on October 16, 2013. The next day, the newly-listed shares traded on the New York Stock Exchange for the first time. At the end of the day, Veeva shares finished trading at $37.16 -- an 84% increase over the IPO price. In this example, Veeva underpriced its IPO by 84%.

This notion of underpricing is strictly theoretical because although some believe the excess capital raised could have profited the issuer instead of its underwriters, the entire subject is moot because it accepts the notion that one day gains are equated with long-term success, which they are not.

In fact, astronomical one day gains tend to under-perform over the long term, leaving investors in the red over many future quarters. The underpricing/ money on the table argument is only valid if the new stock continues to ramp up steadily in the months following its IPO, not when it falls quickly after a fast, steep climb. IPOs that "pop" very often display the disappointing behavior of a falling star.

The statistics about transactions that price in the three basic ranges (above, within, or below) emphasize the need for media support and valuation strategy when planning an IPO: transactions that price above the original file range generate far greater short-term returns (44.5%) compared to IPOs that price within the range (+14.4% returns) or below the range (+2.6%).[7]

The fact that investors bid more than the asking price before the security starts to trade strongly suggests that once the shares do trade, they will surge higher. The key is to maintain momentum over the long term.

The presence of high demand at the time of pricing combined with post-IPO execution largely determines how the stock will perform once it trades. Both factors are integral to increasing the all-important concept of "liquidity". After the shares start trading, liquidity is a key indicator that must be monitored. Maintaining persistent visibility in front of investors and the media is integral to attracting new interest and new stockholders, and is responsible for pushing the demand for the shares, and its price, upward.

A handful of challenges face every IPO. It doesn't matter whether the transaction is a billion dollar blockbuster, or a must-do smaller deal involving a high-profile brand. To be successful, management teams must prepare to battle harder than ever. Equities are an expensive asset class for many investors, especially when volatility is factored into the returns. Worse yet, investor sentiment can change on a dime, and if a deal gets some bad press before or (heaven forbid) during a Roadshow it can be a living nightmare.

In the weeks and days leading up to setting the final pricing terms for an IPO, the reflexive formula of price being a function of expectations and expectations being a function of price is often evident.[8] But it is not a "chicken and egg" situation since marketing is capable of creating a chicken healthy enough to hatch a decent egg. Marketing can, and does, create demand.

IPOs that are "oversubscribed" generate demand for shares that are a multiple beyond the number of shares offered. Over-subscription ensures a broad dispersion of shareowners which achieves a liquid secondary market for the shares; a good situation for any newly-listed firm.[9] But this requires that demand far exceed supply, so marketers must begin their efforts early, well before anything is filed with the SEC to ensure they have every means at their disposal while they are still allowed to communicate freely.

Without seeing the order book, it is virtually impossible to determine how an IPO will perform unless it is known what reaction investors had to management and their story. This provides a clear motive to those going public: impress the investing public at the first opportunity and the likelihood of future success increases considerably.

Communications Strategy

For a transaction to stand out, it is essential that managers prepare diligently for their debut. A firm does not need to prove its business is vastly better than its peers; being "marginally better" can easily be enough to attract new shareholders, such as those that will dispose of current holdings in the firm's competitors.[10] One proven strategy is to prove the firm is better -- in some way -- than others that already trade. Only then can a reasonable degree of control be assured when it comes time to:

a) generate a high level of interest in the transaction; and,

b) avoid common mistakes that surprise investors and inevitably lead to serious consequences to the downside.

The share prices of newly-listed companies can change direction very quickly. This can introduce a very difficult situation for both current and future shareholders should early-stage investors sell recently acquired shares.

News fuels the stock market. Traders can't get enough high quality information. News is why transactions that are marketed early in the process -- before the S-1 is filed -- perform well. By generating news and opinions before the Roadshow, information about the IPO is more likely to appear in publications that are deemed to be credible by the financial community. If successful, the results can be spectacular.

Figure 2: Mainstream Media Coverage for Large IPOs[12]

A phenomenon discovered in 1955 showed that people's evaluation of the merit of a literary passage could be raised (or lowered) simply by ascribing the passage to different authors. In the same way, the financial community's evaluation of the merit of an IPO can be raised or lowered by seeing coverage of the IPO in various media outlets that feature prominent journalists and celebrity investors. Although the financial metrics of two companies may be identical, the perceived quality of the medium through which the message is received (as Marshall McLuhan recognized) has a lot to do with the credibility and value of the message itself.

Perhaps more fascinating is the proof that people change their opinions when others around them disagree. What a person says about something when no one else is around is often starkly different than what he would say when there are others around who disagree unanimously. People bow to social pressure and as few as three people can change someone's mind to agree with a statement that is obviously fallacious.[11] In retail and local media markets, investors and journalists are not immune to the power of popular opinion. Positive coverage of a firm that appears in an influential media channel will positively enhance the perceived quality of the IPO.

Influential investors know what the facts are and are keen to understand why certain parts of the story do not seem to fit. Because the firm may be exposed to criticism during the quiet period, it is helpful to establish an early pattern of habitual disclosure so that followers of the transaction can listen on a predictable and established communication channel.

Marketers of IPOs must be particularly mindful of the threat posed by negative views that can spread soon after filing an amendment to the prospectus. IPOs that generate interest early and establish generally accepted views about certain issues are more likely to turn views into facts, as journalists tend to imitate other journalists, especially those perceived as being better informed or more credible. The traditional media ecosystem has changed as the emergence of stock bloggers and popular investor websites has made matters more complicated, often to the benefit of the savvy IPO firm. Information and analysis once reserved for institutional investors now reaches a much wider audience.

If the possibility exists that an unfortunate scenario might surface because of a future revelation the investing public hasn't yet learned about an IPO or its management team, it is prudent to have a plan in place so that the transaction can be salvaged. The IPO of THE FILM DEPARTMENT HOLDINGS amply illustrates why such a PR strategy is a good idea. The media attention this 2010 entertainment IPO received was so negative they were unable to recover. The firm limped along for months until it finally canceled the offering.

Figure 2a: Opening Day for an IPO as Seen on Twitter. Note the $ tags.

```
•••                Results for $CSLT                    Save
                        Top / All

WSJ    WSJ MoneyBeat @WSJMoneyBeat · 35s
       Castlight Health shares more than double in trading debut. @mattjarzemsky has
       the deets on.wsj.com/1eA5DJY $CSLT
       ▯ View summary        ↰ Reply  ⇄ Retweet  ★ Favorite  ••• More

IPREO  IpreoCapMarkets @IpreoCapMarkets · 1m
       The average #IPO YTD in 2014 has added 16.9%, while the average
       #Technology offering has gained an impressive 71.5%. $CSLT
       Expand                ↰ Reply  ⇄ Retweet  ★ Favorite  ••• More

       Andrew Kim @AdotKim · 1m
       $CSLT now trading over $40 (150%). Keep it coming.
       Expand                ↰ Reply  ⇄ Retweet  ★ Favorite  ••• More

       Aaron Pressman @ampressman · 2m
       At Castlight's valuation, Netflix would be trading at $19,642 a share $CSLT
       $NFLX
       Expand                ↰ Reply  ⇄ Retweet  ★ Favorite  ••• More

       StockTwits @StockTwits · 3m
       New IPO Castlight Health is up 150% right now and here's why that could be total
       insanity --> stks.co/j0OI2 $CSLT
       ▯ View summary        ↰ Reply  ⇄ Retweet  ★ Favorite  ••• More

       Aaron Pressman @ampressman · 3m
       And you thought there was a cloud internet bubble before: $WDAY trades at 37X
       revenue, $BNFT at 15X...Now comes Castlight at 269X $CSLT
       Expand                ↰ Reply  ⇄ Retweet  ★ Favorite  ••• More
```

Those with an existing infrastructure of IR (investor relations) and communications are better positioned to identify "missing pieces" of an investor story and enable tactics that offer solutions. A combination of PR, IR and corporate communications activities are evident at firms raising large amounts of capital.

The Long-Term Goal of Public Ownership

Too many managers focus on "getting the deal done" rather than tending to the vastly more important task of preparing for life as an ongoing publicly-owned company. The best firms use the time to prepare for the demanding level of communications required by new shareholders once the company gains its listing. Telling investors that the firm is ready for the capital markets is not nearly as credible as demonstrating it during the Roadshow and after the quiet period has ended.

Marketing Elements

An identifiable set of marketing materials is permitted and must be produced to assist management and its underwriters to sell a new equity issue. Few companies exploit every opportunity and many do not go beyond the most basic requirement of a PowerPoint presentation.

This presentation, known as "the deck", "color book" or "pitch book" directly reflects the quality of management and the firm's business while providing investors with the information required to inform a purchasing decision. Regardless of the firm's business or industry, the majority of IPOs structure the content of their investor presentations in the same familiar way. It is not advisable to stray from this time-tested and proven format. See chapter nine for more on how investor presentations are structured.

A hastily prepared IPO presentation invites considerable risk. Investors have seen hundreds of presentations and immediately know how much thought and effort went into its creation. If it enables the Roadshow team to convince investors it is a success. To accomplish this, the firm must convey that its growth strategies are sensible, its financial performance is comparable to peers, and that its risks are manageable. The ability to paint an accurate yet compelling portrait of the inner workings of the firm while assuaging concerns about risk are the fundamental components of a solid investor meeting.

Psychology

Institutional investors experience waves of management teams -- the best and worst. Many investors have developed an automatic and involuntary response to certain cues. One experiment found that the amount of smiling, speech errors, speech hesitation, and speech duration as well as the extent of unnecessary commentary causes immediate and automatic reactions that have a powerful effect on cognitive judgments.

Without knowing it, hardwired biases against a presenter can be triggered instantly.[13] For some executives, this means the meeting is over before it begins. This underscores the need to dress, talk and act in a manner consistent with a pattern of behavioral traits that the investor intuitively knows to be credible.[14]

A vast amount of research informs the view that "gut feelings" are vital to establishing trust and confidence in new management teams. In the same way traders make snap decisions to short the Euro and go long the dollar, there is a natural tendency to base predictions on past experience. From a Roadshow marketing perspective, "deep down" feelings have far-reaching implications.

There are other behavioral realities that Roadshow teams should respect. For example, the first piece of information an investor encounters about an IPO could form an impression that sets a direction that changes the interpretation of subsequent information.[15] This is important to keep in mind when meeting investors for the first time. Further research suggests that investors with limited information about a stock are more likely to rely on their feelings when judging whether to buy or sell shares. Marketing can influence the purchase decision by making people more willing to take a chance when other options won't give them the payoff they want.[16]

Roadshow meetings are one hour, during which an investor will ask thirty minutes of questions. This is ample time for the investor to decide whether or not her suspicion is correct that, say, the company's core business is eroding and the offering is being marketed at the top of a cycle before it continues to fall apart. If she believes her questions are being answered defensively, this may provide enough confirmation that her intuition is correct. Then, she will likely decide to pass at the investment completely unless she can short the stock.

Investor Meetings

Face-to-face meetings ("one-on-ones") are a *defacto* requirement for all large institutional investors as they provide a sufficient level of information content required to make an educated determination about qualitative issues. The typical investor looks first at the numbers (e.g., historical performance, margins, balance sheet strength) and then turns to aspects of risks and growth. But growth is rooted in strategy, which is an important qualitative characteristic of any company. In the context of an IPO, strategy is enabled by talent and experience not yet tested in the public market, so it is the investor's task to drill down to determine if she is truly getting the whole story and if management is likely to meet future expectations. She uses the one-on-one meeting to collect evidence.

There are also a handful of very large meetings that are attended by hundreds of smaller ("retail") investors. They gather to eat lunch in a ballroom and listen to management's presentation. This group represents the "sentiment" investor, a critically important segment of buyers when the time comes for institutional investors to sell. Often, this exchange from investment dealer to institutional investor to retail investor can be measured in days or even hours.

Valuation

The amount of capital raised and the price that investors pay for the shares is directly influenced by how much confidence management instills in its ability to:

   i) protect and build on the company's strengths through strategy;

   ii) mitigate, monitor and manage the ever-present risks; and

   iii) stave off competitive threats.

Only after satisfying these criteria will investors think seriously about the IPO's implied valuation and the magnitude of certain discounts that will be applied to proprietary models.

The "range" refers to the lowest-to-highest price that the underwriters will accept for the common shares. If enough investors reach the same conclusion (as in the previous case where management is defensive during Q&A), the range will likely be adjusted downward. Both the price *and* number of shares could be reduced to reflect diminished demand. This is always a bad omen for any deal, especially if the range is revised downward only days before the Roadshow begins. Not only is precious credibility destroyed but genuine interest in the deal implodes, making the Roadshow feel like a patchwork series of meetings with lower-tier investors instead of the heroic conquest it set out to be. It happens all the time.

In such circumstances it is not only the bankers closest to the deal that miscalculated. Equal blame rests on management's shoulders as they likely chose to neglect a serious issue related to pricing rather than confront it head on. The firm that no longer wishes to be private must be realistic about its problems and deal with them. Investors can accept a firm that is slightly broken as long as they are comfortable with management's ability to fix it.

Respect Tradition

Resist the temptation to try a "new" marketing technique. New does not compute with investors and their catalog of previous experiences. If something does not look right, confidence falls. Low levels of investor confidence can spread like a virus, infecting investors attending future meetings. So it is strictly off limits to sing the national anthem, use iPads instead of color books, wear jeans or a yellow suit, utter a single word of foul language, walk around with a hand-held microphone on stage, criticize competitors, high-five in the elevator after a meeting, present with more than three people, open with a joke, be evasive, act defensive, refuse to answer a question, get emotional or mention anything related to human resources. And please refrain from giving a presentation that exceeds twenty-five minutes.

IPOs that are well received often land a large "lead order" in the first two or three days of the Roadshow. These deals stand a better chance at pricing at the midpoint or above the range. The transactions that attract enough interest from a small number of influential institutions make no mistake at conveying their managerial experience and communicating how easily they expect to exploit their competitive advantages. In doing so, investors recognize that a good deal of uncertainty has vanished, so the temptation to wait to express an indicative order of interest is greatly reduced.

The lead bankers view strong early support for an IPO as very favorable and are more likely to allocate shares to those who get in early should the deal meet with similar enthusiasm by others as the Roadshow continues to unfold. These "hot deals" generate substantial interest -- and orders -- early. To have a hot deal, management teams must focus on selling hard from the very first meeting.

Marketing the Intangibles

Warren Buffett summed up the benefits when he said: "no insight is required on the quantitative side -- the figures should hit you over the head with a baseball bat. So the really big money tends to be made by investors who are right on qualitative decisions".[17]

The investment community clamors for information that provides a competitive edge in forecasting the worth of companies and for interpretive data that offers insights into the financials and the future value of the firm.[18] Because today's databases give almost everyone equal access to information, it is almost impossible to get an edge with numbers alone.[19] Several studies suggest that the evidence of return reversals is generated solely by the reversal of the intangible component of returns.[20] In other words, "invisible" assets that are not valuable today -- such as an inexperienced management team, unexplored natural resource, or technological know-how -- may become valuable in the future.[21]

While concrete historical numbers will always be the basis for valuation and comparison, qualitative analysis will remain fashionable until new ways to quantify reams of data -- data that is mysteriously influenced by human behavior -- is discovered. For example, being able to accurately predict the negative reaction of the stock market to the news that President Obama is meeting with the heads of nineteen US financial institutions would represent a highly profitable opportunity.[22] But understanding the speculation-to-reaction relationship may take a very long time, if ever. Until then, Roadshow marketers must focus on high-quality disclosure, sending the signals that institutional investors seek.

The inability of any investor to predict the future is actually good news for well-prepared Roadshow teams. They should count on the fact investors demand the opportunity to look them in the eye during Q&A. This provides one of the only opportunities to change opinions. How managers perform "under fire" and how the numbers "come across" have become increasingly important in an environment that is now more heavily-skewed to judging qualitative aspects of new investments.

The collection and exchange of quantitative information through qualitative or otherwise experiential means increases the overall value of information investors receive. If a connection between the presenter and listener occurs, ("she gets what I'm saying" or "I see what he's getting at"), the quality of communication improves substantially. An engaged audience is more open to accept additional context and concepts in a way passive audiences are not.

There are several proven approaches Roadshow marketers can use to influence and enhance the experience when information is exchanged with investors:

a) Make the IPO relevant by positioning the company during the

pre-marketing (pre-Roadshow) phase.

Early differentiation established through comparisons to existing stocks will promote the development of a nascent investor brand. Historical financial results, key milestones, management team composition, growth objectives and recent successes are all facets from which to draw parallels and other similarities to compensate for the liability of newness. This process incorporates "framing" and "anchoring" techniques, discussed in chapter fourteen.

b) Maximize the exchange of information between management and the investor within the allotted hour.

The goal here is to reduce the tendency of people who do not compensate for missing information even when it is painfully obvious that the information available to them is incomplete.[23] Provide immediate access to supporting data by including an appendix in the color book. Up front, ask investors what issues concern them the most and treat the meeting as if it was the only meeting on the schedule. Use the name of the investor's firm and engage the audience by name if possible. Link core concepts back to investor concerns and highlight the impact on financial performance. Ensure the firm's most compelling features are memorable by instilling them through repetition and varied narrative from different presenters;

c) Optimize the physical characteristics of the meeting environment by establishing desirable ambiance through lighting, furniture, color palettes and various other staging techniques. The sight, sound and smell of an environment affects how people process information.[24] This is similar to the approach used to sell homes by "staging" the interior so that prospective buyers have a memorable and favorable experience during a showing. These methods actually work and can go a long way to forming a positive impression across a broad and influential audience when adopted across a full schedule of meetings.

Volatility Is An Enemy

Benoit Mandelbrot, the pioneer of fractal mathematics dedicated his life's work to quantify turbulence. He believed "roughness" -- or wild volatility -- is a feature of the stock market in the same way roughness is a feature of mountainous terrain.[25] Just as a hurricane can cause airports to close, volatility in the stock market can cause all Roadshow activity to cease.

Unfortunately, Mandelbrot passed away in October 2010 before he could establish the elusively abstract connection behind the seemingly erratic behavior evident in both nature and publicly-traded securities. Forty years of work led to him to ask why unpredictable events such as a massive stock market collapse occur much more frequently than once-in-a-billion-years that the calculated probabilities suggest.[26]

Whether it is the unexplainable whim of some invisible hand or another force we have yet to discover, the launch date of a Roadshow can change in an instant, resulting in deals that get pushed out faster than expected or delayed for weeks or months until conditions improve.

Executives who are not yet adequately prepared to meet investors because two weeks of preparation time have suddenly disappeared can be in for a harrowing ride. CEOs are afforded no leeway for excuses, so the ill-prepared executive who faces investors must submit to a humbling experience. If she escapes unscathed through her sheer wit and interpersonal skills, she is rare and equally lucky. But those who are not ready almost always fail to deliver the signals investors require, which causes major accounts to react tepidly.

An early lukewarm reception tends to ripple through the entire meeting schedule, making things unnecessarily difficult for the duration of the Roadshow. Investors are quick to hone in on specific weaknesses in an effort to gain leverage for the final day when price negotiations occur ("pricing").

In 2010, volatility killed the aspirations of every IPO that came out looking red hot. For this reason, management teams involved with planning a Roadshow must consider communication strategies that will compensate for sudden changes in market sentiment.

Tesla Motors, the most anticipated IPO of 2010, conducted its Roadshow during volatile market conditions. At first, the markets were cooperative but quickly reversed direction, turning sharply downward after the first week of Tesla's Roadshow meeting schedule. But the Tesla team pressed on, enduring the headwinds by riding a considerable wave of momentum they had generated through media coverage at the start of the Roadshow. Much of the momentum was attributable to the announcement that Toyota would participate in the IPO -- an endorsement strategy seen on other transactions such as Blackstone's landmark IPO.

Once the shares began trading, investors racked up 78% gains in the first two days of trading. Things were looking good. But Tesla's huge gains didn't last long.

Less than a week later, the electric car maker's stock got murdered and plummeted back to its IPO price, erasing the fat profits.[27]

But at least the small and unprofitable auto manufacturer made it to the finish line. If Tesla had not been clever enough to anticipate the challenging market conditions and equipped itself with a well-timed announcement, the IPO may have been shelved. Other transactions in the market at the same time were either being postponed or cancelled.[28] It was Tesla's advance planning -- to have the Toyota media release in its pocket in case the market got rough -- that enabled them to survive the rocky trading conditions.

Tesla and its bankers at Goldman exploited a crucial dynamic that exists between institutional and retail investors: attract sentiment investors to buy shares in what looks like a rocket so that institutional investors can flip their IPO allocation. Goldman was well aware that many households with car enthusiasts believed that the stock of the fastest electric car in the world was likely to continue its upward trajectory. We know now this was not the case.

Raising more money than expected is commendable, but investors are valuable assets that are costly and difficult to replace. Despite what many investors will admit, volatility prevents many from being long-term holders. After all, few traders would pass on the opportunity to make a profit of 40% in one day.

This cold reality creates a situation for new public companies that can take several quarters to solve. Stuck with an anemic stock price and the same story as the one told during the recent Roadshow, "underpriced", thinly-traded IPOs are usually forced to wait until some major event creates renewed interest in their fallen star.

Many managers who experience the thrill of being the week's hottest deal should recall Tesla's story as they lumber through their fifth presentation in Denver staring blankly at four fund managers. These guys in Denver are exactly the type of investors that prove very helpful in the future. Tesla, by the way, recovered nicely after two years of volatile, win-loss trading.

The High Cost of Acquiring New Shareholders

The Roadshow is the best opportunity to build an inventory of future shareowners. Interest in the company is at an all-time high and the considerable expense of traveling to meet with investors is covered. It takes work to keep the "smart money" and best analysts interested in the firm. Just as it is costly for any business to acquire profitable customers, acquiring new shareholders after the IPO is also costly. For this reason, it is prudent to establish future milestones and accomplishments that give investors concrete events to look forward to. After initial institutional investors start to defect, the mix of equity ownership changes, which generally results in smaller trades and lower volumes.

A common problem new public companies face is to be stuck with too few shareholders that own a high concentration of stock. This situation severely hampers the ability to create shareholder value and is exacerbated when a selling shareholder retains a large percentage of the shares in treasury (known as a "share overhang"). Firms must spare no effort and expense to ensure the Roadshow attracts and retains a large and diverse base of initial shareholders.[29] This is necessary so that adequate liquidity exists to minimize the effects of a large holder selling into the secondary market.

One way managers can mitigate the effect that a mass exodus of stock flippers can cause is to be cognizant of leaving "money on the table". This is primarily caused by underpricing the transaction artificially low, creating an incentive for IPO investors to flee quickly.

To prevent a high degree of underpricing, firms must make their bankers aware of their sensitivity to underpricing and work to achieve an appropriate capital structure to maximize proceeds and minimize mass flipping. The most important topics to consider are the number of shares issued, degree of senior management's post-IPO retained ownership, use of proceeds, market capitalization, pre-marketing activities, and anticipated valuation range.

Chapter Two

The IPO Marketing Process

Ninety-four CEOs succeeded at taking their companies public in 2012. Not bad, considering the IPO market was on life support a few years earlier.

When the bottom falls out of the broader market, issuers of new equity feel the pain first. Some teams may even find themselves in the middle of a Roadshow when sentiment suddenly turns viciously against the equity markets -- and new issue transactions.

If conditions are judged to be excessively harsh, underwriters begin canceling deals *en masse*. A select few will risk riding it out even though it may mean taking a major haircut at pricing. The transaction most likely to survive a negative-sentiment scenario is the one that had the highest level of investor interest before the Roadshow started (during pre-marketing). In 2008, Visa was the only major IPO to be marketed. It sopped up all available investor capital for the entire year: $18 billion.

For this reason, firms must take advantage of the pre-marketing opportunity and go beyond the two basic marketing requirements that are central to every

Roadshow:

i) the creation of a story; and

ii) the delivery of the story to investors.

The best IPOs go far beyond these two basic requirements. High quality firms with experienced advisors generate media coverage prior to the quiet period, using their precious freedom as a private entity to plant strategic content before it becomes unlawful to do so. In this way, many firms easily establish expectations with market participants that harden as more information is released over time. The ultimate goal with this strategy is to surpass expectations to justify a healthier valuation. At what level the expectations are set and how they are met is the trade-craft discussed here.

The IPO of LinkedIn Corporation (LNKD:NYSE) is one example. As one of 2011's most notable deals, it was also the first "social media" IPO, testing the appetite for future internet companies in the pipeline.[1]

The first week of LinkedIn's Roadshow generated so much interest that the firm upped the range a full $10 to $42-$45/share, representing a 25% increase in proceeds. On the first day of trading, the shares rose as much as 171%

before closing at $94.25 -- more than double the IPO price. LinkedIn's market capitalization reached $9 billion -- tripling the firm's original expectations.

During the Roadshow, media reports surfaced that even billion-dollar institutions were not given allocations of LinkedIn stock. This propelled the perceived value of the shares higher during the Roadshow. This is a good situation but could be a precursor to a one day climax that quickly turns to pain, as was the case with Tesla Motors. Although LinkedIn was not, nor had ever been, profitable, the demand for its IPO and its ultimate valuation was consistent with long-established, better performing peers.

LinkedIn made a good case for establishing a plausible valuation relative to many better known names such as KornFerry, Manpower, Robert Half, Kelly Services, Salesforce.com and Monster. It was also helpful that just two weeks prior to LinkedIn's own IPO, the Chinese equivalent Renren went public and traded at a multiple of 78 times annualized sales.

LinkedIn's IPO was priced with at $45 per share -- an implied value of 17.5 annualized sales -- a bargain in comparison. Seven months later the stock continued to soar at $104.61 per share.[2]

LinkedIn generated substantial media awareness and interest in the transaction before they announced and filed the IPO with the SEC.

There are three distinct phases that define the IPO marketing process: planning, preparation, and execution.

Figure 3: The Three Phases of the IPO Marketing Process

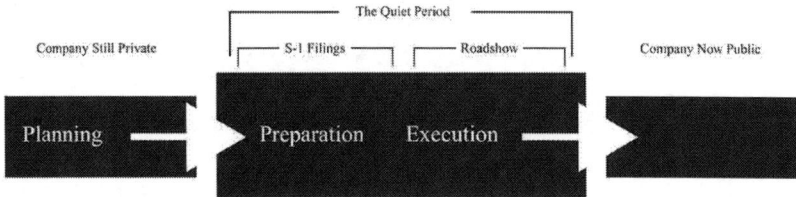

Phase One: Planning

The first phase of the IPO process begins once the drafting of a prospectus (S-1) is underway and ends once the quiet period begins -- which is the same day as the S-1 is filed with the SEC. Writing the IPO marketing plan is a top priority during this initial phase. This plan defines the major marketing objectives, key messages and significant threats.

It also includes a project management time-line that outlines when the following elements will be completed:

a) Competitive research into peer positioning; identification of strengths, weaknesses, threats, and industry issues; and

b) A library of financial graphs and industry data. This library may involve acquiring artwork required for marketing materials such as those used for meeting environments and the investor presentation slides; and

c) A media strategy to build awareness of the company, its managers, products or areas central to calculating valuation; and

d) A new investor relations section on the firm's website.

Once the Roadshow starts it is time to execute the marketing plan. The firm is committed to whatever direction it has chosen, using materials produced in time for the scheduled meetings. Senior management should sign off on the marketing plan with the understanding that its priorities, timing and budget are subject to change without notice at any time prior to the Roadshow.

Peer Group Research

Before the initial registration statement (S-1) is filed, the marketer should learn as much as possible about the firm, its peers and the industry by acquiring and reading every piece of available information. While bankers and lawyers work on early drafts of the prospectus, it is advisable for marketers to be included on the master distribution list so they are intimately familiar with how the content evolves.

Colleagues that possess deep industry experience are also good sources for additional details and context. Background information related to the firm's competitive strengths, marketing strategy and segmentation of financial data is critical to positioning aspects of the IPO story. The firm that successfully captures the knowledge of its top managers also gains the ability to maximize its strengths relative to competitors who aggregate similar information but on a different basis.

Similarly, the means by which information is presented -- by emphasis and order of priority -- can also influence how a story evolves as it is presented to an audience.

It is the marketer's responsibility to work with the facts as they appear in the prospectus. The facts must be combined to create a story that accurately portrays the company's growth potential and related financial performance. There is a standard storyline template discussed in chapter eight.

During the drafting of the story, pay particular attention to the sections related to "competitive strengths", and "growth strategies". Assemble a set of facts with supporting details early so that weaker content can be cut later in the process.

Sources of Research

The investor-targeted content of all competitors must be examined thoroughly. Compile the overall positioning of each peer and the financial metrics used for guidance in a one or two page document. Make specific references and notes about each area of guidance provided by peers: whether they hit their numbers last quarter and what metric they missed on and by how much; did they re-affirm guidance and when?

Ask the bankers to provide you with research reports on all publicly-traded peers and make detailed notes about any operational issues, forecasts or performance data that receive particular attention. Be aware of segmented data -- how lines of business are aggregated or classified; for example, by geography or customer or product line.

Incorporate any specific weaknesses indicated by analysts who follow the firm's peers. To do this, review not only the research reports but also past transcripts and presentations from quarterly earnings calls. Pay particular attention to the Q&A topics. StreetEvents and SeekingAlpha are two providers of free conference call transcripts.

Compile a list of media contacts within your industry and journalists who cover IPOs. Formulate three ideas to pitch to traditional news outlets, including newspapers, magazines, industry-specific periodicals and television. E-mail your story idea using your real name and why the story is relevant. Do not include past events or anything that is obviously company hype. This includes anything that could be construed as a release for the sake of releasing something. Remember: what is said in the months leading up to the IPO sets a tone. Provide ideas and angles that are creative and memorable.

Obtain media coverage. Industry-specific magazines are known to be the easiest if the budget exists to patronize the publication. Make sure they do not appear as "an advertising feature"; the coverage must be an interview or a credible feature about an aspect of the company that is relevant. Do not mention the IPO as the topic could return to haunt the firm. Once coverage is secured, make the link available on investor websites and social media properties such as Twitter or Stocktwits.

Subscribe to websites that publish peer-group information, analysis, or opinion and pay particular attention to social media and investor-only websites and blogs (LinkedIn, Facebook, Twitter, SeekingAlpha). Subscribe to key investor websites and follow the news feeds of individuals who comment on peers. Establish a following on twitter using a name and email address that cannot be traced back to the firm. Generic handles work well when the firm's industry is apparent in the name (e.g. SatelliteMan67, WidgetGal). Use TweetDeck or HootSuite to monitor different twitter accounts and follow all of the people who follow or mention the firm and its peers.

Establish a pattern of disclosure through monthly news releases. Compile a large number (10+) of possible news release ideas and include an abstract of each. Craft the top five and run them by management. At regular intervals, disseminate only the releases that do not violate quiet period rules.

Facebook is one example of a firm that considered media strategy ahead of what was, at the time, rumored to be the largest IPO in history.[3] Led by Morgan Stanley, the world's most popular social media website appeared to adopt public company communication practices while it was still private. Months before the firm entered the quiet period, it conducted private placements led by Goldman Sachs, and formed relationships with major investors around the world. It also leaked strategic information pertaining to its valuation through various bloggers and media outlets.

Although Facebook faced legal threats related to privacy and ownership issues, it was able to witness how investors responded to the valuations of other internet companies such as Groupon and Zynga. Facebook and its bankers knew that last thing they needed during their Roadshow was "headline risk" which could be disastrous. An unforeseen restriction of its service in foreign countries or an unfavorable legal decision related to its legal ownership were scenarios to be avoided at all costs. Investors remember what happened to Google and Research In Motion when China and the Middle East temporarily banned users from accessing those sites.

For good reason, Facebook eliminated every major issue it could before filing its prospectus. It gained insight into how important issues are best "framed" and prepared a story that would support their goal of executing the world's largest IPO. It also participated in the creation of a major motion picture that won *Academy Awards* but was surreptitiously based on framing its legal issues, the reason why Aaron Sorkin of Television's *The West Wing* was hired to write it.[4]

These are bold strategic moves every IPO can learn from, although few firms have the wherewithal to harness the power of the film industry to affect popular opinion. The film *The Social Network* was released before the firm filed its IPO.

Phase Two: Preparation

The arrival of the quiet period marks the beginning of the second phase. This is the time when the SEC receives the firm's initial registration document and the firm can no longer communicate openly with anyone but the SEC.

The preparation phase is when PR execution, communications planning, research, presentation drafting and presentation coaching begins. A great deal of thinking, writing and rehearsing happens in this phase before the Roadshow begins. Most of these activities cease altogether once the Roadshow begins. Let's take a quick look at each of these areas.

The quiet period restricts firms from communicating any relevant information to anyone outside of the SEC through a legal filing (or "S-1 amendment" designated as "S-1/a). When the quiet period is in effect, the firm exists in a bubble. This bubble is meant to protect the firm -- and naive investors -- from being lured by the magic promise of a new listing before the final prospectus is available. This means the firm is only allowed to engage the media on matters that are not material matters of the prospectus. This means that any strategic announcements must be pre-cleared with the SEC.

Public Relations

Legal counsel or the SEC must approve any media interviews before they are published. Groupon initially pulled its high-profile IPO after an internal memo was leaked regarding its transaction, but then later withdrew their withdrawal.

Figure 4: The Film Department Holdings: Not Ready for Prime Time.

Although the media is discouraged to contact the firm during the quiet period, many are not aware, or do they care. So in effect they rely on the firm to cite the quiet period restrictions and explain why the firm is unable to give an inside scoop on the status of the IPO and why the CEO is building a new house.

The quiet period laws partly explain why most major news outlets only publish positive news about IPOs that have not yet priced. The risk and litigation costs associated with de-railing a major IPO are simply not worth it. Investment banks have deep pockets as do many corporate issuers.

Journalists must be 100% committed to stand behind any new material facts they publish about the firm that are not in the prospectus. Most journalists are not in a position to have such knowledge or the time or motivation to prove it. In rare circumstances, though, management may have skeletons that find their way to the popular press with the help of someone with an ax to grind. The CEO of Tesla found himself in such a situation with his ex-wife during Tesla's IPO, as did the founders of The Film Department Holdings. The result was very different for each firm.

Intense scrutiny follows the initial S-1 filing and many firms are not prepared. Those that are prepared capitalize on the extra time they are allotted -- a highly advantageous luxury. Not all bankers prepare their IPO firms for the intense scrutiny that arises from an S-1 filing.

During the preparation phase, a blog can be a dangerous place for an IPO name to surface. Blog headlines have the potential to send unwanted signals as they are often veiled in anonymity. A well-written opinion that sends the message that the firm lacks confidence in its prospects or has a major weakness in its business model can have an impact. Conversely, blogs can also be effective when they are orchestrated with the writer to communicate key data points.

Presentation Drafting

The investor presentation is vitally important to the success of any IPO. As the primary document that allows management to connect with investors, it must be written and delivered with confidence and authority. It is a good idea to develop an insider's deck early -- independently of the slides developed by the firm's bankers. But don't wait until a PowerPoint file shows up in your inbox with the words 'IPO: confidential draft' emblazoned across the first slide. By then it's too late. Important contributions that relate to the structure and emphasis of the IPO story must be submitted early in the process.

When drafting the presentation, keep in mind that investors are likely to be familiar with the firm's competition, but not the IPO firm itself.

Developing a good story is often a process of trial and error. For this reason, it is not necessary to include the lawyers when drafting early versions of the presentation. There will be plenty of them involved later in the process when they are required to sign off on all content as it is appears in the IPO presentation.

Instead, work with the facts as they appear in the prospectus. Prioritize the facts and concepts that comprise the firm's story regardless of how it is logically presented in the prospectus.

Start the drafting process by working up the financial section of the presentation first by developing up to ten slides. Even though this section is the final piece in the IPO presentation (The "Financial Review" section), it is the easiest to figure out. Numbers don't lie. Try to demonstrate a solid period of historical performance of some aspect of the firm. At the very least you'll see what investors will look at first and be able to construct a story around objective data. Use quarterly or annual data -- whatever looks best.

Drafting Sessions

During the drafting phase there will be several conference calls and group drafting sessions. Be cautious and selective when offering feedback or suggestions. Bankers have a tendency to ban those who demonstrate inexperience or unfamiliarity with the content being discussed. It takes only a single errant statement for an individual to be discredited and ignored in perpetuity. Unless comments are supported by well-articulated arguments it is best to refrain from making them.

Start Preparing Early

Managers too often procrastinate, leaving preparatory activities until it is too late. Those facing a Roadshow only two weeks away may be in serious trouble unless the speaker team drops everything and commits to preparing for the Roadshow themselves. There are many good reasons to start preparing early. For one, research shows that inferences of competence can occur within one second of exposure to a face.[5]

As a rule of thumb, executives should run through their presentation at least thirty times alone and half as many times again as a group. More importantly, the entire team including the firm's bankers and consultants must run through Q&A a minimum of five times. Each session reveals kinks that frequently require input and discussion before they can be properly worked out.

Determining the beginning and end of a presentation also requires time. This is when critical impressions are formed with an audience. Investors automatically and involuntarily analyze a presenter's first few sentences until an approximate match to an existing personality profile in neural inventory is complete. As the first and last slide of the CEO's presentation is usually "Investment Highlights", it is important to deliver this slide flawlessly.

People attempt to construct a general concept of another person as likable or dislikeable.[6] Any lull during the listener's cognitive categorical search for a comparative match leads to a mediocre conclusion. In these situations, the CEO may be regarded as a rookie or someone who seems to want to be somewhere else.

Because of the importance of communicating effectively and with purpose, do not wait for "final numbers" or any other reason to delay rehearsing. The most important practice relates to answering the list of the toughest questions. Scheduled this activity with the speaker team as early as possible to avoid calendar conflicts. Videotape the sessions to ensure everyone stays focused. Be critical of yourself but be cautious with others.

Roadshow Preparation Modules

There are two types of coaching involved with preparing a Roadshow team:

one-on-one and group exercises. Each involves interactive simulations, review of video tape and guided interactive exercises.

a) Private one-on-one sessions (x3) with each member of the speaker team. Review the expectations of investors and the various meeting formats. Provide an overview of the coaching methodology, session structure and examples from other similar IPOs. Sessions utilize live video recording and playback and the same technical equipment that will be used during the Roadshow (preview monitor, clicker, comfort monitor, podium). Content and presentation materials are developed and formatted for both one-on-one and group meetings, including speaker's notes and a formal speech tailored for each individual. Written performance feedback and a DVD of each session are provided afterwards for further study by the individual. Various metrics and specific references to material on the DVD expedite speaker skill, comfort and efficacy. Private sessions apply techniques for one-on-one, group meetings and Q&A.

b) Group sessions (x3) include all members of the speaker team and simulate the actual meeting formats encountered over the course of the Roadshow. Speaker team dynamics, Q&A techniques and real-time performance feedback during rehearsal sessions allow the team to gel and grow comfortable with individual roles and responsibilities. Material recorded during previous sessions demonstrates progress in some areas while identifying others that need improvement. Criticism or constructive feedback of individual performances is provided through confidential notes given to each speaker after the session at the time the DVD is circulated.

Prepare To Be Judged

Investors have seen it all. They often make surprisingly swift and decisive judgments that impact pricing and the subsequent performance of the firm's shares.

Right or wrong, everything about management is judged: from the way they walk to the way they talk. The presentation itself -- what it looks like, how much it weighs -- is judged. Clothing and accessories worn by the CEO or other member of the speaker team (watches, rings, jewelry, fancy pens, purses, lapel pins) will inform the investor's process of classification. A ring on each hand could indicate a recent divorce: did she cheat on him or the other way around? From three feet away, investors pick up on minutiae that form clues that turn into judgments.

Refer to chapter thirteen for discussion related to preparing to meet investors.

Phase Three: Execution

The final phase begins once the SEC and the underwriters decide on the "initial pricing range" or "indicative range". The Roadshow is set to launch.

The Roadshow is the final activity in the rite of passage. It takes two weeks to execute and often begins the day after a press release announces that "IPO pricing terms have been set". Printing presses chug away to produce thousands of approved prospectuses that are boxed and shipped to the offices of the lead bank and other members of the syndicate. It is now time to hit the road. This process of traveling from cities around the country (or world) is also referred to as "the dog and pony", "the milk run", or "the boondoggle".

During the Roadshow, two or three members of senior management (also called "The Roadshow Team" or "Speaker Team") meet face-to-face with approximately fifty investor accounts in small private meetings and many more at larger group meetings. Generally, it is the CEO, CFO and an Investor Relations Officer (IRO) who attend the Roadshow meetings. A banker who is familiar with the account will also be in attendance although many institutional investors do not permit bankers in private meetings.

The timing of the IPO ("the window") is shaped by important factors such as other deals in the market, stock market conditions and the release or reaction to relevant economic data or earnings reports. The window may also be determined by the seasonality of the firm's business or timing of an industry event -- such as merger activity or industry earnings period.

The Roadshow

The Roadshow bridges the domain between private and public ownership. Somewhat similar to television's *Amazing Race*, every day features a rapid-fire sequence of at least five one-hour meetings, scheduled back-to-back. These meetings are intense, face-to-face sessions interrupted only by air and car travel. Flying twice a day is common. The Roadshow is the means through which management meets investors in Minneapolis and Kansas City one day before attending meetings in the Dallas area the next day.

Roadshows are known for their ability to push even the most seasoned executive beyond normal limits. Constant pressure from four distinct sources gradually takes its toll on the speaker team:

1) Travel. At the heart of every Roadshow is a travel schedule that, in many cases, would be fair to characterize as maniacal or diabolical.

Figure 6: A Summary Roadshow Schedule

SUNDAY	MONDAY	TUESDAY	WEDNESDAY	THURSDAY	FRIDAY	SATURDAY
10-Jun NEW YORK	11-Jun NEW YORK, NY	12-Jun BALTIMORE, MD	13-Jun BOSTON, MA	14-Jun NEW YORK, NY	15-Jun SAN FRANCISCO	16-Jun
NO ROADSHOW COMMITMENTS	SALESFORCE PRESENTATION Morgan Stanley SALESFORCE PRESENTATION Citi SALESFORCE PRESENTATION Merrill Lynch SALESFORCE PRESENTATION Lehman Brothers	T. Rowe Price Legg Mason Wellington Management Co. Delaware Investments Emerald AM Gardiner Lewis AM ING CLARION NWQ Investments Thornburg Liaming Associates Blackrock Investment Mgmt	Standard Life Investments Columbia Management Wellington Management Co. Fidelity Putnam Massachusetts Financial Services	ING Liazard Johnson Associates Neuberger Berman Atlantic Bernstein	Capital Research Global Standard Pacific Capital RCM Capital Management, LLC BS Investments Mazama Capital Management, LLC SAN MATEO Franklin Templeton Investments	NO ROADSHOW COMMITMENTS
17-Jun	18-Jun NEW YORK, NY	19-Jun NEW YORK AREA	20-Jun CHICAGO	21-Jun NEW YORK, NY	22-Jun CITIES TBD	23-Jun
NO ROADSHOW COMMITMENTS	GROUP BREAKFAST MEETING Goldman Sachs AM OCH - Ziff Fifth Park Capital Mgmt Morgan Stanley Investment Managers Kingdom Capital Mgmt Mexico Capital Citi Land UBS Global Asset Mgmt.	Tralstat/Hunter Global JP Morgan Asset Management Janus Capital DINNER MEETING	Magnetar Capital UBS O Connor Atlantus Bernstein GROUP LUNCH MEETING UBS Global Asset Management (US)			NO ROADSHOW COMMITMENTS
24-Jun	25-Jun CITIES TBD	26-Jun NEW YORK, NY	27-Jun	28-Jun	29-Jun	30-Jun
NO ROADSHOW COMMITMENTS						

2) Mental exhaustion. Often the result of intense focus or boredom. It can be torturous to present the same set of slides and answer the same questions again and again.

3) Logistics. Seemingly innocuous details such as the location of luggage,

lobby security, and the efficiency of pick-ups and drop-offs in each city make a huge difference. The smoother the logistics, the less wear and tear management endures. Flawless logistics require significant planning and experience so that changes can be accommodated in real-time.

Many executives suffer unnecessarily because they simply don't eat and drink enough throughout the course of an entire day. Who is responsible for buying food and drinks? And what's on the menu? Who will ensure an adequate supply of nourishment is always available in the cars used by the Roadshow team? The task of ensuring management has enough to eat and drink usually requires a committed resource, but is well worth the expense for $300+ million IPOs.

Intense Scrutiny

Consider this: how long have you sat silently in an uncomfortable chair without checking your phone or fidgeting? Have you ever just sat still and done nothing for forty minutes straight? How about sixty minutes at a time, six times a day for two weeks? That's a typical Roadshow. When a manager is not presenting, she is doing nothing.

Somehow you'll find the strength within you to remain looking attentive and interested over eight hours of back-to-back. But it can be absolutely brutal. Plus, you can't help noticing that your colleague looks better than you at doing nothing.

None of this is lost on the investor. They pick up on the smallest details. They have to: a lot of capital is at stake and you are sitting directly in front of them. Keep this in mind as you prepare to be scrutinized during the Roadshow.

Expectations and Levers

In contrast, macro-level scrutiny can cause anxiety because it is largely beyond the firm's control. Once the firm files its IPO documents, anything the media says about the firm is fair game and defending the firm is unlikely if it doesn't already have plans in place.

When the firm goes public, it becomes owned by a demanding new set of stakeholders. Rarely do investment bankers warn management of how much attention shareholders actually require once the firm is public. Every move is parsed and analyzed in an attempt to gain a better understanding of how future performance will measure up to expectations. Management may become obsessed with achieving growth in order to satisfy the insatiable appetite of equity investors.

Aim Low and Hit High

Wall Street's focus on growth should provide enough incentive to compel firms to build in ample "wiggle room". This is accomplished by setting expectations through targets the firm knows will be much lower than the final result. If revenues will be $20 million, announce a guidance target of $19 million. Or less.

Perhaps the best way to think about how to pull off such a feat without being too obvious is to examine the various "levers" at the firm's disposal. These controls are used in an appropriate and legally acceptable manner but can be useful and sometimes necessary when adjusting financial results. Identify what levers exist and what impact they have on certain results. Some will influence net income, others revenue or operating cash flow. The classification of certain expenses and investments are popular levers, as are the arbitrary value of mark-to-market assets. When times are good, some management teams quietly decrease the value of impaired assets so they can increase them later. This is the controversial realm of "financial engineering", a topic few want to talk about and fewer will admit to, but it is a widespread and pervasive practice.

Some companies rely on an accounting category often referred to as "one time", "non-recurring" or "special charges" so that rather awkward pear-shaped results can fit neatly into a round hole. There are many companies that appreciate the benefit that non-recurring items provide.

Other Preparations

In addition to presentation skills, Q&A, coaching, crisis planning, scriptwriting, and investor messaging, it is prudent to think about ongoing disclosure commitments.

What will the firm say once the quiet period ends? Does it have a plan to release news after the lockup period expires (180 days)? Lockup agreements go a long way to ensuring an element of stability to the IPO's stock price during the first few months of trading. When lockups expire, restricted people are permitted to sell stock, which can result in a drastic drop in share price due to the huge increase in supply of stock.[7] A disciplined approach to preparation will ensure that areas central to the IPO's ongoing success are addressed.

There are a dozen aspects to Roadshow project management and preparation. The components of the critical path are presented below.

Table 1: IPO Roadshow Project Management Activities.

1. Development
> Research
> Working group interviews
> Historical media analysis
> Project brief
> Master messaging brief
> Strategic memorandum

2. Content & Creative
> Acquisition of branding materials
> Acquire photography
> ID graphic elements
> Wireframes/3D
> Animation: logo

3. Investor Relations

Website content
Disclosure policy
Vendor selection
Database development
IR plan development

4. Public Relations

Crisis overview
Messaging strategy
Strategic memorandum
Pre-IPO media outreach
Listing release
Boilerplate development
Post-IPO media plan

5. Roadshow

Working group distribution lists
Roadshow - Europe
Roadshow - USA
New York
Boston Group Lunch
San Francisco Group Lunch
Coordinate investor profiles
Finalize hotel and working contracts
Send out Personal Profiles
Rooming Key List
Baggage Lists
Confirm catering details

Confirm accommodation needs

6. Supplies

Name badges
Speaking notes for each speaker
Assembly of packages for meetings
- French (Canada)
- English
- US (no green sheet)

7. IPO Presentation

Presentation outlining
Speaker coaching
Creative production
Q&A formulation and training
Finalize scripts and presentation

8. Roadshow Presentation Materials

Initial briefing to discuss materials
Design direction submission
Presentation drafting
Presentation production
Print slides

9. Rehearsals & Coaching

Management individual rehearsals
Management group meeting rehearsals
Final full dress rehearsal
Salesforce presentation
Roadshow Day 1

10. Production & Technical

Confirm set requirements
Establish full technical requirement
Confirm suppliers & technicians
Design set
Security for group meetings
Walk in music – selection
NetRoadshow: confirm recording details
Table tents
Venue signage
Color books

11. Measurement

Media coverage analysis
Internal de-brief
Client and banker feedback
Budget Reconciliation

12. Content & Creative

Discuss and develop 'core' messages
Design handout materials
Present all design material
Receive and apply comments
Sign off all design materials
Creation of final artwork for printers
Sign off all final artwork

Chapter Three
The Speaker Team

Every IPO involves a broad cross-section of professionals known as the "working group". This group consists of investment bankers, lawyers, accountants, consultants, and the senior executives of the firm work together for months to prepare the launch of a new public company. Yet despite the large and collective effort, there are no guarantees that any given deal will be successful.

Within the working group is the speaker team. This is a small but important crucially important subset of the larger working group because it consists only of the executives that attend the meetings in the Roadshow schedule. Also known as the Roadshow Team, these two or three senior executives grind away each day for approximately two weeks meeting with scores of investors in cities scattered around the continent and beyond. Responsible for bringing the story to investors, each member of the speaker team discusses specific content pertinent to investors when delivering the IPO presentation.

The Roadshow Team

The Speaker Team almost always consists of the firm's top two executives: the CEO and CFO. Some circumstances dictate that a COO or other specialized executive also has a speaking role. Independent board members rarely participate as they lack the granular knowledge of the firm required by investors.

For a few good reasons, keep the speaker team to the smallest size possible, regardless of internal politics. Presenting thirty slides with three or more people can be awkward. To investors, too many speakers looks a bit like a game of whack-a-mole since someone always seems to be either standing up or sitting down, which creates substantial interference to establishing a connection with audiences.

However, there are special situations that require four or more executives to attend the investor presentations, especially during Q&A at the large group meetings. With transactions involving private equity sponsors or other types of share offerings that feature a selling shareholder -- such as a "carve out" or "spin-off" IPO -- it is not uncommon for an outbound CEO to join a recently hired CEO on a Roadshow. The outbound CEO generally stays behind at the parent company and assists his successor at the newly forged public company unit with answering questions related to the reasons why the parent company has decided to spin off the business unit into a standalone entity. Outside of this framework of specificity, however, it is generally not a good plan to have the former head of the operating unit travel with the new chief executive because of the potential dynamics between the team members. Investors are very sensitive to interpersonal relationships and are highly skilled at detecting friction between members of the speaker team.

Prior to the Roadshow, colleagues working in finance, accounting, sales and corporate development support the speaker team. The ability to quickly track down or develop information that can be used in the prospectus, investor presentation and speeches is very helpful. A single graph can sometimes provide a much needed missing piece in a story that without it would remain puzzling.

The speaker team is the most important component of the broader working group as they meet with investors and run the firm once it is public. They are the leadership team of the new public entity, so they also have the highest vested interest in seeing the IPO executed successfully. The Speaker Team will continue to engage investors beyond the IPO by maintaining ongoing contact with the investment community. The methods, programs and discipline the team adopts during the IPO process are paramount to influencing share price valuation over the long run.

Members that are already familiar with investors may feel more confident in their ability to arouse interest through the narrative of their presentation. This can lead to overconfidence that results in more pressure for the relatively experienced executive, as she may be expected to outperform her less experienced co-presenters. Personal overconfidence may also cause some individuals to be less receptive to coaching and the demands imposed by thorough Roadshow preparation. An executive with minimal experience (or none at all) can be coached to perform at a level consistent with investor expectations if adequate time is allotted.

Although the emphasis of each speaker team member is different, the CEO always talks longer than the CFO, covering roughly fifteen slides versus five for the CFO. The total duration of the CEO's speech is between twelve to eighteen minutes out of the total twenty-five to thirty minutes of total talk time, excluding Q&A. This differential of six minutes of talk time between the CEO and CFO equates to75% of the formal portion of the investor presentation.[1] After the speaker team has presented to a dozen or more live audiences, much of the superfluous verbiage and repetition will have disappeared from the presentations. Indeed, by day three of the Roadshow, all speaker team members will know not only their own presentations inside out, but the presentations of their colleagues also. Many teams will learn that just four or five slides form the heart of the story and become adept at delivering a very powerful abridged version of the presentation, which frees up valuable time for Q&A.

The CEO

The firm's chief executive is the recognized leader of the speaker team. As the foremost character, the chief executive must ensure the investment story resonates with audiences. The CEO is absolutely confident in his role and speaks with experience and confident ease. People feel and trust the CEO's presence and character. The CEO satisfies the needs of viewers for a strong leader and will continue to attract an ever-growing audience as long as favorable reviews keep coming.

The archetypal chief executive resembles a character already familiar to investors; self-confidence and cool temperament are apparent.[2] Wilting under intense pressure does not occur, as the CEO's sole focus is solve the problem at hand and provide assurances that the situation has been fixed.

Investors will make judgments about the chief executive's credibility within minutes (or seconds) of meeting the CEO. Some investors may have pre-conceived notions created through a conversation with a colleague or investment banker. They also have a good idea of what they expect a successful CEO to be like. In a complex process known as "belief updating", how a CEO acts in a meeting -- including their responses to questions -- are involuntarily evaluated and codified in an effort to reveal where the CEO fits in relative to the observer's concept of a peer group.

In the context of an IPO meeting, if the investor experiences someone who is a little naive and perhaps overly friendly, this initial encounter becomes an "anchor" which sets the stage for further interaction with management. In what Warren Buffet calls "the price of excellence", the trait of *intensity* is one that conforms to investors' general expectation of how a successful executive is supposed to behave. Investors use similar traits as the basis for interpretation and do not expect or even care about how friendly a CEO is, as long as intensity is present.[3]

It may seem that the initial frame of reference of a naive, overly-friendly CEO is not a favorable starting point, but the CEO who understands this is much better equipped to "update" this belief in the very first few seconds of his initial encounter with investors. The prepared CEO will create the impression of being more polished than expected. He'll smile once but rarely again and maintains the look of someone who is comfortable and in control. The investor gets a sense that it is the CEO who is trying to read her and does not appear to be self-conscious or concerned by what she might think about that.

As the first few seconds and minutes are vital in the belief-updating process, any sign that the CEO is naive and inexperienced will confirm an unsatisfactory pre-judgment and make it much more difficult to change the investor's feelings towards the CEO or CFO they are meeting.[4]

Investors are experts at detecting the smallest cracks in confidence. They have developed sharp skills that allow them to recognize signs of uneasiness unknowingly displayed by a presenter. By nature, CEOs are confident -- they have to be -- but they walk a fine line between displaying too much or too little confidence. Many recent examples provide evidence of the overly confident CEO whose company quickly went bankrupt after giving a televised statement that was meant to assuage fears. Lehman Brothers, Bear Stearns, CIT Group, and GM are but four examples. The display of overconfidence had the unintended and opposite effect.

Overconfident statements often signal that something must really be wrong. Executives that change their ritualistic pattern of behavior and mode of disclosure risk triggering heightened skepticism from those looking for signs to confirm the hypothesis that something is wrong at the firm. The lesson here, compliments of Nassim Taleb, is the best way to control people without offending their sensitivity is to be exceedingly polite and friendly.[5]

The CFO

No other member of the Speaker team must adhere to a stereotype more than the CFO. One study found that 845 companies, or nearly 10% of those listed on the NYSE, AMEX and NASDAQ had to restate their financial statements.[6]

All companies are under intense pressure to meet quarterly earnings forecasts; newly listed firms even more so. Some are aggressive with their treatment of certain financial results that can cause problems in the future. Investors must get a strong sense that the CFO is not likely to pursue actions such as "managing earnings". It is well known that management incentives, the value of stock options and the results of competitors are all reasons why CFOs are tempted to fiddle with unaudited numbers. Although a great deal of accounting classification is perfectly legal and completely within the bounds of GAAP (generally accepted accounting principles) investors want to know whether the CFO is the type who has, or is likely to, re-classify certain questionable expenses or defer revenues for the sake of hitting forecasted ("guided") numbers.

There are signals -- red flags -- that investors are acutely sensitive to and will try to uncover the existence of during a Roadshow meeting. Over-optimism is a blaring signal.[7] This is because CFOs should treat good or bad news with equal weight. Numbers are simply numbers, and nothing else. There is no tolerance or excuse for a CFO to exhibit exuberance or use promotional language or superlatives at any time. There is an immediate loss of credibility to the CFO who characterizes financial performance as "great" or "fantastic". These words should never be uttered by any experienced CFO. Instead, adjectives such as "solid", "positive" or "above expectations" are much more appropriate.

Some investors will have done a fair amount of homework ahead of each meeting. They will have combed through footnotes and scanned for accounting oddities in the prospectus. The polished CFO knows this and will know her numbers cold so she can easily justify the reasons why certain metrics are presented on a non-GAAP basis. She is always composed and answers questions in a matter-of-fact way, no matter how malicious the question was intended to be.

More than anyone else on the speaker team, the CFO must take steps to prepare for the hot seat. Above all else, investors require a solid and trustworthy CFO because there will come a time when her credibility is essential to maintaining trust in the company and the belief that the firm will perform well.

The CFO is the main supporting character; her integrity is essential to instilling confidence in the firm and its governance structure. At critical times, she can save the day through her adept command of granular numbers and ratios. She does not waver; what others describe as good or bad are merely variations of a theme defined by expectations. She knows she may be under-appreciated but does not want the spotlight because she knows the focus belongs to those who generate revenue. She does not exude excitement or disappointment in front of others although privately she may be her own worst critic. She handles the most detailed questions with incisive responses that never cross the boundaries of disclosure. She understands risk thoroughly and actively defends against it by controlling everything she can and protecting what she cannot. If something can be measured, it is.

In certain industries the CFO is often substituted with a Chief Technology

Officer or Chief Medical Officer. Financial services firms generally employ a Chief Risk Officer (CRO) in addition to the usual audit and compensation committees. The CRO is often required to attend meetings with certain investors as well as attend the Q&A session at large group meetings in New York, Boston and San Francisco. With the exception of biotechnology and certain technology firms, attendance is generally mandatory for the CFO during the Roadshow.

Other Actors on the Speaker Team

Apart from the CEO and CFO, other presenters may also be necessary to include on the speaker team, but exercise caution when proceeding with more than three presenters. Making other company executives available to answer specific questions during the Q&A period is acceptable even if the executive does not have a formal speaking role.

Companies pursuing an IPO should expect to hire an investor relations officer (IRO) prior to the IPO Roadshow. The CFO's daily schedule will simply be too demanding to deal with constant phone calls from small investors. The IRO can take much of the workload away from the CFO by answering many of the questions asked by retail investors. The IR officer also maintains a database of current investors and prospective targets. Some new public companies hire an outside IR firm, but it is much better over the long-term to have a dedicated, experienced employee that maintains ongoing contact with the investment community and its network of service providers.

The IRO rarely has a formal speaking role but rather attends meetings to make contact with the investors and analysts she will be working with once the firm is publicly traded. Many organizations will refer investor calls to the IRO who is authorized to speak on behalf of the CEO and CFO on a wide range of topics.

Investment Bankers

The investment bank responsible for leading the transaction is similar to the director of a motion picture. The key decisions -- and there are many -- involving the plot, casting roles and the story itself are ultimately decided by the lead banker. What parts of the story are emphasized or downplayed is mostly their call; the form and shape of the story and how it is presented reflects their preferences because the bankers know the investor audience far better than the firm.

The investment banking team usually appoints three or more people to work with the firm on a day-to-day basis, with some of them rotating in and out of the picture. Firms will speak to their lead banker with regular frequency, especially during the marketing preparation phase. The senior banker will have one or two investment banking analysts working under them to perform tasks such as sourcing data, preparing graphs, writing key-takeaways for slides, or providing feedback to the firm. At certain points, the head of the lead banker's industry group (e.g., FIG, software, real estate) will provide feedback on the firm's deal and its marketing considerations.

For example, if the firm is a financial services company operating in the insurance sector, the lead investment banker will have significant knowledge gained on other similar or recent transactions and will likely lead the process from start to finish. Along the way, the lead banker works with the head of the industry group to ensure the most valuable information and perspective as possible is incorporated and available to create a sharp and differentiated IPO story.

Equity Capital Markets

If investment banking can be compared to a film director, Equity Capital Markets (ECM) could be likened to that of a film producer because this role is focused on flawlessly executing the production with limited risk. ECM is an important function at every large investment dealer. ECM sets the timing for launching the IPO and oversees the production of anything related to the Roadshow and its scheduled components (e.g. meetings, conference calls, hotels, flights). They work closely with the investment bankers and the syndicate desk throughout the entire process but are very involved once the Roadshow begins.

ECM provides daily feedback on the market and what investors are reacting to with respect to the broader market and the transaction itself. Working under ECM is the Roadshow Desk, which ensures all logistical and production requirements are carried off without a hitch including all air and ground transportation, accommodation, meeting rooms and audiovisual equipment required to complete the schedule of investor meetings. Large deals that involve big brands or very high profile management teams may retain an external Roadshow consultant to assist with the preparation planning activities, such as the author's firm SKY | Alphabet.[8]

Equity capital markets' (ECM) is a division within the investment bank and is especially important because it is responsible for the timing and execution of deals. They also monitor demand on a daily basis. ECM personnel interface with other investment banks to avoid conflicts in marketing schedules; this is why several multi-billion dollar IPOs aren't launched at the same time in tepid markets. ECM ensures the supply of transactions does not exceed investor demand for new equity issues.

ECM personnel are 'big picture' thinkers and have executed hundreds of transactions and understand the subtleties and hot buttons that were successful (or not). With access to real-time intelligence through the trading desks of other firms, ECM has information that can influence pricing.

Although ECM does not regularly contribute granular suggestions to presentation content, they do provide clear direction regarding sensitive issues about which investors are likely to be concerned. It is important to listen carefully to any feedback ECM provides, as they are familiar with the differentiation between your IPO and others that are in the market currently or have raised capital recently.

Chapter Four

The Research Behind the Marketing

Exhaustive research must be conducted before marketing strategy, competitive positioning or growth tactics are formulated with confidence.

Research begins with understanding the firm's financial data. Historical financial performance (quarter by quarter for as many consecutive quarters as possible) provides objective indications of relative weaknesses and strengths. Only by analyzing the wealth of information captured in the firm's historical balance sheet, cash flow and income statements will the marketer see the same things investors will see. Many investors augment data from the prospectus with their own information.

Investors are also known to manipulate and process vast quantities of performance data through analytical software and staff trained in forensic accounting methods. Information is central to any IPO so a significant supply of competitive data exists at websites maintained by securities regulators: *Edgar.Sec.gov* in the United States and *SEDAR.com* in Canada.

Thorough research is necessary to produce perspectives that are vital to formulating a communications strategy that will successfully counter objections. Groupon's CEO was surprised to learn of the overwhelming negative reaction his firm received after they filed an accounting amendment to their S-1. In response, he stated in an email to employees "we just didn't realize there would be so many skeptics". In the world of IPOs, there is never any shortage of skeptics.

Only after a thorough analysis of the universe of information that exists on an IPO and its peers can a marketer identify legitimate angles to exploit through a combination of presentation scripting, branding and other forms of messaging. It is critical that investors understand the firm's unassailable competitive strengths as well as the apparent weaknesses that shape long-term financial performance.

Formulating a communications strategy to accomplish this objective starts with gathering unassailable facts about the firm -- facts that are credibly aligned with business objectives. When discussing major weaknesses or threats facing the business, explain how the risks are mitigated.

The firm's desired positioning should reflect the intersection of strength, weakness, risk, and opportunity. Specific qualities of each aspect should support the argument for an equity security valued appropriately and consistently with identified peers.

To establish valuation parameters, it is necessary to position the IPO among a group of already trading, better-known competitors. Be realistic about where the firm ranks among them. By comparing key financial metrics and conducting a thorough and critical analysis of less objective criteria (such as recent valuations of similar or recent IPOs that may or may not be in the same sector), the marketer will understand the components inherent in the valuation range. A very useful search of SIC (or NAICS) codes and the financial metrics of constituent member firms can be performed at *Nasdaq. com/investing/dozen*, a variety of valuation metrics are listed.

Define The Prime Directive

Developing a communications strategy starts with defining one "must-stick" message. Perhaps the firm wants to be known as the leading low-cost producer poised to enter high growth markets. Or perhaps the firm desires to be positioned as a technology leader set to provide new products to massive, under-served markets. Or, maybe the firm wishes to secure a reputation as the newest, high-margin producer of luxury goods with a strong brand name that is rapidly gaining popular acceptance. Yet another example is the IPO that sees value in being perceived as a market leader through its portfolio of patented therapeutics aimed at providing a better answer for a neurological condition that is prevalent worldwide. A final example is the startup firm that has recently attracted highly experienced and proven talent positioned to do battle in an unexplored high-margin segment.

Once the prime directive is identified, the data and information to support the desired positioning must be identified and located. Aggregate all objective information and data related to the transaction's strengths, growth strategies, opportunities and threats into a document titled "Messaging Architecture".

This document will also include subjective opinion and perspectives to create an information set that captures all necessary evidence to support the firm's desired positioning. Any and all information that can be used to create and strengthen the marketing messages will exist in the Messaging

Architecture document, as well as the arguments that will be used to defend against doubts that surface during the Roadshow.

A Shortcut to Messaging Architecture

The messaging architecture document defines and prioritizes the universe of facts so that the company's most salient features come alive. They are logically connected so that the acceptance of one message contributes to the overall positioning of the company. They are comprised of facts related to operational or financial performance. They are derived from the prospectus and support management's strategies for growth and managing risk.

As the presentation materials evolve, the architectural structure of the messaging is a valuable resource to the working group. Any risks that investors are likely to identify must be confronted directly by clearly articulating how the company confronts each challenge and threat. Strategies related to growth must be supported by concrete evidence that the company's positioning and distinct capabilities underscore its ability to execute its plans.

Investors also want to know when certain milestones or accomplishments will occur so that the firm is accountable if it fails to meet its goals.

After reading the entire prospectus, back to front and front to back, copy and paste any information pertaining to each of the four areas (Strengths, Growth Strategies, Opportunities, Threats) into a document with the appropriate section headings. Include the page number from where it was pasted. Make sure you use the current prospectus in PDF format so it is easy to copy and paste.

Once this raw categorization has been completed, a healthy mix of subheadings, paragraphs, charts and data points will exist. Tighten the document by removing any unnecessary wording.

Now, review past presentations and presentations located on competitor's websites or SEC filings (found at *Edgar.SEC.gov*). Make notes about anything related to the information in your master document. For example, if you discover that your competitor's primary growth strategy is to further penetrate low-margin, high volume markets, make a note beside any of your growth strategies that are consistent or run counter to their strategy.

Scan the internet for further discussion on your IPO or business. There aren't many websites that offer free analysis of IPO filings but *SeekingAlpha. com* and *IPOdesktop.com* are two favorites. For years, Francis Gaskins and John Fitzgibbons, Jr. have been publishing metrics-based analysis of IPOs. They often expose serious flaws regarding transactions in the pipeline. If Gaskins has commented on your filing, you'd better hear what he has to say.

At this stage, you should have a document entirely sourced from the S-1, augmented by publicly available sources researchable by anyone on the internet.

Adding up the Risks, Threats and Weaknesses

To begin shaping the messaging it is helpful to ask several questions: what are the key objections investors are likely to have? In plain language, what are the arguments against the firm's valuation, growth prospects or ability to execute? Do concerns exist about the firm's competitive positioning and ability to defend against competition? What about the sustainability of financial results?

What are the firm's clear strengths relative to its peers? How do specific key financial metrics stack up? Do young markets or new products demonstrate legitimate areas of growth? Is the company a low-cost producer? Will growth generate additional revenues that will drop to the bottom line (operating leverage)? Are past capital expenditures starting to generate results? Is the company in the right place at the right time? Does the firm's brand translate to significant pricing power?

Considering both the negative and positive qualities supported by comprehensive research, what are the primary features of the company? What can be said that will withstand close scrutiny? What is the main point? What can be said to support this main point?

Figure 6.1: Sample Messaging Architecture

Overall Desired Positioning

Similar to its US peers but with higher growth potential rates, NewCo, Inc. is the only digital radio satellite broadcaster serving the world's largest and fastest-growing markets through its control of, and $1.2 billion investment in, technology, content and spectrum allocation licenses for commercial use in India, China, Western Europe, and covering 130 other countries outside of North America, South Korea and Japan.

Investor Positioning

NewCo is a US-based satellite digital radio company similar to Sirius or XM Satellite that has the exclusive rights, technology and content to broadcast in the world's largest markets outside the US.

Media Positioning

Since 1994, NewCo has operated in a highly-regulated, highly-scrutinized environment. NewCo has successfully undertaken stringent due diligence conducted by qualified, independent third-parties including the US Department of Defense. NewCo has thoroughly and absolutely disclosed all aspects of its business. As a point of fact, through a recapitalization last year, NewCo bought out its former investors' interests. Former shareholders are no longer involved with the Company whatsoever.

Key Strengths and Supporting Statements of Fact

The Company is the only FCC DARS license holder in attractive, long-term growth markets outside of North America.

In 1991, the Company received the first DARS license from the FCC for broadcasting satellite-based digital audio radio and is the only company currently providing DARS outside of North America, Japan and South Korea. The company is currently licensed in the 1467 to 1492 MHz portion of the L band.

-- Cite cable growth rates in India, China, Western Europe

-- Cite cellular growth rates in India, China, Western Europe

NewCo has a fully-operational technology infrastructure in place similar to that of the operators participating in the US' digital satellite radio duopoly, but with much more progress relative to their infrastructure at the time of their IPOs.

The company has invested $1.2 Billion in assets consisting of two geostationary satellites, AfriStar (launched in 1998) and AsiaStar (launched in 2000); the associated ground systems that provide content to and control the satellites; and the receivers owned by customers.

NewCo has commenced the commercial roll-out of its service in India with 21 channels of content.

Addressable market: 70 million people and 14 million households.

Initial targets include the most affluent segments of India's population living in India's top eight metropolitan areas

Markets under-served by AM and FM radio

Low cost operating platform.

Low subscriber acquisition cost relative to US peers

Lower content development and production costs

Lower variable costs

The Company's management team consists of recognized leaders in the satellite industry, with particularly deep experience in India.

The CEO – Pioneered the development of satellite-based digital radio services (DARS) and has been involved with the industry since its inception. The CEO was involved in the development of both geostationary and low earth orbit satellite systems in the mid 80's. Mr. Samara was also instrumental in the international allocation of broadcast spectrum for DARS. The CEO is one of the principal founders of XM Satellite Radio, and was responsible for hiring its top executives and overseeing the development of its business plan.

Growth Strategies and Tactics to Achieve Success

India – continue to drive subscriber growth through a continued roll-out in India's major urban centers

Penetrate higher income segment and early adopters

India – Build the NewCo brand and awareness of its digital radio service

Integrated combination of outdoor advertising, experiential marketing, and point of sale displays

India – Expand sales and distribution network

Follow cable and cellular adoption model to expand relationships with key retailers and other sales outlets

Drive continued progress in China to full commercial roll-out

Most populous nation: 1.3 billion people, 360 million HH, 8 million cars

Relatively underdeveloped radio markets

Indefinite broadcast license issued by China's MII (Ministry of Information Industry) subject to annual review

Broadcast technology infrastructure in place through state-of-the-art uplink station in Beijing (ASIAStar)

Established contractual relationship with state-owned third-party representative (CHINASat); largest satellite operator in Asia; three year option to extend past August 2005

Agreements in place with local receiver manufacturers – Tongshi and Tesonic

Memoranda of understanding with several third-party providers of content

2 patents awarded, 5 patents pending

Exploit mobile DARS opportunity through regulatory franchise position in Western Europe

Maastricht 2002 plan consistent with AfriStar's coordinated frequency range

200 million automobiles

With Analog Devices, develop automobile compatible mobile receiver and service

Continue mobile DARS system tests

Further preliminary negotiations with major European automobile manufacturers

Establish necessary partnerships for DARS in Europe

Negative Perceptions and Marketing Challenges

1. Historical shareholders – involvement of recognized names associated with national security

2. Historical media coverage citing financial and operating performance prospects that have not materialized

3. Past challenges with executing the business plan

4. Lack of internal financial controls

Tactics to Address Negative Perceptions and Challenges

1. Take a strong and definitive position on the subject. See "Overall Desired

Positioning – Media (Crisis)". Establish the individuals who may be in contact with the media and restrict all contact with the press to these individuals. Yanor has a team on standby to take calls and handle inquiries.

2. A quick internet search using standard research tools available to any media outlet produces past articles that contain quotes from management regarding expectations on operating performance and consumer demand. Although investors will be more understanding than the media, credibility could be sensitivity with some outlets and, more specifically, reporters who are already familiar with the Company. Therefore, it is important to shift the messaging mix and responsibilities to include more members of the management team.

In terms of architecture, it is recommended that the CEO be the creative and visionary voice of the Company, while the CFO be responsible for commenting on all aspects relating to the Company's operating and strategic performance. It has not yet been determined what role the COO should play in shaping the Company's profile with the business and trade press going forward.

3. According to documents widely available and inferences from the S-1, The Company has experienced periods of "stopping and starting". Although the most recent period of limbo (2003-2004) can be credibly attributed to a necessary period of re-capitalization and restructuring, it is difficult to ascertain exactly what issue, if any, was responsible for periods of downsizing and an inability to gain traction with subscribers. To counter this, it is worthwhile to emphasize the business plan as it exists today and identify clear and achievable "milestones" for investors. The identification and guidance given by the Company with respect to these milestones will be crucial for the Company's credibility once it is a publicly-traded security. It is extremely important that any forward-looking statements be achievable and that the Company begins to build a bank of goodwill with the financial media and investment community.

4. As the S-1 indicates, at the present time there are inadequate internal controls. It is therefore important that the Company provide full disclosure on its methodology, progress, and anticipated date of achieving the necessary conditions for it to be deemed SEC/Sarbanes-Oxley compliant and to make investors comfortable that it will be able to meet its reporting obligations as

a public company.

Sources Used in the Messaging Architecture

A particularly effective method for organizing the messaging architecture is to divide the various classes of information into three distinct, color-coded binders. The content of each binder is then distilled before synthesizing the summary of each binder together into the final Messaging Architecture document. The binders are as follows:

1) Red Binder: All publicly available information about the firm, including data in the prospectus (S-1) and amendments, and mentions in competitor's regulatory filings;

2) Black Binder: Transcribed one-on-one interviews with bankers and management team;

3) Green Binder: Parsed and analyzed perspectives and opinions from analyst research reports and investor websites regarding the firm's peers and the industry.

Once these binders are full of research, the information in each binder must be sorted into four broad categories: strengths, growth strategies, opportunities and threats.

The Red Binder: Legally Vetted, "Objective" Content

To establish benchmarks, review all recent filings of peers, including all 10-Q (quarterly reports), 10-K (annual reports) and 8-K (press releases) submissions.

Revenue growth, cash flow, net income, debt, and asset values are all measures used to compare data in IPO filings with those of known peers.

Answer the same questions investors will ask: how large is the firm, relative to others? What are the salient highlights of its balance sheet, cash flow and income statements? What do the financials of peer group firms reveal? How much larger could the firm company become? Is there demonstrated growth? What drives or inhibits growth? Are margins or market share expanding? Is there evidence of declining performance in any key measure?

The financial statements are the basis of any credible communications strategy because historical performance data must support the desired positioning. If numbers alone do not support the prime directive and its underlying investment thesis, other elements that are more subjective must be considered to build a strong -- but perhaps not the strongest -- case. One method is to apply multiples based on identified peer group averages for certain categories to subjective categories such as growth possibilities, brand strength or anticipated changes in the competitive landscape. Finding credibly sourced benchmarks and related data can require considerable effort. However, it is well worth the effort because the smaller the difference between the firm's current positioning and its desired valuation, the fewer multiples and subjective themes will be required.

The Black Binder: "Subjective" Content: Interviews

The bankers working closest to the deal must be interviewed to understand the mechanics and thinking behind the firm's valuation. Although few relish the idea of being recorded on audio or video tape, it is highly advantageous to record the interviews so they can be transcribed.

Fifteen minutes is all it takes to interview a single banker. There are generally two or more bankers must be interviewed. It is beneficial to hear the various unique views without a wider audience listening in. On co-led deals, be sure to ask each lead banker to participate; whether they do or not is up to them.

The goal of the interview process is to capture the thinking and views about the key strengths and weaknesses of the deal so that, as a group, you can make informed decisions regarding what is important and what is not. For this reason, when conducting the interviews it is better to use a conversational tone rather than pursue a formal line of questioning.

This approach helps to uncover information and unpleasant issues that may be lurking beneath a calm exterior. Bringing all serious issues to light will enable the development of a thoughtfully considered investor presentation while addressing the key threats along the way. Gain as much insight as possible to augment the information contained in prospectus and add context to the main concepts already identified.

Preface the conversation with "I want to know four things: what you think investors will have a hard time with, what the consensus will find interesting, where the growth will come from, and why would investors want to participate now rather than in the secondary market? Is it valuation, portfolio re-balancing, flight to quality or a new alternative, or what?"

Keep the interviews with the bankers separate from the firm's management. Confidentially and one-on-one, interview the CEO, CFO, IRO and any other speaker team members involved with the IPO.

Interview Question #1: (Weaknesses/Threats/Risks):

What's going to sideline this IPO? What are serious negatives about this deal? Honestly, what are the possible snags going to be? What negative views or opinions are we up against? What are investors going to be the most critical about?

Do not ignore obvious shortcomings about a transaction. If there is a glaring weakness, think of it as an essential component that defines the character of the IPO marketing. It is future upside. Deficiencies and areas of improvement represent challenges to overcome. Investors need to understand the difficulties because the firm instantly becomes more valuable once they are mitigated or eliminated.

To ignore faults is strategically unsound because it infers the firm is perfect which implies it is also fully valued. And why would any investor want to invest in a fully-valued company? Isn't down the only direction to go? Hubris and overconfidence are prevalent in deals that perform poorly once they start to trade.

If the answer to these questions is "nothing" or "not much really", either the deal is going to be tough or the banker doing the interview is declining to participate. Even the best deals have some risk, some hole, some glaring fault. All of them do. Most operational concerns are fixable, and fixed quickly through IPO proceeds. Growth objectives are more difficult to achieve if the strategies behind them are impaired.

Question #2: (Opportunities):

From a competitor's perspective, what attributes make the IPO firm superior? What keeps competitors up at night when the firm goes head to head against them? What are the firm's opportunities?

Playing 'Devil's Advocate' generally produces better, more relevant and focused answers than simply taking the same side. You want to encourage debate and find out about the strengths that truly provide the company with a distinct competitive advantage.

Question #3: (Growth Strategies):

Is this Company going to grow and how will it, exactly? Over the next year, how fast will it grow? What could impede growth?

Questions regarding growth are often forward-looking. This means the answers invite forecasts about the future performance of the firm. If growth isn't specifically addressed in the presentation, it will invite investors to probe for answers to where it will come from.

The difference between what the bankers believe of the firm's growth prospects relative to management's belief may reveal important disconnects.

Question #4: (Strengths):

If the firm had unlimited capital and resources what would it do? How fast would they execute? What would they do differently?

This is a very interesting question and often opens new avenues of discussion. It provides good insight into whether the bankers think the Company can execute and, in effect, how good they will be as a public company.

People often try to modify the question ("you don't mean unlimited -- that's not possible" or "obviously the Company will never be in this position") but the answers and the detail behind the answers can be revealing.

The Green Binder: Analyst Reports and Online Research

Collect and review as many analyst reports as possible that relate to competitors and peer group companies. Although this will amount to a hefty assortment of material, it is important to understand what "guidance" peer companies provide and what their strategies are -- from a disclosure, growth, and operational perspective. The firm must understand the stated outlook of its peers, as well as the markets they operate in, their competitive advantages, threats and risks.

In the green binder, classify all content into four categories: guidance, risks, opportunities and growth strategies.

Bing It

After combing through the prospectus and analyst reports, source and analyze as much data as possible about the firm's industry and its peers. Use as many sources as possible, such as subscriber-only databases such as Nexus-Lexis, Bloomberg, and Highbeam.

Now, even small investors seek ideas and perspective about the IPO pipeline from active portfolio managers and research analysts contributing to websites such as SeekingAlpha.com, IPOhome.com, finance.Google.com, investors.Yahoo.com, and the trader's favorite, StockTwits.com (a site that substitutes the familiar hashtag (#) with a dollar sign e.g., $AAPL instead of #AAPL).

A good place to start online research is by visiting finance.Google.com. Google has done an excellent job of providing the retail investor with real-time data, discussion groups and stocks that until recently was only available to professionals or those with an online brokerage account. Make a list of all companies in the firm's industry and download as much information as you can about each peer, including any press releases, transcripts, presentations and articles. You should also visit Edgar.SEC.gov (or SEDAR.com in Canada) to download any regulatory filings over the prior two years.

Ask your analyst to provide you with the research reports on all peers if the firm does not have direct access to them.

Marketers should count on the fact that savvy investors will dig up all available information about a pre-IPO firm and its top managers through their access to massive proprietary news databases, peer group analyst reports and specialized websites and social media sources that provide insight into the firm's business. In some cases investors also have access to former employees, competitors and vendors and will not hesitate to look to them for information.

It is worthwhile to visit the message boards on finance.Google.com and biz.yahoo.com to learn what the investment community is saying about the firm and related stocks. Much of the content is speculative nonsense, but there may be some valuable perspectives, including the identities of active contributors.

Twitter is another source to find information on IPOs and stocks. Twitter is the fastest, cheapest source for real-time information about stocks and rumors. Twitter has a large community of traders who share information and opinions around the clock. Many financial reporters use Twitter to send out breaking news and links to primary sources. Most of the users are mature professionals so it is largely free of spam and riffraff seen on message boards. You can 'follow' or 'unfollow' as many users at any time which is a key feature of the Twitter application. Visit StockTwits.com or download Tweetdeck to perform searches on a stock, specific subject or other users who are interested in relevant topics.

The marketer will only be well informed about the best possible competitive positioning by conducting a thorough and complete review of every available piece of information on the firm's peers.

If one clear positioning does not exist, write down two or three possibilities. There are likely only a few themes essential to achieving your desired positioning. By combining a select few themes, you will create powerful concepts that are easier to understand than a myriad of individual facts.

These concepts will be central to establishing substantive differentiation that is necessary to a legitimate valuation.

You should now have three perspectives based on the same set of questions: one view gleaned directly from the prospectus, another from the bankers and management team, and the third from analyst reports and online sources.

Developing the Messaging Architecture

At this stage, three binders of material are available. This is enough context and material to enrich the primary material from the prospectus. Now it is time to synthesize the facts, commentary and opinion.

Binder by binder, topic by topic, aggregate the content from the prospectus, interviews and peer group research into each of the four subsections. Keep the content from each binder in its own color until the final stage.

There will be disparities -- some will be large but inconsequential -- while others will be too glaring to ignore. Make a note of significant areas of contrast as investors will also note similar disconnects.

Remember, you can't use anything that isn't published in the prospectus, so classify any strengths, growth strategies, opportunities and threats that aren't in the S-1 under a new heading such as "vestiges".

You now have a master document divided into five main sections: strengths, growth strategies, opportunities, threats, and vestiges. All content (aside from vestiges) is derived from information that was sourced legitimately through hard facts, opinions, war stories, speculation or conjecture. The content of the fifth section titled vestiges will either be absorbed into one of the four primary categories or dismissed.

Organizing the Universe of Content

This content will be extremely useful when it is time to write the IPO presentation. But for now, each of the four areas must be prioritized and ranked in order of importance. Use whatever scale suits you to order items from the most to the least important (e.g. 1-5 or A-Z). Prioritize content that relates to financial performance, market opportunities, and revenue generation.

Similarly, rank content that is aligned with the banker's interviews higher than other data. Threats that are widely recognized as dangerous would rank above others in the 'threats' category.

This broad collection of information must be shaped into a sharp, one page document: the key marketing fundamentals of the IPO. Hone each section until it can no longer be tightened. Remove superfluous words, duplication, and unnecessary complexity. Simplify things as much as possible without losing any of the intended meaning. Spend as much time as it takes to get it right.

You should now have a document that has triple-filtered the marketing language by category. You've identified every useful strength, growth strategy, opportunity and threat supported by layers of facts and context so they can be presented as concisely as possible. There will always be outstanding issues not directly addressed in the prospectus, but these topics should still be raised nonetheless.

The document and its history of revisions provide an auditable trail of topical breadcrumbs leading to how and why certain decisions were made.

Circulate the messaging architecture document to management and the bankers and schedule a conference call to discuss its contents. Your goal is to use the same group that contributed to the document to gain consensus about the precise order while refining the language of each message.

Relationships and patterns should emerge from different classifications. For example, material that appears under "strengths" will relate to certain "threats".

To clarify what may appear to be overly theoretical, imagine that your company is the leading provider of round widgets by revenue, because you have a new patent on its design. For the last year, you have commenced sales in three countries that exhibit clear signs of steadily growing demand.

Using this as an example, you might write under strengths: "The leading producer of round widgets in attractive markets" and then list all of the many facts that support this statement. List the qualities or characteristics of financial performance, operations, capacity, and patents that protect your widget.

Now, play Devil's Advocate. Hash out what arguments could be used to poke holes in "the leading producer of round widgets in attractive markets". What could an investor take issue with, which would render the claim useless because of its apparent lack of credibility?

Investors hone in on statements that contain words like "leading" and "attractive". Are you really leading or one of the leading? If you are really "the leader" because no one else sells an alternative, then be prepared to clarify that through supporting facts. Cognitive research indicates that people need time to process information and even more time if they are unclear or have questions about the reliability of information. The upshot of this is that the next point you make will probably be lost if investors are silently pondering "are they really the leader?" while you continue to speak.

Similarly, ask exactly why the markets are "attractive"? Why are they fast-growing? Are they really that profitable? Are the barriers to entry very high?

Prove beyond any doubt that every major strength put forward is unassailable and incorporates opposing points of view as they relate to risk and credibility. You have to assume investors are going to uncover every major threat or already know of them. Maintaining a contrarian mindset is good practice if only because you may not be aware of information that an investor knows about a competitor. Private equity investors often own or have owned a similar business and may have unique insight through their access to private data about that portfolio company.

Overly confident statements that push the line a little too far can have serious consequences. With a highly structured story that relies on messaging to support an overarching positioning, things can fall apart if one of the logical steps is removed. Consider the theoretical case of a well-known competitor that announces plans to compete against you while you are on the Roadshow. Not only is this dirty pool, but the competition is introducing a new, lower cost triangular widget that functions the same as your round widget but is useful in more applications. This fictitious example demonstrates the need to identify any information that could be used to unravel your messaging and the valuation you are seeking to establish.

The story of Zillow suing Trulia during its Roadshow isn't fiction. In September 2012, already public Zillow sued its competitor Trulia while Trulia was on its Roadshow. Citing patent infringement, Zillow filed a lawsuit one week before Trulia priced its offering. At the same time, Zillow also completed a secondary offering that was twice the size of its own 2011

IPO -- a strategy clearly designed to mop up investor capital and reduce the appetite for new shares in Trulia, a direct competitor.

As you continue to refine your story and tighten the components (the strengths, threats, growth strategies and opportunities) the messaging architecture will gradually take shape as more information flows in from the working group as they continue to review the document.

Returning to the widget example, perhaps someone on the board directors knows that the competitor is working on the better widget but it has yet to be commercialized which could take at least twelve months. Then the question becomes: how long will the competitor's widget take to come to market, best and worst case? Is there time or any way to prevent the adoption of the alternative design? Are there any facts or information that can assuage concerns in the minds of investors? Perhaps the round widget patent is ambiguous enough to tie up any alternative design in court for years. You'll need to consult the lawyers to find out if legal action is a viable option and include the determination and its impact in your messaging and prospectus.

Facebook had a legal overhang with respect to who rightfully owned the patent covering its software. The dispute delayed the IPO until it participated in the approval of a feature film that essentially put the matter behind them in the court of popular opinion.[1]

Using the over-simplified widget example, you can identify language and concepts related between your strengths and threats. Since your competitor has no official product announced yet, avoid mentioning it specifically. But you should make a point of saying if new competition should enter the market, you are well defended for sound reasons over a precise and identified period of time.

The key is to gain as much context and argumentative support around the four areas that shape the IPO story.

Valuation Risks

The primary set of risks to every firm going public are those related to valuation. Assigning a value to the company's shares is often the motivation for pursuing an IPO in the first place. Management teams at private companies see their publicly-traded competitors trading within a price band and often believe they deserve similar valuations.

The peer group's price band provides the first frame of reference for valuing IPO shares. Discussions with investment banks ahead of an IPO often begin with ("we are worth more than this firm because..."). Since comparable publicly-traded peers trade at valuations based on historical information that are absolute and quantifiable, the process of valuing a new, unknown business going public introduces the academic but important concept of a "risk premium". This premium represents what investors are willing to pay for IPO shares when an identical alternative already trades.

The risk premium introduces two important concepts. First, drawing a comparison -- or at least making a connection -- to publicly-traded peers by invoking similarities of market size, position in the cycle or growth opportunities between the two firms is highly advantageous. Second, the degree to which management chooses to be aggressive or conservative with its growth targets and implied multiples of valuation will alter the risk premium investors are willing to pay.

The risk premium is calculated by discounting key metrics related to future financial performance. To alleviate the natural tendency to discount unknown and unproven firms, marketers must make a strong case that long-term cash flows are sustainable and that they can successfully execute their growth strategies. It is vitally important to demonstrate that permanent revenue streams are not transitory. Private companies in fast-moving industries or with short operating histories or significant intangible assets present additional risks to investors.[2]

Should investors understand and agree with logic behind an IPO's price and its market capitalization, that's good news. But should they disagree with the valuation methodology or the discount that has been applied to sources of future revenue, the result is likely to be an IPO that prices at a larger discount than expected. In these cases, many managers wish they had ratcheted down initial expectations by setting a lower price and then closing the transaction in or above the range. So setting the initial price range ("the offering terms") is crucial. In the first few months of trading it is better to be build on a lower price than trying to get back to black because the shares have fallen below the IPO price.[3]

A systematically-composed messaging architecture should withstand considerable scrutiny and critique without the entire structure falling apart. Because of the risk premium applied to new companies, complete transparency is not possible. Ensuring that those most familiar with the finer details of the business are engaged in the messaging process early will reduce uncertainty about risk and strengthen management's credibility.

Legitimize Valuation

The primary objective of any IPO marketing effort is to establish a plausible level of valuation for the firm. To accomplish this, marketers must be familiar with popular valuation methods so they can calculate the firm's objective value and determine what multiples might be helpful to achieve the desired price target.

The first step is to list the comparable multiples of peers (e.g. revenue versus share price, earnings versus share price, cash flow versus share price) and analyze each metric to find weaknesses or opportunities. For example, on what basis are peer group firms most often valued? What are the key issues central to each competitor's valuation and how did they overcome them? Rank the firm's performance based on this publicly-known data as it relates to each metric. Think about how the presentation of non-GAAP financial data and operating metrics might be useful for reconciling certain discrepancies.

Intangible assets can be a contentious issue because the values ascribed to such assets are subjective. Are they "marked-to-market"? If so, what is the accounting methodology used? If assets are not marked to market, be sure to rationalize why they are not. Cite specific quantifiable facts and qualitative information relevant to both sides of the argument as it pertains to valuation. Whenever possible, include examples from publicly-available sources to bolster credibility. Investors weigh data that has already been established more heavily than an opinion offered by a management team trying to execute an IPO. See chapter nineteen for more discussion on valuation.

Assumptions

Investors are sensitive to how the assumptions used in the non-GAAP treatment of financials, growth estimates and other guidance targets. Even though assumptions play an important role in how growth strategies, strengths, opportunities and threats are articulated, be overly cautious and conservative when working with assumptions.

First, all assumptions must be legitimately sourced and appear in the S-1. To the trained eye, forecasts related to rates such as GDP growth, compound annual sales growth, margin expansion, churn, adoption, customer acquisition costs, and return on invested equity can be met with a high degree of skepticism. If a particular number or strategy is based on an assumption that doesn't feel right to an investor, it is not worth the risk to include it unless it is adequately explained. An investor will not only discard the proposition but will also question your credibility, creating a larger problem.

Inexperienced CFOs may see the firm's base-case valuation scenario disintegrate because a variable factored into the firm's valuation was discredited. If just one investor is successful at challenging a base assumption, so will many others.

For this reason it is imperative that any third-party facts, research or forecasts in your S-1 be sourced from well recognized names in your industry. Organizations such as Forrester Research, McKinsey & Co., national trade organizations and non-profit research groups are much preferred to names that are not recognized or, worse, known as companies who publish pay-for-play data. But even these sources are preferable to management's own estimates.

As the success of equity IPOs are largely predicated on growth prospects, utilizing sources that are easily challenged will increase the risk premium. Investors usually have access to top-tier research and proprietary benchmarks on every industry so carefully consider how any prospective differences can be reconciled before incorporating semi-reliable data in key assumptions.

Chapter Five

Roadshow Marketing Elements

A Roadshow is a series of back-to-back meetings that are designed to stimulate a favorable impression with investors. Everything is fair game when it comes to positively influencing perceptions, but adjustments can be difficult to make once the Roadshow begins.

On the day before the Roadshow, color presentation books are approved and printed and the team is videotaped for an internet broadcast that is available for the duration of the Roadshow. Any changes regarding the content and graphics of the investor presentation are no longer allowed. But other materials -- such as creating the 'right' atmosphere at a large group meeting in New York or London -- still present opportunities to instill the right message.

The range of marketing elements is often limited on smaller transactions (<$200 million) to presentation design, video production and prospectus graphics. Large transactions (>$500 million) tend to stand out because limitless marketing budgets permit a much broader range of creative possibilities, such as custom meeting environments and branded staging. Regardless of the size of new issue, most transactions would benefit from additional marketing spend as the first impression made with investors is crucial and will be an opportunity lost if not intentionally seized.

The Investor Presentation

A surprising number of IPO presentations look the same. They use identical typefaces (arial) and other stylistic conventions such as identical large blue arrows and bar graph styles.

The result is numerous "look-alike" presentation decks from IPOs led by other banks that safely assume the format is a winner through its legibility. The rule of thumb for one-on-one presentations is that only footnotes should require the reader to squint. At group meetings (which use plasma-type displays or projection onto a screen) it is imperative that people sitting at the back of the room be able to read every word on the slide, with the exception of footnotes.

Carefully consider the use of graphics and images in the IPO presentation, S-1 filing or new investor relations (IR) section of the firm's website.

Looking like other transactions in the market is a reasonable approach. Make a decision about the firm's creative direction -- the content and images that will appear on the firm's new website (including the use of management portraits and product images) -- six to eight weeks before marketing begins.

Generally the bankers like to 'own' the master presentation file but will release it so that graphics can be added. Don't bother adding a fancy Photoshop background too early in the process -- work with black and white text for as long as possible.

Until the working group is comfortable with the content, continue to edit the file using black text over a white background. This will save hours of time and will decrease the frustration of lawyers and others who want to mark up the file manually. A design proof consisting of a few sample slides included in the appendix is enough to make everyone comfortable with the process.

Attaching an alternate color version that shows the graphic look and feel of the presentation can also be very helpful as deadlines are likely to change.

It is common for investor presentations to be revised dozens of times, so managing the change process by including time and date stamps is critical. Appending *"final_final_for_sure_Final_IPO.ppt"* is not a disciplined approach when it comes time to track down changes that were missed in the "official" final file. Instead, try an ISO-friendly numbering system ("Project_Daylight_rev056_13_sep_2013_001.ppt").

It is important to clarify who is responsible for producing the PowerPoint presentations used by investors two weeks before the Roadshow starts. It is not unusual for an investor presentation to go through a major transformation during working group sessions, so make sure a PowerPoint expert is available at these meetings.

Although it is customary for the lead banker or roadshow coordinator to ensure that an adequate supply of prospectuses and flip-books are available in each city at each meeting, the experienced marketer makes arrangements in case Plan B is required.

It is a very good idea to print a box of fifty color books that are pre-shipped to each continent addressed to a hotel where management is sure to stay. An even better solution is to determine the tail number of the private jet that will be used for each leg of the Roadshow and arrange to have an emergency stash of books and prospectuses stored in the cargo hold. Ensure the investment banking analyst and all members of the speaker team are aware that this stash exists as it should removed from the plane and transfered to the trunk of a car every time the team lands in a new city. The materials aren't very useful in the back of a plane if the team finds itself short of flip-books.

Speaker's Notes

Each member of the speaker team should hold one or more personal copies of speaker's notes for use during the one-on-ones. These notes should be bound into each executive's one-on-one presentation (also known as the "flip book" or "color book") so that the notes accompany the presentation.

The Formal Speech

Each member of the speaker team should refer to a typewritten script available to read from during the large and small group meeting presentations. These speeches must be formatted to reflect the preferences of each presenter. Font size and style, line spacing, page breaks, method of emphasis (e.g. passages distinguished by bold, all caps, double underline or larger bold type with an underline) will vary according to individual tastes, as will any handwritten notations that management wants to include in the flip-books and speeches.

Introductory Video

Some firms believe that producing a corporate video that plays prior to the final presentation will help sell the transaction. This is rarely the case, so don't bother with a video unless there is something to say that you can't say yourself (e.g. a key executive cannot attend the Roadshow or there is a serious issue -- such as a bankruptcy -- to confront). Familiarity with the firm's television advertising or other media can also be a sensible reason to create a short video. Familiarity ranks second only to pleasantness in recall performance.[1]

Many years ago corporate videos were a popular approach, but the practice has waned considerably. Investors view most videos as a waste of time. Rather than resort to a corporate video, they believe it is management's responsibility to articulate the strengths of the firm. For firms that believe a video is helpful, the content should reflect the investment highlights and be less than two minutes in duration. It must convey the strength of the management team and its experience, and the size of the firm's opportunity.

Incorporating video within the presentation is a different matter altogether. Embedding video is an effective way to demonstrate something that would take much longer or might be incomplete if only static graphics or speech were used. Zeltiq Aesthetics used video to reveal how their 'coolsculpting' anatomical tailoring works during their 2011 IPO.

The Meeting Environment

Investor meetings vary only by size, audience type and the ability to access the meeting venue itself. Gaining access to a location before the scheduled meeting time is a key feature when considering technical equipment or branded elements aimed at enhancing the meeting experience. Anything not already in the room must be loaded in, set up and tested.

Management teams should use a prudent level of visual support (PowerPoint slides and "scenery"), aural reinforcement (tone and cadence) and visceral awareness (the presenter) to connect the presenter with listeners. Features of the experiential environment (ambiance, variety, palette) may also establish credibility and promote retention or recall.

"Walk-in" content such as a logo animation or music that plays as investors mill around the registration area prior to taking a seat in the meeting room can be an effective way to frame certain issues or familiarize the audience with key messages. The use of anecdotal, graphic or aural material can also strengthen the impact of the story.

Figure 7: Make use of unused space as an opportunity to convey messages

Design and produce physical objects and other sensory stimuli to reflect the firm's brand and key messages at both the small and large group investor meetings. Determining what elements are to be produced ahead of the meeting schedule will enhance the meeting environment so that investors are assured a pleasurable experience. Many ideas and executions will not be possible due to the ever-changing nature of Roadshow schedules; exact dates and venue locations change constantly, and are often not known until a week (or less) before the actual event. For this reason it is prudent to produce standard sized sets and other components that will fit into almost any venue.

To get a better perspective of what is practical to produce, refer to chapter sixteen.

Chapter Six

The IPO Marketing Plan

Every IPO must overcome at least one marketing challenge: the "liability of newness". Since 1965, scholars have recognized that the legitimacy of an organization is correlated with its age.[1] As soon-to-be public companies have yet to demonstrate their true value in the capital markets, firms turn to the only viable solution when fundamental changes to the business are not an option: marketing.

Marketing is the only way an IPO can achieve its maximum valuation. Marketing is the primary generator of information and ideas that surround a securities transaction -- before, during and after the new listing is achieved. At its most effective, marketing solves difficult problems associated with the perception of risk and reward. To achieve these goals, it creates criteria that would otherwise not be measured or considered if the marketing effort had not occurred.

Effective marketing consists of three ingredients. First, a sound knowledge of the investor audience; second, the ability to clearly put forward one main idea; and three, the ability to apply strategic messages over time. Psychological messaging techniques commonly referred to as "priming" or "framing" are often used to make the most creative production and experiential strategies. Taken together, marketing strategy and execution exploit the opportunities that exist to solidly position a firm during its capital raising Roadshow.

The marketing of an IPO is only as good as the strategy that drives it. Strategy dictates the form and function the marketing is expected provides. It defines what signals are required and when. It also defines the rate and volume of information flow between the firm and the outside world. Strategy will dictate if some messages are repeated while others are completely restricted. The best marketing is invisible, completely transparent to most investors.

Gift Wrap

In a sense, IPO marketing is like a layer of gift wrap around a common corrugated box of historical information. Firms must package and present all knowledge related to the firm's history of operations, financial results, and management team in a way that is known to be attractive to investors.

Strategy defines the color, thickness, transparency and other qualities of the wrapping paper, or in this case, the story. But that's not all. Marketing also determines the box the information comes in. As some children learn at an early age, big boxes are more likely to conceal a low value item than what they communicate at first sight.

Marketing strategy must be carefully considered because once the Roadshow starts, the clock stops. There is no more time to produce or create much of anything. All materials to be used at the Roadshow meetings (e.g. signage, name tags, table tents) must have already been produced before the first meeting in the schedule occurs.

For example, at large group meetings management is seated at a "head table", facing the audience. This table is three feet in front of an overhead projection screen where the slides are displayed to the audience. A professional technique that works well is to apply graphics to the front of the head table (usually a logo or tagline). This requires something known as a "surround" to be built, which consists of three pieces of painted wood or other substrate that wrap around the front and sides of a standard hotel table (six foot), a size used by hotels around the world.

Figure 8: Graphics on the Head Table Maximize Messaging Opportunities.

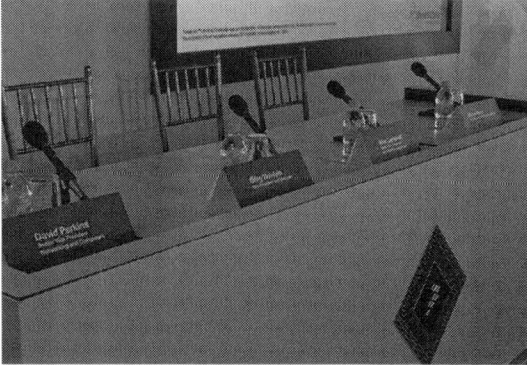

The surround must be painted before it is crated and shipped to wherever the meeting is being held. Once on site, components of the set require assembly (usually) by union carpenters. The entire process takes about a week or two, depending on how long it takes for everyone to agree on what artwork should appear on the front of the desk. The complexities and large size of many working groups can delay decisions related to producing artwork for many weeks or months, so it is best to start the creative process early. This way there will be enough time to ensure professional components are created to convey a high quality meeting environment, as these items are not available from the local inventory of any hotel.

To ensure the availability and proper installation of any special items such as colored linens or seat covers, the marketer must coordinate with the hotel or have the items produced by an external supplier.

Certain IPOs are successful for the same reason that certain consumer products are successful: they clearly differentiate themselves from the competition. We know that price, position, promotion and packaging work together to stimulate a consumer's buying decision at the grocery store. Similar forces also exist in the capital markets. Whether the buyer chooses to buy again after the initial trial depends on how agreeable the experience was and if the product met expectations.

While the vast majority of retail investors are satisfied with superficial qualities, institutional investors are not. Institutional investors want to know what is inside an IPO -- whether it has the right ingredients to surpass alternatives offered by better-known brands. The IPO scholar Jay Ritter modeled almost 7,600 IPOs adjusting for "market style" -- a method that calculates the three-year return based on the difference between an IPO and a style-matched firm -- and determined that returns generated by style-matched firms was 8.9% better between 2001-2011.

More markedly, in the 1999-2001 "bubble" era, investing in an already-listed public company with the same financial characteristics (book value) would have returned 58.9% more than subscribing to the IPO and holding it for three years.[2]

Marketing is largely responsible for setting expectations with investors in a market where so many alternatives already exist. But once the firm's stock starts to trade, management must deliver on its promises or face the consequences.

To set initial expectations, marketers count on the power of first impressions. First impressions are a very effective means to establish an image consistent with the IPO's valuation or proposed price. This is done by elevating the brand and providing clear proof of the attractive benefits -- the investment highlights -- when investors experience the brand for the first time.

But not everyone takes what the firm says in its marketing at face value. To determine what is true and what is window-dressing, investors try to "reduce information asymmetry". This is an academic term to describe how investors seek to become as knowledgeable as management about certain critical topics.

Investors that make the correct bet after meeting management face-to-face during the Roadshow stand to either make a lot of money or avoid losing a lot of money. Before the meeting occurs, some investors will have well-informed opinions about the IPO firm: its industry, competitive position, financial performance and management team. A reasonable snapshot is available through blogs, investor-only websites and sources of paid content (such as Bloomberg). But genuine insight can only be confidently gained through private one-on-one meetings with the firm's top executives during the Roadshow.

To investors, an IPO firm is relatively unknown and opaque. After a sixty-minute meeting, all must be adequately transparent.

The Communications Plan

To determine what aspects of the firm are emphasized, be certain that the communications plan consists of a healthy mix of good growth prospects, credibility enhancers, and defense tactics.

The marketing plan should detail who is responsible for the writing and design of the various elements that come into play over the three phases (pre-marketing, quiet period and post-IPO). Over the schedule, key themes should emerge. Driven by just one or two dominant messages, emphasize those aspects of the firm that are most likely to fuel growth, profit, and improved competitive positioning.

IPO Project Management Activities

Pre-Marketing

Research

Write the investment highlights

Develop messaging architecture

Crisis public relations planning

Develop media contacts database

Media monitoring and registration with popular investor websites

Develop investor section on company website

Speeches at industry events

Quiet Period

Create investor presentation

Determine the "look and feel" of the firm's marketing materials

Produce graphics for S-1 and meeting materials

Provide coaching for Q&A and presentation skills

Finalize speeches and speaker's notes

Achieve readiness

Roadshow Execution

Management travels to dozens of cities to meet investors

Audio-visual production

Branding at large group meetings

Organize Q1 conference call

Post-IPO/Declared Effective

Official pricing announcement

Ring Bell/Attend listing ceremony at NYSE or Nasdaq

"Go Live" with the new 'Investor' Section of the Firm's Website

Announce date of first quarterly earnings call

Issue official guidance

Release ongoing news

Communication Objectives

A typical communications plan for an IPO that reduces asymmetry and engages investors includes the following objectives:

1. Act like a public company by talking like one:

i) Maintain an investor mindset.

ii) Provide concrete proof that the firm is likely to be worth more in future quarters than it is now.

iii) Establish a consistent pattern and style of disclosure.

iv) Focus on the most important products or markets.

v) Frame important issues and threats. Discuss them openly.

2. Maximize valuation:

The primary objective of many firms is to raise the most capital possible during the IPO. Since the value of a given firm going public company usually hinges on one or two central issues, firms must provide concrete evidence related to the numerous components integral to valuing assets, future cash flows, and other metrics. An effective media strategy identifies the components early and seeks to influence opinion by establishing frames of reference and opinions with a broad audience about certain metrics.

For example,

"The microblogging service [Twitter] was valued last month at about $10.5 billion by GSV Capital Corp."[3]

The fact that the average investor has never heard of GSV Capital is irrelevant. What is relevant is that a $10.5 billion valuation has been established in a nationally syndicated news piece before Twitter's initial IPO filing. The anchor has been set.

Widespread acknowledgment and adoption of facts and opinions related to valuation substantially ease the necessity to persuade investors, because an important segment -- the retail investor -- already believes the data is true. This approach is much preferable to dealing with a contentious issue that is difficult to argue within the limited time constraints of an investor meeting.

3. Instill confidence.

Higher confidence translates to a lower perception of risk. As an investor processes more information, the stock price becomes more informative and the remaining uncertainty is lower.[4]

Instilling confidence in the firm's ability to generate permanent levels of future cash flow is always a responsible communications strategy.

To cut through, firms need to communicate signals clearly, frequently, and consistently. Set realistic expectations with investors.

During one-on-one meetings, certain firms clearly stand out among others also parading before investors. Language, posture, attitude, and personal style of the speaker team are all subjective attributes not found in any prospectus, but these qualities could override objective investment criteria.

The Strategic Brief

Once the universe of peer group and company information has been compiled, the IPO communication strategy document is the next task to complete. It need not be long; two pages will be enough to identify the key messages, arguments to major objections, communication tactics, and timing of activities. These elements aim to successfully position the IPO, achieve objectives and identify solutions to anticipated challenges.

Over three distinct phases, the communications strategy should outline all activities related to PR (public relations), social media (*Twitter*, investor websites and blogs), IR (investor relations), advertising and event branding. Planning ahead is necessary to neutralize future challenges with a plan that does not antagonize regulators during the quiet period (phase two).

There are two primary types of strategy: the prospector and the defender. Defenders perceive a stable and certain environment and thus seek stability and control in their operations in order to achieve maximum efficiency. Defenders have narrow product/market domains and defend them aggressively. In one study of NASDAQ biotechnology IPOs, the consistent communications of a defender strategy positively impacted thirty day initial returns.[5]

How aggressively firms use marketing to drive share purchases will impact the discount investors apply to the new company. It can be a delicate balancing act between gaining enough visibility to stimulate interest but not enough to trigger the feeling that the firm is hyping the stock ahead of its IPO. For this reason, use a broad base of communication mediums with varied content and messages specific to each. A poorly executed marketing program may leave a bad taste in the mouth of the investment community which will likely prompt a public thrashing that can be difficult to recover from. This is why a finance-oriented approach to communications is sensible as concrete and specific numbers provide an objective degree of comfort.

Communication Issues

Because much about the IPO firm is unknown, investors are at the mercy of only two documents: the S-1 document and management's IPO presentation. Only large or influential institutional investors participate in face-to-face Q&A, a critical third informational component not available to retail investors.

Astute investors will track amendments to the S-1 filed with the SEC to understand what content was changed and to divine the reasons for the change. Tracking these changes can be very illuminating, but is not possible through confidential filings under the JOBS act.

Because some investors conduct comprehensive pre-Roadshow research prior to attending a one-on-one meeting, it is in the best interests of the marketer to determine what information is publicly available about the firm, and what opinions exist. This is similar to the 'discovery' process lawyers conduct before trial. Should uninformed opinions surface that are based on limited data, it is important to know their source.

Once a firm files to go public, internet searches on the firm will skyrocket. According to the popular media website Mashable, Twitter's IPO filing was viewed 15,293 times while Facebook's IPO filing was viewed only 1,027 times. Whether or not this is accurate is irrelevant; what is relevant is that Mashable users appear to be more interested in Twitter's IPO than Facebook's 2012 IPO. As this example demonstrates, Bloggers are opinion makers that can shape important aspects of demand by drawing inferences that may not be fair.

Knowing what -- and who -- is out there before the S-1 is filed enables the IPO marketer to coordinate a defense. Consider defense before offense, as it often protects the firm while advancing communications objectives at the same time.

Conducting the Communications Audit

An audit consists of gathering all publicly-available information that exists about the firm. This includes any mentions in the news, websites, social media properties (*Twitter, Facebook, Pinterest, Tumblr*); biographies or quotes from the management team; and descriptions of any public-facing activities that involve the company.

Simply cut and paste every single mention of the company into a document and footnote the URL or source of the content. Be certain to review analyst research reports covering the firm's peers, as distinct and credible perspectives will emerge.

The first page of the audit document should summarize the findings of the data and cite specific references to support any claims made. At times, the findings may be controversial and disagreeable to the CEO. For example, if the message boards on Yahoo and a couple of other investor websites were openly critical of management's lack of experience, this would be a cause for concern for the marketer. In such cases, it is prudent for the marketer (who is also the messenger) to take her findings to the CEO personally and say "I know this may not be a big deal but it's out there. I know it has no merit because of the retail nature of the site where it appears, but I wanted to bring it to your attention because it exists and it's my job to warn you about risks like this. I think a good way to deal with this is to have you speak at an industry conference so we can get your updated biography out there and re-visit the content on our website about you and the rest of the executive team."

Risk and the Liability of "Newness"

Every IPO communications strategy must consider factors related to risk. It is widely accepted that the aversion to loss strongly favors the avoidance of risks, by as much as two and a half times that of the pursuit of gains.[6]

The two primary features of every IPO are "newness" and "risk": the quantitative and qualitative aspects of each must be carefully considered.

Investors no longer evaluate risk in terms of a company's underlying fundamentals, but have augmented their assessment with a behavioral approach to better understand sentiment risk.[7] New risk-based portfolio management approaches have been instituted across the industry in an effort to minimize losses over discrete time periods.

Investors will search for comparables to better understand the unknowns that will be comprised of risks and uncertainties. Risk can be measured, uncertainty not.

In an attempt to reduce the uncertainty around new companies and management teams, investors and the financial media feed each other information (e.g. "...one fund manager attending the Roadshow said..." or "...Scott Sweet of IPO Boutique said..."). The ensuing dialog usually reveals one or two critical issues.

Perhaps the most difficult issue to tackle relates to the true valuation of the firm: "is it really worth a $10 billion market cap?" Another popular issue relates to the firm's expected future performance relative to better-known peers. A far less troublesome problem is the apparent outrage of the CEO's instant wealth due to the IPO. Fortunately, there are many examples of even more prosperous CEOs to tie back to.

But if an accounting debacle or apparent flaw in the business model is documented in the media, perceptions can be irrevocably altered. The only thing investors really trust is audited numbers, and if the firm is perceived as engineering their numbers, investors will take notice and conclude that the proverbial wool is being pulled over their collective eyes. For this reason, firms should work back to front when thinking about communications strategy: start with the financial statements first and end with financial targets.[8]

The size of the gap between the financial statements and the firm's performance targets ("guidance") will dictate the character, direction and force of the marketing.

To expand on these concepts one at a time, *character* relates to the marketing's 'personality type'. If the marketing could be expressed as a personality -- such as a celebrity, family member or some other character -- what label comes to mind?

For example, could the marketing be described as geeky or jocular? Conservative or renegade? Given these limited choices, geeky and conservative are much better alternatives. That is, unless you are a well-known consumer brand defined by your jocular or renegade qualities, such as Urban Outfitters. The decision is also predicated on the audience and its needs. If an institutional investor has to spend an hour listening to someone they are actually considering a multi-million dollar investment in, with whom would they be most comfortable?

The answer is that investors would prefer to invest in a manager they already know and trust; someone who has made them money before and who has the proven ability to run a public company. These are the most desirable characteristics to investors. But very few managers can pull off playing the trusted, already proven and profitable character because very few managers have yet to run a public company. In the absence of past profits, investors look to the future and other value-creating aspects such as management's past track record as they prepare to make a decision to invest in a new public company.

Marketing Personality Types

The marketing's personality is defined largely by the firm's creative direction and the force of content it wishes to emphasize. Five types of content are prevalent: financial messages, operating highlights, growth strategies, brand strength and management experience. The force of the marketing refers to how prevalent or noticeable each quality is. It can range from absent to understated to aggressive.

As in physics, there is also a time component underlying the marketing's personality. Messages and the force with which they are communicated change over time. Every transaction faces certain challenges (or threats), so it is prudent to recognize these threats early so that layers of messaging can be executed at various intervals.

An effective IPO marketing plan instills credibility, competitive differentiation and value. There are six individual objectives that are supported by a variety of strategies to achieve their purpose:

1. Establish management credibility

2. Arouse interest in the firm

3. Set a consistent pattern and tone of disclosures

4. Establish and defend valuation inputs

5. Establish the basis of growth expectations

6. Define boundaries of risk

Management dictates what investors will focus on through its PowerPoint presentation, but any transaction will benefit from clearly defining the boundaries of risk while maintaining a conservative posture about underlying growth assumptions.

Enhance Management's Credibility

One research study indicates that people rate the credibility rating of another person when they have seen a face more than once, even if the viewer does not remember seeing it.[9] Just one prior encounter is enough to increase credibility ratings, even after several weeks have passed since the initial impression. This points to the need for one basic requirement to be fulfilled: ensure that good pictures of the company's top managers are available on the firm's public-facing website, accompanied by detailed biographies.

Management biographies are essential to establishing a baseline of credibility. Information about board members is also a good idea. It is more efficient to include them below biographies of the firm's top executives. Solid corporate governance is viewed favorably, so emphasize executives with a background in finance or independent board members. Include evidence that each executive has the skills and experience necessary to lead the firm to the next -- and much more demanding -- level.

Another method to strengthen the visibility of management's experience is to create new opportunities and situations that feature management. For example, simply following the CEO around at a special event with a photographer and copywriter could result in useful material. Consider gathering historical footage, including clips of televised interviews and company meetings and make the content available on *YouTube* through *Twitter* or *Facebook* and other social media channels such as *Tumblr*, *Pinterest, Instagram, Mashable, Slideshare, PassFail.com* and *Scribd*.

If the firm maintains a blog, consider opening it up to the world or allowing access to Facebook or LinkedIn profiles on a read-only basis. This is not a solution for most firms, but affords a solid opportunity to make an impression.

Repetition is a powerful variable in effective communications, because it is not really a repetition effect but a recognition effect.[10] When combined with signals that are related to credibility (retained ownership and competitive dominance are but two), the results can be satisfactory.

Repetition rings truer than statements that are new. A contradiction rings falser than new statements. It is the appearance of contradiction, rather than the fact of contradiction, that predicted how people rate truth in some studies. Statements called "old" ring truer than "new" statements, even if the classifications are wrong (e.g. the statement called "old" was just called old, but was actually new).[11]

Timing of Disclosure

What is to be disclosed about the firm and how frequently? Many IPOs increase their disclosure ahead of the initial S-1 filing. Some firms go from zero press releases to one or more per month. Investors will notice the change and make assumptions about what the firm is trying to achieve. Research shows that issuing firms dramatically increase their disclosure activity, particularly for the categories of disclosure over which they have the most discretion.[12] A generous application of disclosure across different media will reduce the tendency to take such disclosures with a grain of salt. As already discussed, be mindful of message drift and contradiction.

Public companies that maintain a consistent level of disclosure tend to experience price increases before a secondary offering (not an IPO), and only minor price declines at the offering announcement. Those that substantially increase their disclosure activity in the six months before the offering also experience price increases prior to the offering but suffer much larger price declines at their announcement to issue equity. While the sudden disclosure increases may be interpreted as "hype", it is still successful in lowering the firm's cost of equity capital.[13]

Being in the spotlight introduces risks. One study concludes that visibility negatively influences reputations; the greater the scrutiny of the firm by the press, the worse its reputation.[14] Many new firms do not have the historical burden of significant historical information so are better positioned to make positive impressions.

Arouse Interest in the Firm

If the firm features one particular quality that a wider audience might find appealing for whatever reason, this is often enough to gain coverage with local media and industry-specific publications. A wildly successful recent IPO by a similar business is often enough to stimulate interest. As long as the horizon to filing is far enough away, a campaign to aggressively educate readers can be implemented. Provide a raft of details and photos of management in customer environments or foreign markets to validate the effort while providing online search results with relevant material. Winning new contracts with high-profile clients can make for a good pitch to a journalist if the end goal is to create jobs or promote a locally-developed technology.

If a new product introduction is planned, make sure the media is invited and guarantee interviews with top managers who are coached to consistently repeat key messages and facts about the company's strengths. Do not make forecasts and maintain a strong air of humility because the same journalists may be required under very different circumstances in the future (e.g. missed earnings forecast).

The firm's website should clearly dimension the size of its markets and the opportunities based on the needs of customers today and in the future.

Provide broad details about the firm's operating units and ensure the search capability is working properly so the site can be navigated quickly. Investors do not want to hunt down information so avoid making them click too many times to find what they need.

Articulate Growth Strategies

No one wants to give competitors an advantage by divulging company secrets but communicating the firm's aspirations in a way that makes employees and customers proud to be associated with the company satisfies all stakeholders, including investors.

Consider the use of "we said it, we did it" statements that prove management has a track record of executing its plans. Evidence that confirms a history of strategic performance is worth the effort.

Attend industry conferences and make the presentations publicly available. Investigate what conferences are planned in every market the firm operates in and highlight the ones that pertain to risk or financial management. Review the dates and purpose of each event and attempt to secure a slot so that management can present. Like a Roadshow, diligent preparation is paramount to success, so be sure to retain any outside help so the presenter is comfortable and performs well. Post a link to the event's external website and include the podcast, presentation or transcript of the event excluding any portions that could be misinterpreted.

Highlight important affiliations and alliances. Include any appropriate copyright text or get approval from related parties before "going live" and posting it for public consumption. Describe the partners with language devoid of embellishment; strategic relationships should not incorporate a promotional tone. There is a degree of risk attached to associating with external entities in case circumstances change, so it is prudent to downplay the importance and the firm's reliability (or survival) on key partnerships or customers.

The Three Most Important Signals

The term "signal" refers to information that is imbued with meaning known to be relevant to investors. Signals are especially important in areas defined by asymmetric information -- when management (or the investor) clearly knows more than the other party.[15] Another way to think about signals is that they are a valuable means to gain a better understanding of some aspect of the IPO business that management is much more familiar with than investors. High quality disclosure during an IPO requires as many as six convincing signals.[16]

Making things more interesting is that analysts and institutional investors regard signals differently when they think about the positioning of a given company. A 2002 research paper summarized the different signals that are most valued by analysts and institutional investors. Surprisingly, each group assigns entirely different values to the various signals.[17] As measured by both degree of importance and relative performance, what is important to one group is irrelevant or not important to the other.

Three signals emerge as the nexus between these two primary audiences: ratios, growth projections and management quality. Track record is excluded as a signal because the IPO firm has yet to establish one except in very rare cases. So the quality of management provides a sufficient proxy of the firm's quality for both investor and analyst audiences.

The same research also suggests institutional investors place the most value on signals related to ratios, transparency, nature of the firm's industry, growth track record, and the firm's own growth projections as indicators of high performance. The quality of management was cited as the most important requirement, but as a performance indicator it is less valuable than the signals previously referenced.

Analysts, on the other hand, indicated that the same signals used by institutional investors provide very little value as performance indicators. Instead, analysts focus on the relative importance of the signals themselves. Analysts indicated that signals related to strategy, growth track record, ratios, the company's own growth projections, and quality of management to be the most important requirements when determining the positioning of a firm.

Ratios

When formulating communications strategy, make note of exactly what ratios are most appropriate for the firm's industry and its target valuation. Work back the numbers as they factor into inputs towards calculating net asset value, enterprise value, price/book, book/market, or whatever valuation method is appropriate to get a feel for what metrics provide the most flexibility (or highest quality "levers") for future needs. Valuation is discussed in chapter nineteen.

For example, investors are interested in new equity issues that have a distinct competitive advantage in large and growing markets. The first question to ask is: exactly how large is the market opportunity? This is an essential measure to state immediately -- on the first or second slide. Does a credible reference point already exist in the prospectus? If not, this is a high priority item to acquire.

Before the quiet period, it is necessary to establish a legitimate dollar figure that sums up the firm's opportunity in markets where it currently operates or plans to enter in the foreseeable future. As we saw with the Facebook and Twitter IPOs, information related to market size and valuation can easily become an accepted statement of fact that the firm can exploit as a legitimate target enabled through its growth strategies.

Other metrics investors seek to understand relate to timing and capital investment. How long will it take to grow the current business to a very conservative (achievable) target level? How much capital and business development will be required so that management can look investors in the eye and say emphatically "this is a very solid, very conservative opportunity achievable with the proceeds from the IPO"?

To get a handle on these metrics, work the numbers back to understand what is realistic based on the current state of the firm, its historical sales and margin growth, capital expenditures and other metrics until the right balance is achieved between where the firm is currently, where it wants to be in the future and how long it will take to achieve conservative growth objectives.

Other Signals

Investors rely on other financial and non-financial signals that provide incremental information to predict the future success of an IPO. For example, the quality of management can be determined, in part, by the percentage of ownership they retain in the IPO after the firm goes public.

Research shows that investors place the highest value on the CEO's equity holdings post-IPO. The CEO's level of retained ownership sends the strongest signal to early stage investors seeking to legitimize valuation more than any other factor. Entrepreneurs who bring their firms into the public markets tend to maintain the pre-IPO performance of their firms.[18]

Similarly, the firm's corporate governance structure communicates valuable information. The number of independent board members translates to the degree of monitoring the firm is likely to receive, as does the composition and size of the audit committee and how often it meets.[19] To investors, these aspects of management quality determine the degree to which a firm is able to identify, control and mitigate risks.

Other qualitative characteristics related to management strength can be evaluated by assessing the firm's growth strategies and business potential. Are the firm's strategies for growth well articulated in large and well defined markets? Or are they positioned merely as growth opportunities with no tangible strategies? Investors require hard facts supported by precise numbers. Vague statements are heavily discounted.

Another signal relates to the amount of news coverage a firm has historically received. This is a sign of perceived future demand, an important consideration because demand directly influences liquidity following the IPO.

Quantitative Signals

Financial aspects of the firm also contain signals that are interpreted. The number of accruals (fewer is better), share of market, book to market calculation, cash flow and free cash flow per share contain clues about how fairly valued the firm is relative to others.

Other quantitative signals include the use of IPO proceeds. What percentage of the proceeds will be used for general & administrative purposes (G&A), one of the vaguest categories of expense? Or, are the proceeds earmarked for specific uses such as debt repayment, capital expenditures or research & development? Each of these categories can be interpreted in various ways but specificity is important.

Since investor signals are correlated, the marginal value of any of them drops with the number of signals aggregated.[20] However, investors consider the following criteria when making an IPO investment: overall business potential, composite quality of top management, and level of competition.[21] Investors are cautious of the claims associated with hyping an IPO, but are particularly responsive to valid signals of value.[22] Both retained ownership and pre-IPO capital and debt levels are linked to IPO valuation.[23] IPO marketing must reduce the risk premium. Those that are successful with establishing a new category -- a hybrid or blend of peer qualities -- can change the pricing range based on optimized multiples.

Aping the Attributes of Others

One study found that issuing firms conditionally structure their IPOs based on various features of recent offerings.[24] Since uncertainty causes buyers to discount valuations, high quality firms can benefit significantly *ex ante* by adopting attributes and activities that reduce quality uncertainty.[25] Initial return is one example of an *ex ante* uncertainty that is positively related.[26]

To illustrate, let's look the successful IPO of Zillow, an online real estate data portal. Fourteen months after Zillow went public, Trulia (TRLA:NASDAQ), a direct competitor to Zillow, also went public with a similar valuation and was able to attract similar success. Both of these transactions were widely deemed to be 'hits' because of the small number of shares floated, rather than the health of their businesses, as both firms were historically unprofitable.

But the average investor would have no way of knowing why these firms had such successful IPO launches, and may have instead been attracted to buy shares in the secondary market based on alternative explanations.

Brand Value

Brand value estimates are significantly associated with the value of the firm's equity securities in the capital markets.[27]

Brands are one of the most valuable intangible assets that a firm can possess. In the context of marketing an IPO, the process of managing an investors' entire experience with a soon-to-be listed firm is governed by experiential marketing. By creating an environment that is memorable, meaningful and has aesthetic appeal, brands can distinguish themselves from peers and command higher prices.[28]

Why Go Public Now?

Investors are always curious to know the answer to the question "why take the company public now?" This is because the answer reveals factors that relate to the timing of an offering, another important signal. The timing of a transaction can be driven by management incentives, the state of the market, the business itself, and the motivation for raising capital.

Some equity transactions are the result of a parent company "spinning" or "carving" out a division, business segment or operating unit. This type of IPO -- the carve out -- serves as a good example for illustrating the range of possible motivations and issues associated with the timing of taking a company public. In this scenario, the larger entity disposing of the asset seeks to raise capital by maximizing its stake in the business. Private equity firms and large corporation regularly spin out companies from their portfolios.

Examples include General Electric's carve out of Genworth Financial and Motorola's spin out of Freescale Semiconductor in 2004. Freescale was then taken private in a $16.7 Billion leveraged buyout in 2006, but returned to the capital markets again with a $4.6 billion IPO in May 2011 (FSL:NYSE). In April 2014, GE filed to spin off its insurance unit in a standalone IPO.

After these spin-offs were completed, both parent companies continued to reduce their ownership stakes while shares in the new publicly-traded entities climbed higher. By the time General Electric sold its final 10% stake in Genworth in 2006, the shares had risen 67%, contributing a very healthy return on equity for the former parent.

Distinct classes of IPOs have a significant impact on investor perceptions that must be realistically evaluated and addressed by the Roadshow marketing. With spin-outs, there are a multitude of questions: the current state of the industry cycle; health of the business and ability to generate superior returns as a stand-alone entity; management's ability to execute without support from the parent; the effects of retained ownership by the parent company (known as "overhang"); the firm's capital structure (debt levels, ratings quality); and likely receptiveness of a new brand unknown to consumers (e.g., Freescale was unknown before it was spun out of Motorola as it was simply an unbranded operating unit).

These are all relevant questions that weigh on the minds of investors when a parent company or private equity owner seeks to capitalize by selling all or part of its holdings through a new equity issue. The underlying questions relate primarily to calculating valuation (is the business worth more or less than before and why?) and management's strategy and ability to create shareholder value in capital markets where other larger, better-known competitors already operate.

The Investor Audience

The communications plan must recognize that two types of investors exist: the institutional investor and the retail investor.

The institutional investor is "the professional" with the ability to buy large blocks of stocks held in portfolios. Hedge funds, money managers, mutual funds and asset managers are all distinct classes of institutional investors. Typically, institutions are allocated the majority of shares purchased in an IPO. Low levels of institutional interest almost always translates to poor pricing and anemic trading volumes if and when the stock gets listed. Institutional investors look for an informational advantage over the party on the other side of the trade (e.g. the retail investor that will go "long" versus "short").

The retail investor is anyone who has a brokerage account; they may not be a licensed securities professional. A retail investor can be a private equity fund, a very wealthy individual or an out-of-work bus driver with an e-Trade account. Retail investors are also referred to as "sentiment investors" as they are more prone to sell at losses due to reasons related to fear and not the firm's fundamentals. This is why the behavior of retail investors is quite distinct from the trading behavior of institutional investors.[29] When good news hits about a stock, institutional investors buy 9.7% of the time while the retail investor buys 16% of the time. The pros are also able to short stocks while the average retail investor cannot.

Institutional investors are assumed to be "well-informed" as they can access high quality information immediately. They have a clear advantage over the individual who makes a decision based on second hand, manufactured news. The dynamic between these two investors is important during an IPO because the professional will expect to transfer risk (e.g. sell their IPO shares) to the amateur who is buying because Jim Cramer recommended the stock on television. The entire stock market operates on the concept that institutional investors will profit from the knowledge and restraints imposed on retail shareholders.

If institutional investors perceive that an IPO will be a "hot deal" with the average Joe, they are much more inclined to participate because the opportunity to sell their shares profitably is increased because of the built-in perception of demand. Retail investors don't usually use "limit orders" to buy shares; they just want to own them or sell the shares. This creates an opportunity for investment dealers that have a large retail base with an integrated trading operation.

Over the course of a trading day, share prices can fluctuate 10 or 20%. It's the institutional traders that will sell high after buying low during a trading day to the retail investor. This institutional-retail relationship is a well-established ecosystem that major buyers of IPOs count on.

The percentage of institutional to retail ownership has a major impact on market capitalization. Zillow is twice the size of Trulia even though their financial performance is identical. But Zillow's institutional ownership is 88% while Trulia's is only 39%.

Table 2: The Effect of Institutional Ownership on Market Capitalization

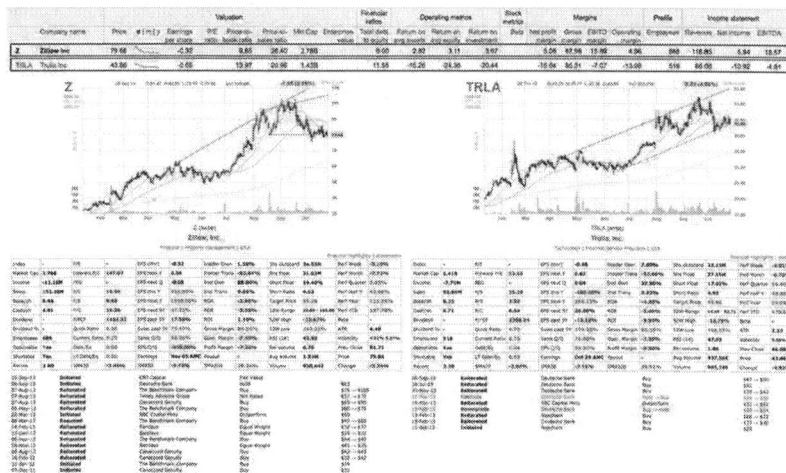

News Timing

Be definitive about communications strategy and decide what news can be generated before the first filing so it establishes a pattern of disclosure with institutional investors. The pros have tools to search databases of news, radio and TV coverage about any company and will extract every bit of publicly available information about an IPO in which they are interested.

Firms that want their IPOs to be successful must be certain to plan for ample news flow before, during and after the IPO starts to trade. Strategic partnerships, new ventures, new products, and other growth catalysts will be of interest to news outlets that are following the IPO and its progress. Although press releases with promotional language survive surprisingly well and are often picked up and quoted, use this approach with caution.[30]

Most news about IPOs is good -- 98% of the articles that appear about upcoming deals is positive.[31] The savvy marketer will plan a program of strategic announcements clustered around the IPO to get both investor types interested: the retail investor about the IPO and how wealthy they might become, and the institutional investor that gets excited about certain ratios and the fact that retail investors are excited.

Communication Channels

Social media has expanded the number of media channels. The emergence of internet-based outlets poses risks while offering opportunities never before available to marketers.

While favorable coverage in *The Wall Street Journal* still guarantees success for any IPO, several websites that cater specifically to traders and institutional investors offer marketers an attractive alternative to traditional media. Blogs and Twitter feeds are now often the source for news picked up by traditional media. It is the availability of so much free information -- from expert opinion and analysis to real-time commentary from hedge fund managers -- that make the monitoring of some websites a necessity for the IPO marketer.

Messages are dispersed through a variety of media over time. Like a pinball, they may bounce around hitting various websites while taking on various forms such as a rumor published on someone's blog, a tweet on *StockTwits.com*, or comment on an online article maintained by *Forbes* or other popular magazine.

During the Roadshow -- the "official" marketing period -- the investor presentation and meeting environments afford the greatest opportunity to instill messages with investors and influence opinion. Once the Roadshow begins, all amendments to the S-1 ("prospectus") have been submitted, reviewed and approved by the SEC. It is common for managers to be unknown or not particularly credible as they have been working at a private company. This is why marketers should tap other media channels to establish and subsequently solidify credibility ahead of the firm's first SEC filing.

Management teams that already possess a high level of credibility are off to a good start. Usually it is a prudent strategy to build confidence in the management team ahead of the S-1 filing through management interviews or opinion pieces in trade or financial publications. If management compensation is aligned with shareholders and others industry executives, credibility will be further bolstered.

Traditional News Outlets

Newspapers, industry periodicals, and television news programs represent most of the channels in what is known as "traditional" media. Creating and disseminating a press release that catches the attention of a journalist or editor is one way to access these channels. Speeches at industry conferences and events are other traditional venues a firm can consider to get messages out. More frequently, social media is a way to get the attention of mainstream journalists.

The Company's Website

The firm's own website is the first place investors expect to locate information about the firm. Although investors may discount the credibility of information because of its biased origin, it is still important to be clear and emphatic about the company's strengths and advantages. Include case studies, customer testimonials, employee stories, fact sheets and financial information that can be easily viewed and downloaded. The easier it is for investors to access information, the better. Monitor any website links contained in press releases to understand the source of the traffic accessing these sections.

Investor Sites

It takes time and advance planning to exploit the opportunities offered by the collection of online investor-focused sites. But the reward is worth it. By taking the time to register multiple identities on popular sites before a situation arises that demands attention, the awkwardness of posting as "a new member" is reduced. The ability to respond to another's anonymous posting that cites erroneous information about the IPO is enhanced considerably. Multiple identities (more than one account on a popular website) afford the opportunity to play "good cop, bad cop" by a single marketer. This can be valuable if the bad cop decides to switch sides at a critical juncture. On a site such as *StockTwits*, this can mean the difference between success and failure at positioning a company with traders and investors.

Many investor sites provide the functionality of notifying registered members by email if news about the firm appears. This makes monitoring easy, and allows the marketer to monitor others who are watching similar stocks. But this functionality is invaluable when it comes time to respond to an unfair criticism or uneducated opinion. Without the ability to respond, the firm is handicapped considerably. Every IPO firm should have the ability to defend itself and exploit other salient points about its business. One company, HootSuite, provides a social media monitoring application that is very helpful. TweetDeck is another application that makes the task of monitoring multiple accounts much easier.

It is not recommended to use a company email address for surveillance and response activities, as this could come back to haunt the company should other members of the site discover that it is the same company that is commenting about itself. Of course, full disclosure by the firm that it is responsible for any public postings is always recommended, but any activity carried out before the initial S-1 filing is unlikely to have any legal ramifications.

Social media has become a rich source of information for both institutional and retail investors. While the *Average Joe* is busy combing through search results consisting mostly of old news from traditional news outlets, the Wall Street crowd cuts straight to sites that cater only to investors, like *seekingalpha.com*. Evidence shows that retail investors spend far less time on investment analysis, engages in public trading, and typically rely on a different set of information sources from their professional counterparts.[32]

Retail vs. Institutional Search Behavior

An actual example illustrates the difference between retail and institutional search behavior and how the quality of information returned to each varies significantly.

In the weeks leading up to the highly anticipated IPO of the social media gaming company Zynga, a retail investor enters "Zynga IPO" in a Google search. Google returns ten links. One of the top results is an article from *Reuters*, a trusted name in business news. But the other links are from sources at least one month old. The retail investor, however, does not take the time to conduct a search for more recent information. So the retail investor simply clicks through the links, satisfied with stale results.

Let's look at how an institutional investor conducts the same search. Instead of using Google to search, the professional investor searches directly on the website of *SeekingAlpha.com*. The results are markedly different. The search yields four links to very recent news items, including a concise analysis of Zynga's recent S-1 amendment (IPO filing).

SeekingAlpha.com also provides the option to review transcripts, articles and 'market currents' mentioning Zynga. Registered users on the site can also post responses to articles written by other users and the site's contributors. No major news outlet would ever publish such analysis for free because doing so could expose the publisher to serious legal risks.

In this example, the most recent link produced by *SeekingAlpha* reveals commentary from Francis Gaskins, a long-time IPO analyst whose views influence a wide audience, including analysts and investors.[33] His analysis incorporates data from early filings of the S-1 (S-1/a); the same information that is being reviewed by the SEC in the weeks leading up to the final filing and kick-off of the Roadshow. Mr. Gaskins is known for his thorough, by-the-numbers examination of IPO filings and their comparative valuations.

Prior to new legislation knows as the JOBS Act, every firm that filed a registration statement also provided the public with free access to all of the information appearing in its financial prospectus. A provision of the JOBS act provides firms with revenues under $1 Billion to file confidentially so that the prospectus is kept a secret until 21 days before the Roadshow. Before the Act was passed, it was easy to compare recent revisions to the S-1 with past revisions to identify what content was revised at the SEC's request. Deleted passages or expanded entries provide valuable clues about the nature of SEC comments.

The final version of the prospectus consists of any and all information pertaining to the firm's business, operations and strategies -- pretty much everything anyone would want to know. With the Zynga example (which went public before the JOBS Act came into effect), Mr. Gaskins highlighted an amendment made to a new filing from Zynga which is exactly the kind of information investors seek during the "pre-marketing" phase. Gaskins' headline says it all: "Zynga is Going to Have a Hard Time Justifying Its $14 Billion Valuation".[34] Gaskins provides convincing evidence to support his opinion, which is enough to cause heartburn at Zynga headquarters. Here's what else Gaskins had to say about the inclusion of a new, non-GAAP financial result against a backdrop of deteriorating results:

"Whenever a company boldly creates its own accounting conventions, investors question whether it's just a restatement to pull the wool over investors [sic] *eyes...As for Zynga management and its consultants, imagine showing quarterly income of only $1.4 million and a $14 billion valuation at the same time? At a $14 billion valuation, Zynga is an obvious short."*

Perhaps this analysis didn't get picked up during a Google search, but institutional investors didn't ignore it. The very next day *The Wall Street Journal* published an online article titled "Reason to Worry Before Zynga's IPO" that concluded the company's restatement is "a red flag for investors since it suggests folks may be growing tired of Zynga games". A five minute video attached to *The Journal*'s article featured two analysts raising new questions about the strength of long-term cash flows and the appropriate multiple of the game developer's earnings stream given the condition that its games are losing popularity.[35] To them, the questionable accounting maneuver suggested Zynga revenues may have already peaked, which changes the initial valuation assumptions Zynga used. Gaskins warned investors a few months earlier about Zynga's numbers in his regular column at *SeekingAlpha.com.*[36]

Another very popular site for investors and stock traders is the social media site "Twitter". Free registration at *Twitter.com* provides access to an enormous resource of individual opinions from analysts with cult-like followings, links to little known blogs, and exposure to what's being said in real-time. On Twitter, entering Zynga IPO in Twitter's search bar produces a lengthy list of "tweets" (or links) that are summarized by a short description from the "tweeter" (author) who posted the link for anyone in the world to read. (A tweet may not contain more than 140 characters, so including a link to an external website site is a workaround to the restriction).

Not surprisingly, Twitter reveals that sentiment towards the Zynga IPO has incorporated new information related to valuation. Roughly half of the twenty tweets relate to declining profits and users, reasons Zynga should not go public, and several explicit references to a "50% price cut". The remaining tweets are non-Zynga specific, offering general information about the overall health of the IPO market.

Going one step further, the links provided by negative-sentiment tweeters uncover an array of new perspectives all of which argue a case for a 50% price reduction to the IPO. Data that was consistently cited included a rather unfortunate reference to a 95% drop in prior year revenues and earnings multiples of peers that are clearly worth more. Groupon was forced to cut its IPO in half for similar reasons.

Firms should expect bad news to travel fast, so communications strategy must be realistic about the obligation, timing and details of announcing bad news. One school of thought is that sooner a firm announces bad news, the better, but this approach may have disastrous consequences if incorrectly executed.[37]

Zynga's Post-IPO Misfortunes

After successfully completing the largest internet IPO since Google, Zynga met with terrible misfortune -- much of it attributable to a combination of poor communications and timing. The world's largest internet gaming company priced at the high end of the $8.5-$10 range and closed at $9.50 after its first day of trading on December 16, 2011.

That was the last time the firm would do something right. Two months later, Zynga announced it would proceed with a secondary offering -- a highly unusual move because the IPO lockup period had not yet expired. At around the same time, the firm announced it would exceed analysts' expectations for the 2012 fiscal year. As a flood of new shares diluted IPO investors, Zynga's stock tanked. A flurry of class action lawsuits followed, alleging the firm had violated the lockup restrictions.

In November 2012 -- less than a year after Zynga's $10 IPO -- the share price hit $2.12. The CFO resigned, leaving behind an unqualified disaster. By November 2013, the share price remained well below its offering price, trading at $3.62 per share.[38]

Figure 9: The rise (and fall) of Zynga

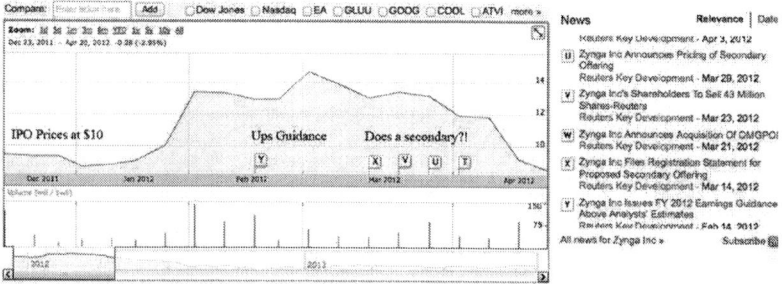

Chapter Seven

Pre-Marketing

"Pre-marketing" refers to the period when the firm is still private and has not yet filed IPO documents with regulators. The pre-marketing period ends once the firm files its initial registration statement (S-1) with the Securities and Exchange Commission (SEC). Once the S-1 filing occurs, the firm moves beyond the pre-marketing phase and enters "the quiet period". The quiet period can last a very long time -- at least until the stock starts to trade -- so experienced marketers use the pre-marketing phase to their advantage.[1]

Legislation known as the JOBS Act has relaxed securities marketing practices considerably, giving firms that have not yet filed an S-1 (preliminary prospectus) substantial flexibility compared to those that have already entered the quiet period. During the pre-marketing phase, the firm's communications are not monitored or restricted. This allows important information to be established through news releases, the firm's website, magazine articles, podcasts, industry presentations, or any other media channel the firm chooses.

Pre-marketing is the only time an IPO firm will be able to plant seeds of credibility and make strategic disclosures before it is unable to say anything that could overtly help the IPO. With total discretion to communicate what it wants -- whenever it wants -- firms should ensure the essentials are in place before the SEC starts to monitor all communications disseminated to the public.

Knowledgeable marketers focus on sending signals known to be valuable to investors. This is because the financial community is focused on determining what's *inside* a company pursuing an IPO; characteristics related to intangible qualities such as strategy, competitive strengths and management experience are often high priority topics for pre-marketing treatments. Most of the information created during pre-marketing is ignored until a firm announces its intention to go public, so embedding specific information ahead of the announcement is a solid opportunity.

The fact that every material piece of information about the firm will soon be publicly available is a primary consideration when deciding how much emphasis is placed on certain aspects of the firm. What a firm says during pre-marketing must not contrast the truth when the facts are eventually revealed in the prospectus. Similarly, the level of understatement a firm adopts (e.g.

non-promotional versus promotional) during the quiet period can generate goodwill when the time comes for investors to judge the firm for themselves.

Regardless of the hype (or lack of coverage) an IPO receives before its Roadshow, investors will assess a transaction based on the information available to them about whether the company is likely to perform better (or worse) than its peers. In the same way new consumer products are evaluated, investors are experts at reading labels. In the case of a new equity issue, the label consists of data related to the firm's financials, business opportunities, management team and competitive positioning. These labels are reliable signals.

Before filing an S-1, marketers must ensure the firm has successfully established adequate information about various valuation inputs. Enough information must exist to form the impression that management is competent and experienced enough to run a public company. There are many examples of management teams that do not convey competence. This is unacceptable in an environment where social media delivers powerful reach and frequency. Should the CEO commit a PR fumble prior to an S-1 being filed, corrective action is required immediately.

Understanding News Flow

Journalists adapt and build on key themes from other journalists, duplicating messages while adding various promotional elements. Investors like to see positive headlines about companies about to go public in the news. Even if some investors don't believe "the spin" they know many others will. Ample research supports this assertion.

Revisions to the IPOs offering price (the "range") are positively and significantly related to pre-offer publicity. This widely acknowledged fact is supported by evidence from a team of researchers that the greater the number of news articles prior to going public, the larger the price revision and underpricing.[2]

Marketers should compile a list of all media contacts including journalists and editors of popular investor websites and major media publications. This list must be maintained and updated until the firm's stock starts trading and it is time to issue guidance and announce the date of the company's first public earnings call. Maintain a separate list of investors that are met throughout the Roadshow.

A 2008 study of 514 pre-IPO and 401 post-IPO media articles found only fourteen instances out of more than 13,000 firm-day observations in which a company received two media mentions on a given day. No company received more than two mentions a day.[3] During the pre-marketing phase, firms going public should establish a consistent pattern of disclosure through a program of news releases, disseminated to newswires at a predictable time and at regular intervals. The tone and style of the releases should also be considered and consistent from release to release. A conservative, non-promotional approach will help to establish credibility, especially with announcements that are clearly positive. Quotes from the CEO or CFO are also helpful to audiences interested in management's communications style. References to financial performance using specific, concrete examples will help legitimize the statements by reducing ambiguity.

It has been shown that promotional language from press releases survives remarkably well in press publications. Most often, promotional elements (PEs) end up in news reports because their host sentence has been copied verbatim; however, even when this sentence is edited, the PE stands an almost 50% chance of turning up in the publication.[4]

Marketers must identify the timing of when publicly-traded peers release quarterly results so they can make plans to release their own results during the same period. Although private companies are not required to host conference calls to discuss quarterly financial performance, having the logistics in place ahead of time will be helpful when the time arrives. Because of the JOBS Act, it is much more common to see private companies adopt public company communication practices ahead of an IPO.

Table 3: Sample Table of Earnings Releases

To Re-Brand...or Not?

Pre-marketing tactics are primarily focused on enhancing credibility. For this reason, some companies choose to "re-brand" the company with a makeover aimed at looking more professional. If a new CEO has been hired to guide the company through an IPO, she may elect to re-brand on the basis of reflecting a new era in the firm's history. Take care to reflect restraint so that it does not appear as if millions of dollars have been spent on a new logo, even though this may be the case.

Investors may view overtly impressive re-branding attempts as unnecessary window-dressing ahead of the IPO. Investors have no problem with websites that are not chock full of bells and whistles. Maintaining the same identity throughout the IPO process conveys a sense of fiscal discipline and emphasizes the firm's preference for substance over sizzle. New signage and logos suddenly appearing on real estate owned or operated by the firm could be construed as fiscally inappropriate, and are often better left installed after the IPO.

Re-branding activities are often associated with a new CEO, a major change in strategy or a business unit separating from its parent company. For all but a few industries, minor tweaks to the company's look and feel are usually enough. Investors couldn't care less about a new logo or how business cards look, so don't undertake such an exercise on their behalf. Allocate funding to other areas that create shareholder value, such as adding a new investor relations executive or updating the firm's website with investor-oriented materials and infrastructure that will ease the transition to public ownership.

Update the Firm's Website

Once the company goes public, an "investor" section must be added to the firm's website. Knowing ahead of time what content will appear in this section will prove to be very beneficial. Wait to post this new section until the company completes its IPO, after its registration statement is declared "effective".

Create a "news" section that features links to the firm's press releases and other information that is beneficial to the firm but comes from external sources. According to one researcher, growth in traffic to an IPO firm's website in the month of the Roadshow has been shown to be positively and significantly associated with initial returns, with an economically significant effect.[5] If the media or investors would not have otherwise located the valuable posted information on their own, they will find the links useful. Examples include highly-specific industry analysis, reports, blogs or "inside" information from non-insiders. Firms should also consider including a brief synopsis about the external information so that outsiders are aware of what aspects are particularly informative or have value within the context of the firm's operations or strategies. Post and monitor this new section immediately.

The firm's website should also have a public calendar to display the dates of management presentations at industry conferences, links to senior management's social media accounts, and other interesting dates (such as anniversaries of patent protection and other corporate milestones). It is essential to include comprehensive information about the board of directors and the audit, risk and compensation committees. Augment the information provided by individual board and committee members with thought-provoking interviews. Biographies should include recent pictures that convey management as experienced professionals wearing clothing that is consistent with the expectations of investors.

Conveying the firm's most important messages and providing relevant links or data can contribute meaningful levels of confidence at a time when the firm most needs it.

Register with Investor Websites

Social media can have a profound impact on how an IPO is received. A huge number of investor-only websites, blogs and news feeds provide a wealth of opinion and analysis that can shape how a deal is portrayed to a much larger audience.

Not all bloggers have the status, prestige, or extensive network ties enjoyed by mainstream journalists, but a few can trigger cascades in the adoption of particular opinion or practices.[6] This is because during the quest for information, investor-centric blogs and websites often publish valuable information. As new information becomes available from more sources that are widely available and therefore socially verified and reinforced, the initial source disappears.[7] Both the cumulative prior and the recent attention a firm has received increase the likelihood it will continue to attract attention.

Marketers should monitor investor websites and other social media channels during the pre-marketing phase. By registering with sites using email addresses and identities not affiliated with the company, comments related to the firm can be monitored without unnecessarily exposing the firm. The decision to react to a posting -- and how -- is up to the firm to decide.

Always use caution as any action taken is irreversible; public postings are not typically removed.

One recent example is that of HootSuite's CEO Ryan Holmes who was apparently misquoted in a recent local news article. The article quoted him as saying:

"I want to build a billion-dollar company and take it to an IPO [or] exit, enable the financial independence of 50 people around me and build something disruptive, like how Netflix disrupted the traditional movie rental industry or how Apple rewrote music."

After seeing his quote in print, Mr. Holmes was forced to tweet a clarification:

"For the record I said ipo/exit, but thank you."

During pre-marketing, corrections such as this should not be necessary as it only highlights confusion surrounding the firm's abilities to clearly communicate future plans -- a skill vital to maximizing long-term valuation. In subsequent encounters with the press, Mr. Holmes exhibited a much higher level of preparation.

The mechanism for monitoring and responding to published articles must be established prior to the pre-marketing phase so that false or blatantly misleading material can be corrected before gaining traction with wider audiences. Consider any posted comments with an eye to conveying a fair and balanced approach so that a historical review of the member's comments does not reveal any intent at any time to promote the company or the offering.

Marketers with access to IT support may procure the basic infrastructure necessary for confidential and secure identity protection. The better solution is to use an external entity (e.g. PR firm) that simply executes whatever the marketer desires. Few lawyers or senior executives would sanction this approach, but it is consistent with how certain high-profile deals are pre-marketed using preferred PR firms that enjoy cozy relationships with influential journalists and media personalities.

Jim Cramer of MSNBC's *Mad Money* and Andrew Ross Sorkin of the *New York Times' DealJournal* represent two of the most powerful individuals in financial media. They comment regularly on IPOs. Taken together, their audience is so large that much of what they say is regarded as truth. With enormous amounts of capital at stake, IPOs must be mindful of how critical issues are framed by controlling the messages -- and the media -- to the extent that they are able. Jim Cramer's stock-picking accuracy is 45%.[8]

Chapter Eight

The Investment Highlights

Investors have limited time and attention. They cannot fully evaluate every IPO marketed by every syndicate. Instead, investors rely on shortcuts to evaluate many investments, especially during busy periods of new equity issuance.

Typically, the first PowerPoint slide delivered by the CEO is titled "Investment Highlights". The content on this slide serves as a reliable shortcut to investors as it describes the "major moments" of the investment story. Because the investment highlights slide is a staple in every IPO presentation, it is particularly useful to gauge management's level of preparation and sophistication.

Apart from positive media coverage and a legitimately credible management team, a transaction's "investment highlights" provides reliable clues to predicting how a transaction will price. The investment highlights slide and others that form the Roadshow story are available to anyone interested in viewing the firm's Roadshow presentation for free at *www.RetailRoadshow.*

com. This website features Roadshow videos of deals being currently marketed to investors, although not every transaction chooses to participate.

On this extremely helpful site, users can watch Roadshow teams delivering their speeches accompanied by the same slides that institutional investors see in the daily face-to-face (one-on-one) meetings. The slides change automatically as the presenter progresses. Investors rely on this internet-based version of the Roadshow when assessing a potential IPO investment. This allows observers to choose *ex ante* how to allocate limited attention.[1]

Sky Alphabet, an IPO consulting firm, analyzed the investment highlights of 107 IPO presentations between 2009 and 2011. The results indicated that the content of the investment highlights opening slide is positively and significantly correlated with the success of the offering.

There are many aspects that are beyond management's control when marketing an IPO. Other deals in the pipeline and conditions in the broader market are just two examples. But the form and content of an IPO's investment highlights are within the control of every Roadshow team. Investors are aware of this, and expect firms to understand the value of this slide as a shortcut to them. It must include signals that directly reflect management's experience and the quality of the IPO story itself.

The number of highlights, number of words used, and presence of extraneous information (such as "sub-bullets") convey signals to investors. The investment highlights provide a vitally important introduction by outlining the essential features of the company and its opportunities. This slide is the high-level introduction of the entire IPO presentation, so great care must be taken with its crafting. It is not unusual to see the Roadshow presentation revised more than thirty times.

Because the investment highlights slide is a traditional convention that investors expect to see, it should not be surprising that 33% of all IPOs that were canceled did not include an investment highlights slide.[2] Only 11% of IPOs that priced within the range neglected to include the traditional opening slide.

These findings suggest that it is wise to adhere to the tried-and-true formula of opening and closing with the investment highlights slide. The fact is, if the investment highlights slide is not included, there is likely to be other essential content also missing. This slide is recognized as a template that provides investors with a high level summary of the IPO story and its underlying investment thesis.

Do not use any other title but "Investment Highlights". Four firms in the sample chose to ignore the standard nomenclature and all four priced below the range. Derivating from the familiar "Investment Highlights" by substituting "Summary", "Compelling Attributes", "Pre-Commercial Highlights" or other variation is not at all recommended. The investment highlights is a recognized and respected title for the slide and should not be worded any other way.

Empirical data and knowledge gained through direct experience support the assertion that investment highlights are best when they are direct and concise. A slide full of tiny words and little bullets can be confounding and unacceptable to investors who are familiar with experienced public companies that communicate exceptionally well. Specifically, firms should avoid using "sub-bullets"; a common reference to content appearing directly below a primary highlight, and may be slightly indented and set in a smaller font. There is ample evidence to suggest that sub-bullets are to be avoided.

Although it may be tempting to add further information to further explain or add detail to a highlight, firms in the survey that included extra verbiage suffered the consequences. Deals that used two or more sub-bullets ("subs") on the highlights slide almost always priced poorly. Of the twenty companies that used one or more subs, eighteen priced poorly with many cutting their deal sizes substantially. This suggests that sub-bullets are a proxy to firm quality and indicate inexperience on behalf of the management team or its bankers.

The offerings of successful US-based companies usually include the investment highlights slide as the first slide in the CEO's presentation (immediately after a banker reviews the "Offering Summary"). Other successful offerings starting with "Company Overview" or "Corporate History" are usually from China; US deals that price above the range rarely start with anything but the highlights.

Inserting a slide or two before the highlights is a risky communications strategy. All firms marketing to US investors should include the highlights as soon as possible. Ten IPOs in our sample chose to insert one or more slides before the investment highlights and priced at the bottom of the range or worse. Another eight priced at the top of the range or better.

Of the eight IPOs that priced at the top of the range (or above) and included a pre-amble to the investment highlights, one was the best performing IPO of 2010 (Financial Engines). With this transaction, the CEO opened with a slide that was titled as a question: "Who's Managing America's Retirement?" This introduction was followed by two more slides before the highlights. This approach worked well because the question was effective at capturing interest immediately because the audience wanted to know the answer.

These highlights are a snapshot of the story so they must be as concise as possible to arouse interest without introducing any element of confusion. No more than a total of six highlights are recommended. The massive IPO of General Motors consisted of just three.[3] The content of subsequent slides should reveal the facts that support and strengthen the veracity of each highlight.

The investment highlights should distill the S-1 into four or five concise statements or "bullet points" (e.g. "Market Leading Provider with Significant Scale in Employer-Sponsored Child Care" or "Attractive Industry Fundamentals with Favorable Demographics").[4] The investment highlights should not be simply lifted straight from the S-1. The optimal number of highlights does not exceed five. For some reason, many firms choose to list eight or more highlights. These transactions, on average, do not price as well compared to those that use fewer highlights. Research shows that humans cannot handle, discriminate or reliably transmit information involving more than five distinct categories.[5]

Each highlight should capture a reason why investors should consider the firm as an investment opportunity. The best highlights are emphatic statements that include numbers and other non-subjective content. They should establish clear differentiation by articulating the firm's strengths, opportunities and strategies. They not only build on the language and concepts of the S-1 but also justify the firm's valuation.

One after another, the highlights should build a strong case for the primary reasons to invest in the firm at the time of the IPO. These highlights should appear on one slide, in order of importance. The most important consideration is always the first highlight, followed by the second reason and so on. Investors see this slide twice during management's presentation.

The investment highlights appear at the beginning and end of every IPO presentation. Like bookends, the investment highlights are a kind of parenthetical index to a story that unfolds within. New equity offering presentations usually use this convention of starting and ending with the investment highlights. Investors expect management's opening salvo -- and finale -- to be delivered succinctly and with an assured sense of confidence.

The investment highlights convey the potential of the business by defining its markets and the firm's position in those markets. Only the most essential competitive strengths are included. Concrete evidence of a solid defensible position ("barriers to entry" or "first mover advantage" or "opportunities of scale") are complemented by why the firm is positioned for future growth. Include the most attractive financial characteristics relative to publicly-traded peers, if possible. Highlights that the firm's competitors can match or exceed are considered low priority and are often discarded at some point before the final slide deck.

Use as few words as possible to articulate the investment highlights. Avoid using paragraphs consisting of full sentences, extraneous words ("we are" "our competitors") or ambiguous language ("nimble business model", "great hardware", "attractive practice economics", "agile DNA"). Each and every word must be clear and direct with its intended meaning; precision reduces subjective interpretation.

What constitutes a "large" market varies from one investor to another. Be concise as possible from the outset by precisely specifying the firm's total potential opportunity, leadership position in key markets, irrefutable competitive advantages, growth strategies and most compelling financial attributes.

Start by Defining the Size of the Opportunity

The first investment highlight should clearly convey the precise, legitimate size of the market opportunity, preferably in dollars. It must be dimensioned with as much precision as possible, backed by a source cited in the prospectus. Firms that have not yet submitted an S-1 should consider tracking down this critical data point with a view to including and exploiting it to the fullest. Big numbers -- billions -- will arouse investor interest immediately.

A large market number is particularly effective to introduce as an opening data point because people tend to anchor to whatever number they hear first. A large number translates to a large opportunity, paving the way for a successful presentation to an engaged audience.

Danny Kahneman, the pioneer of behavioral psychology, conducted several fascinating experiments in the 1970's which identified several seemingly irrational patterns of behavior related to decision-making. For example, people tend to "anchor" to any number they are given even though the number may be wildly inaccurate. This produces an effect known as "representativeness", which refers to the tendency of people to work with the last number stored in memory, because it is quickly and reliably available.[6]

Representativeness is easily demonstrated by asking a group of people if the average household income of Turkey is more or less than $200,000 per year, and just how close is it to $200,000? The vast majority of responses will be concentrated within plus or minus 20% of the anchor ($160,000-$240,000). But, in fact, the actual figure is only $6,000. Retail investors are much more likely to fall prey to this approach, as stock promoters of tiny companies know ("Don't miss out on this fifty cent stock headed to fifty dollars!").

To provide investors a clear sense of the scope of its core business, the second highlight should address the firm's core competency and its markets, and a clue to where its growth areas exist.

The third and fourth highlights should articulate features involving the firm's leadership position and strength, growth strategies, ability to execute and control risk, and essential industry-specific attributes. For example, a technology company might reference patents or intellectual property rights, while a drug company may highlight progress with its clinical trials or strategic partnerships. The firm with relatively strong financial results should weave in a metric that substantively differentiates itself from peers.

To round out the investment highlights, the final point (or at most, two) should capture the firm's financial health, growth trajectory or other demonstrable trend driving current and future performance.

Taken together, the highlights encapsulate a multitude of facts and concepts that are described at length in the prospectus. The "messaging architecture" (described in chapter four) categorizes the main topics investors are interested in and condenses the many facts into as few words as possible. Condense ten (or more) strengths, weaknesses, threats and financial performance into just four or five powerful points. Structuring the highlights so that they convey five key messages requires considerable thought, time, and experience. So it is the first area of the presentation to tackle. As seen in Figure 10, there is some flexibility to re-order or mix content found in section 2, 3 and 4.

Figure 10: The Investment Highlights Message Model

1	Size of the opportunity ($) or (global) or (# customers)
2	Core competency & markets
3	Strength of product & position; growth strategy
4	Industry-specific feature
5	Financial attribute

The beginning of presentation is the only time management can be certain everyone is listening. This is why the objective is to hit investors hard from the start. This is for several reasons. First, information that has the greatest effect is information that is presented first, which is attributable to the "primacy" effect on judgements.[6] Second, audiences are most attentive during the first thirty seconds and are the most interested in what management has to say.

The first investment highlight often begins with words like "large/largest/ the largest", "leader/leading/the leading" followed by a very brief summary of the firm's business, market or industry. The IPOs of Maxlinear and Groupon cut right to the chase from the first highlight: "3.2Bn addressable market" and "Enormous market" set the stage for deals that priced above the range.

Maxlinear did not have the benefit of widespread interest in its IPO so they wisely defined their opportunity precisely instead of opting for another alternative that could be open to interpretation. The IPO of Convio led with "large, under-served market", while Nexsan Technologies opted for "large and growing digital-age storage market". These opening ambiguous statements hurt both firms. Convio priced below the range while Nexsan's IPO was pulled.

The first two bullets must clearly differentiate the firm and its most attractive features. If the first highlight causes the audience to think "that is interesting" or "I did not know this company was so big/strong/well positioned" it is likely the rest of the presentation will be well received. The first two points are critically important.

It may also be useful to understand that the order of evidence of two positive pieces of information followed by two negative items result in greater downward revisions of initial likelihood judgments than the order of two negative items followed by positive evidence.[9] This is why IPOs that face significant and well-known challenges often begin with highlights designed to confront the serious objections.

Companies emerging from bankruptcy or those with highly leveraged balanced sheets (lots of debt) often use this approach of tackling the issues head on from the beginning.

Delphi Automotive's first highlight was "Successful transformation into a premier global automotive supplier", a direct reference to changes at the firm since its bankruptcy in 2008. General Motors employed a similar tactic by using just three highlights stacked within a triangle that pointed upward: "New business model/Leverage to global growth/Significantly lower risk profile". GM knew the success of its enormous IPO hinged on conveying how major alterations to its business would defend against the risks that contributed to its bankruptcy just two years prior.

Avoid "Management Experience" as a Highlight

The investment highlights of many IPOs incorporate a well-known "fluff point" that usually appears as the final highlight. "Experienced Management" (or a similar derivation) is often tacked on with the hope that investors will accept the assertion at face value and award management points for credibility. This is rarely the case. Instead, statements such as "Experienced team with value-maximizing platform" or "Experienced senior management team with nearly 20 years of industry experience on average" are ignored or even arouse concern.[8] But for some reason, many firms make the mistake of adding this superfluous content anyway, diluting other legitimate and effective messages.

For these and other reasons, "experienced management" should not be included as a highlight. The majority of IPOs that included a highlight alluding to management's experience priced below the midpoint, or worse. Only 4 deals in our sample of 107 companies that referenced management as a highlight priced at the top of the range or better.

This practice of including a subjective statement about management -- in a presentation delivered by management itself -- has become so widespread that most bankers consider it redundant and a waste of valuable time. It also introduces considerable risk should investors disagree with the talking points that accompany the cliché.

Choosing to include experienced management as a highlight is like a new driver telling the guard at a border crossing that he is an experienced driver, even though the guard is fully aware that his license is restricted. Management may have been successful at running the firm while it was still private, but this is not the same as running the firm once it is publicly-owned.

"Experienced management" attracts attention to a subjective issue that should not be debated at a time when management is actively trying to prove its worth. When used as the final investment feature -- as it often is -- it provides a weak ending to a story that may have been developing nicely. By the time these words are spoken, investors will have already judged management's experience. If they believe other executives running comparable firms are decidedly more experienced, the story can take a wrong turn. All previous highlights become compromised and investors become less interested in sitting through twenty-five more slides.

Another obvious liability is that achieving past success at a public company in no way guarantees future performance at a different firm; there are often too many variables to make the connection with complete confidence.

But if a reference must be made to the talent, experience or track record of management, consider it as a separate slide before the investment highlights. Or include it as the second or third highlight; any position except the last. It can also be combined with another relevant message. For example, Mattress Firm Holding Corp. opted for "Experienced and invested management team" to emphasize their post-IPO ownership stake, an important signal that indicates alignment with shareholders. Chatham Lodging Trust worded things a bit differently: "Management aligned with shareholders ($10 million concurrent investment at IPO price)".[9]

Writing the Investment Highlights

To determine the best investment highlights, identify the firm's most important competitive strengths and growth strategies. What really gives the firm an advantage over its competitors? Why is the firm successful now and what will drive growth in the next year? Be specific. Gather as many hard facts as possible that can be used as evidence. Determine the exact size and scope of the company's markets -- by geography, product line or consumer type -- whatever it takes to dimension the opportunity credibly.

Examples from successful IPOs include: "Leader in a large market driven by powerful trends"; "Global leader in our segments with market presence in ~100 countries"; "Trusted intermediary in highly fragmented and massive markets"; and "Evolution of financial services industry driving large market opportunity".[11] The theme of leadership in a large market is an effective way to introduce the firm. It arouses interest in the story because investors need to understand the details so they can gauge the various probabilities of success, failure and risk.

It is often difficult to pin down credible data to determine the size or growth rate of markets. "Management's best estimate" is only valuable if the base assumptions are derived from credible sources.

Another approach is to assume the firm has all the capital necessary to fully exploit the most profitable opportunities. How would it maximize revenue and margins?

Crafting powerful investment highlights is much easier if you have the views and thinking already articulated in your messaging architecture. This platform of content allows you to quickly make clear-cut decisions as to what stays and what goes; what's important and what is not. As one researcher observed, the highlights should provide the "kernels" or major moments of the story, linked to minor moments that anticipate future kernels or refer back to previous ones.[11]

The Investment Highlights Shortcut

1. *Make a list of the top five things about the firm.* No more than five.

One quality is industry-related (e.g. the industry has been growing at 15% CAGR for the last five years; the addressable market is $• billion;). Two of the five points are growth-oriented, specific to the firm. (e.g. how or why the company expects to grow its revenue, market-share, cash flow or net income). The final two points are finance-oriented (e.g. cash flow from operations is increasing; net debt is decreasing, cost per gross subscriber addition is decreasing, or operating leverage is increasing, for example).

2. List three or four or facts that support the top five strengths of the company. Take the facts directly from the prospectus.

3. Ascertain how much education the investor requires about your industry on a scale from 1 to 10. This will determine how far you should drill down. A sophisticated investor with deep industry knowledge ranks an 8+ and will require substantial detail.

4. Make a list of major weaknesses. Examples include new product introductions, diminishing margins, higher operating costs, executive compensation, or a high percentage of secondary shares on offer.

5. Distill this list of facts and concerns down to a single page of paper and circulate it. One page is much more helpful than twenty-five pages of PowerPoint.

One by one, ask your management team and bankers their thoughts on what the most salient, pertinent and "packageable" aspects of the firm are and why investors will be interested. Determine if the lists of other team members are similar to your own. Debate the issues.

The bankers will have the most valuable input regarding the strengths and challenges of the transaction. With both sides engaged, you will have developed a definitive list of messaging inputs.

Now re-order and prioritize the messaging for the strengths, weaknesses, opportunities and threats and find three or more references in the prospectus that support each of the four areas. Be sure to include specific references to financial performance whenever possible. Now try outlining five investment highlights.

Never mind the factual details that support them for now. You want to try and hone these highlights as much as you can, sharpening them so they are powerful and undeniable. The investment highlights are really the *raison d'etre* for the IPO, so they become a critical focal point for discussion and the genesis of the investor presentation.

Run the newly revised and refined list by your management team and get their input before circulating it to the banking team. Schedule a conference call and discuss the proposed investment highlights as a team.

On the conference call, discuss and justify each investment highlight. Determine the precise language of each point so that you know exactly what content appears on the opening slide.

When you drift into adding verbiage to the investment highlights you lose focus and so will your audience. They will know you couldn't agree on the five main points and that you don't have the acumen to write an effective IPO presentation. These transactions price poorly.

Visit *RetailRoadshow.com* and review the current IPOs being marketed and search for presentations that list many highlights. These same transactions are likely to feature slides that are difficult to read. You will also see presentations that stand out through their clarity of communication and concise investment highlights.

The Collaborative Process

It is common for highlights and other content to become compromised either because it is simplified, understated, or made "safe" in order to keep the process moving along. Establishing a consensus view can be difficult as some parties may have their own motivations for wanting to see the story structured in a certain way. If it is still early in the process, it can be best to return to fight another day. Gaining buy-in from the wider working group is paramount to a successful transaction.

If the highlights are not compelling or differentiated enough from those of the firm's peers, they must be modified until they are. They are that important.

Once the investment highlights are completed, the introduction and conclusion of the presentation are also done. Now it is time to tackle the story that unfolds between them. Twenty-five slides will be sufficient to paint a complete picture of the IPO and its potential, not including "fluff" slides like the "title" slides that feature management's name or the legal slides that list the disclaimers (such as the "safe harbor", "forward- looking statements" or "GAAP reconciliation" slides).

Behavioral Considerations

Cognitive psychologists have long recognized that people are more likely to remember the last thing they heard. For this reason, conclude the highlights -- verbally or on the slide itself -- by demonstrating that management is legitimately aligned with investors. This will send a very strong and positive signal. If management can show they have "skin in the game" by disclosing substantial personal investments beyond the lockup expiration period, this says much more than "experienced management team" ever could.

Executives that stake their fortunes on the outcome of their public debut should tell investors this from the outset, as surprisingly few managers are willing to accept the same risk they expect from investors.

A study on the topic of truth-telling involving 325 university students indicates that statements that are repeated ring truer than statements seen or heard for the first time. This is why it pays to start establishing core messages early in the process and to repeat the investment highlights more than once over the duration of management's thirty minute presentation to investors.

Bias plays a major role in how the investment highlights -- and the story itself -- is perceived and received. The same study also concludes that statements that repeat affirmatively biased facts (e.g. what the CEO says jives with what the audience remembers to be the truth) ring truer than statements where there is an appearance of a contradiction rather than the fact of contradiction. Affirmatively biased facts were also found to ring truer · than new statements. This is remarkable, since teaching investors something brand new appears to be more difficult than building on a weakness or even positively denying a negative.[12]

Three Themes

The investment highlights set the stage for the IPO story by outlining the firm's most salient features. There are key themes that are evident in the highlights of the best-performing IPOs. They include:

1) The firm's leadership position in large, growing or otherwise strategically attractive markets; and

2) Specific characteristics that differentiate the firm from its peers; and

3) The barriers to entry that protect the firm against emerging competition.

Transactions that perform well over the long-term set precise expectations in the minds of investors about the firm's managers and the business opportunity while demonstrating an ability to manage risk.

Examples of Investment Highlights

Financial Engines ($127.2 million): 1. Leader in a large market driven by powerful trends; 2. Scalable, proprietary investment technology platform; 3. Substantial growth; 4. Predictable, recurring revenues with high operating leverage.

MaxLinear ($89.6 million): 1. $3.2Bn addressable market; 2. Leveraging core CMOS RF technology across multiple markets; 3. Highly differentiated radio architecture for SoCs; 4. Top-tier customers & diversified revenue base; 5. High-growth, profitable financial model.

Qlik Technologies ($112 million): 1. Expands addressable BI market; 2. Disruptive in-memory associative search technology; 3. Compelling customer value proposition; 4. Scalable global infrastructure; 5. SMB to enterprise; 6. High growth, ramping profitability.

Demand Media: 1. We are targeting a large market opportunity; 2. We create quality content at scale; 3. Demonstrate high return on content investment; 4. Proven business model operating at scale

Nielsen Holdings: 1. Comprehensive understanding of what consumers buy and watch; 2. Global leader in our segments with market presence in ~100 countries; 3. Consumption-based, measurement science intensive; 4. Syndicated product set with significant scope and scale; 5. "Mission critical" measurement and

analytics; 6. Unique competitive advantages that are difficult to

replicate; 7. Proven track record of growth and economic resilience.

From S-1 to PowerPoint Slide: Modeling the Investment Highlights

The following example illustrates how the "key strengths" and "key

strategies" derived from an S-1 can be manipulated to produce investment

highlights. Although the content of any S-1 could be used in the model,

the actual investment highlights of MaxLinear's IPO presentation closely

approximate the ideal output from our model.[13]

Table 4: Populating the Investment Highlights Messaging Model

Size of the Opportunity
Worldwide market for silicon tuners and demodulators is projected to be $2.4 billion in 2010 and $3.4 billion in 2013.
Key Features
Proprietary, CMOS-based Radio Architecture Technology
High Signal Clarity Performance
Highly Integrated CMOS-based RF Solution
Low Power
Scalable Platform
Space Efficient Solution
Key Strategies
Extend Technology Leadership in RF Receivers and RF Receiver SoCs
Leverage and Expand our Existing Customer Base

| Target Additional High-Growth Markets |
| Expand Global Presence |
| Attract and Retain Top Talent |

Table 5 (below) shows how we translate content related to the size, key features and strategies of the firm by combining its most attractive attributes to approximate the five major highlight types (shown in bold).

Highlight #2 addresses the firm's proprietary technology while indicating there are multiple markets that comprise the $3.2 billion market opportunity.

Highlight #3 sums up the various features (low power, signal clarity, etc.) by categorizing the entire group as "highly differentiated" while making reference to SoCs --an industry-recognized acronym for "Systems on Chips".

Table 5: The Investment Highlights -- After Refinement

1	**Size of the opportunity ($) or (global) or (# customers)**
	$3.2 Billion Addressable Market
2	**Core competency & markets**
	Leveraging Core CMOS RF Technology Across Multiple Markets
3	**Industry-specific feature**
	Highly Differentiated Radio Architecture for SoCs
4	**Strength of product & position; growth strategy**
	Top-Tier Customers & Diversified Revenue Base
5	**Financial attribute**
	High-Growth, Profitable Financial Model

The remaining highlights (4 and 5) are primarily attractive financial features. Although "top-tier" is not found in the prospectus, it conveys the point succinctly without stretching the bounds of materiality. Maxlinear's IPO priced above the range.

The $82.5 million IPO of Country Style Cooking Restaurants, a China-based company, provides another illustrative example.14

Table 6: Sample Messaging Model Using Country Style's F-1 (Foreign Prospectus)

Size of the Opportunity
China quick-service restaurant sector: 13.1% CAGR '04-'09 ($37.4 Billion - $69.4 Billion) / 10.3% CAGR YTD -'14 (Est. 2014): $113 Billion.
Competitive Strengths
Delicious, everyday Chinese food of consistent quality Leading position in existing geographic markets with great potential for expansion
Highly standardized and efficient operations
Large customer base, frequent visits by repeat customers
Dedicated and experienced management team
Strategies
Further penetrate existing markets and expand into selected locations
Further drive comparable restaurant sales growth and profitability
Continue to provide quality food and develop new menu items to attract more customer visits
Further improve standardization and operating efficiency
Further enhance our brand recognition

As table 7 (next page) indicates, once the raw inputs of the investment highlights have been tightened, the result is a concise combination of compelling attributes that can be fully explored over the remainder of the presentation.

Table 7: Country Style's Investment Highlights -- After Refinement

1	**Size of the opportunity ($) or (global) or (# customers)**
	Favorable industry growth
2	**Core competency & markets**
	Leading position in home markets
3	**Strength of product & position;**
	High customer loyalty and strong brand recognition
4	**Industry-specific feature**
	Highly standardized and scalable business model
5	**Growth strategy**
	Multiple growth opportunities
6	**Other**
	Passionate, dedicated and experienced management team

Although the firm's F-1 cited attractive growth data, it seems likely that they opted for "favorable industry growth" as highlight #1 because the exact addressable size of the market is impossible to pin down accurately. Instead, they invited investors to judge for themselves. Regardless, the enormous size of the segment makes the approach appear more credible once investors saw the industry data on the next slide.

Scalability, standardization, loyal customers and brand recognition provides enough support for the claim that the firm has multiple growth opportunities.

A slide just before the highlights showed impressive financial results, negating the much weaker "experienced management team" cliché that followed.

Chapter Nine

The IPO Presentation

Management's presentation to investors must tell the IPO story and tell it well. As Akerlof and Shiller point out in *Animal Spirits*, the CEO who is able to tell a great story might also be considered to be a great leader as "great leaders are...first and foremost the creators of stories".[1]

Investors view the IPO presentation as a proxy for the quality of management and the company itself. As a story-telling medium, no other marketing element of the Roadshow comes close.

Every investor encountered on the Roadshow will hear management's story and see their PowerPoint presentation. The manner by which investors evaluate the equity offering often depends on how skilled the managers are at conveying the investment thesis and opportunity for growth while reviewing the slides. Even though great stories are simple, even the simplest ones have multiple layers of context. Doing an effective job at uncovering the layers while keeping an audience focused on the big picture takes a great deal of practice.

The optimal IPO presentation runs twenty-five minutes and consists of thirty slides.[2] The majority of presentations involve both the CEO and CFO although one other member of senior management may also form part of the "speaker team" during the Roadshow. Each member of the speaker team presents a well-defined section of content.

Information from the firm's prospectus always forms the basis of an IPO presentation but it must be structured and organized in a way that is familiar to investors. The IPO presentation is a genre in its own right, as it has its own social and historical aspects of rhetoric that other perspectives do not.[3]

Characteristics of an Effective IPO Presentation

One study identified a framework for describing various types of messages based on an extensive list of characteristics compiled from examples of effective communications.[4] Two qualities of the framework are applicable to the genre of investor presentations: the fact that the content contains material that is both informational and relational.[5]

The informational material satisfies a strict set of criteria that pertain to the science behind a Roadshow meeting: the need for content that is focused, logical, organized, rigorous, precise, controlled, technically correct and accurate.

On the other hand, the art of a Roadshow meeting lies in the presenter's ability to relate with an audience. From a relational perspective, investor presentations must also be credible, believable, plausible, open, candid and honest.6

Follow Tradition or Pay the Price

There are two rules that define a long tradition of successful IPO presentations.

The first is that a Roadshow presentation should not exceed thirty minutes in length. Some investors consider it rude to cut into valuable Q&A time, which is supposed to be thirty minutes -- or half -- of a one hour private meeting. Such meetings occur in the investor's own offices, so violating tradition on another's turf is not viewed favorably.

The second rule is based on tradition but should also be regarded as a strict rule: begin and end with the "Investment Highlights".

For all but the most anticipated offerings (the IPO of LinkedIn, for example), it is not advisable to deviate from tradition in any way.

Unfamiliar approaches are not easily accepted or welcome. The presentation must follow a clearly defined structure with a recognizable beginning, middle and end to the story. The middle section of the story -- the heart of the new equity investment thesis -- must be clearly identified as "growth strategies" and must not appear anywhere else but in the middle, before the final section titled "financial overview". The IPOs of Walker & Dunlop and HomeStreet deviated from the norm when they elected to cover growth strategies after the financial overview. Both IPOs were pulled.

Both the presentation's content structure and physical form should also conform to a long tradition of how new equity presentations are formatted: 8.5" x 11" landscape format, coil bound. This is what institutional investors expect to see.

For no other reason than the fact the speaker team will deliver it hundreds of times, the IPO presentation must be as good as it can possibly be. The slides are critical to success and must stand on their own merit, without the usual benefit of accompanying explanation, narrative, or voice-over.

The best teams are ready to turn in a solid performance from the first meeting on the first day of the Roadshow. This is when the investment banks gather to attend the inaugural kick-off meeting known as "the salesforce presentation".

Main Goals

The presentation must provide arguments and substantive proof to define and support four key aspects of the firm. These four characteristics must reflect the firm's:

1. Most valuable and enduring strengths in large or (fast) growing or profitable or predictable markets/segments or (new/hybrid) categories; and

2. Attractive valuation and growth metrics through the various inputs related to visible, persistent long-term cash flow and revenue streams. Emphasizing, demonstrating, inferring or otherwise exploring data and financial concepts through comparing or contrasting similarities or differences between other firms is a reliable means to establish concrete and advantageous differentiation; and

3. Business potential and the core growth strategies and associated tactics that will generate sustained levels of shareholder value through the

achievement of stated objectives and milestones; and

4. Ability to actively identify risks and mitigate threats from competitors or known market forces.

These four essential elements of an effective IPO presentation appear in order of importance, not the order in which they appear over the course of the presentation itself.

Dimension the Opportunity

Every company going public must demonstrate at least one clear competitive advantage. From the outset, investors want to know what that advantage is and the precise size and scope of the opportunity the firm intends to exploit with the advantage.

Investors are also keenly interested in how prone the company is to competition -- existing or otherwise -- and if they are leaders, by what margin do they lead? Investors appreciate the precision conveyed by dv/dt-type of explanations that precisely convey not only the rate of change, but the *rate of the rate of change*.

The firm that generates revenue from online subscribers provides a good and typical example. Let's say year-over-year revenues have increased sequentially three years in a row from $79 million to $120 million and then to $243 million in year three -- or a leap from 52% to 102% year over year. Sounds pretty good, but it begs the question: is that it? Is it the top of the cycle? One additional data point tells us it is not. In the first quarter of the fourth year, revenues are up 110% over the prior year's comparable quarter. This might be enough information for the retail investor, but the institution wants to understand the variable components that are driving the growth -- are they profitable and enduring? Are the highest margin components of the business driving growth or are individual subscribers in foreign markets driving the growth? In short, where's the growth?

The numbers cited above were taken from LinkedIn's IPO presentation, which demonstrated that its Hiring Solutions business contributed a greater and greater percentage of revenue on a quarterly basis, although the firm's two other lines of businesses -- premium subscriptions and marketing solutions were also growing, but not as rapidly.[7]

Investors need to understand the single most important reason why management believes its competitive advantage is so compelling and why it deserves their investment now. This is where the firm's growth strategies enter the picture.

Telling The IPO Story

No fairy tale has ever been written with bullet points. The story that managers attempt to tell during an IPO presentation is no different. When drafting the IPO story, use full sentences rather than trying to combine a series of bullet points. Talk it out. You can reduce the story to bullet points once you have crafted a beginning, middle and end that flows. It is easier to write long and cut short rather than expanding from stray thoughts and messages. For the marketer that adheres to tradition, the beginning, middle and end of the IPO story is clear-cut and well defined, eliminating the guesswork.

Investors require a clear rationale to invest in new companies and managers. They must be convinced with authoritative logic that an IPO is worthy of attention because of a combination of characteristics. The presentation must be clear with its intent and focused on the primary goal of ensuring investors get the main point of the equity story: growth.

After the meeting is over, investors must remember the one or two messages management attempted to instill -- the "key takeaways". Whether investors agree with the exact content put forward largely depends on management's skill level and the tools it uses to convey the transaction's most salient features and key messages.

A proven method to stimulate investor interest during the Roadshow is to demonstrate that a high level of media awareness about the offering exists. This indicates that sufficient retail demand will exist beyond the offering.

It is also advantageous if the story keys off the success of what other peers have done, but with a new twist or improvement. This approach of leveraging the success of others will hasten the understanding and acceptance about the issues central to both the IPO's pricing and the decision to invest now or later.

Growth is at the heart of any equity story, so the growth strategies must exude true merit. The substance of each individual strategy must be tangible and supported empirically. The degree of authority with which the IPO presentation is delivered determines the extent of how the information relates to its audience. Although the story itself is conveyed with authority, the tone and language used by a CEO differs from the CFO.

Research shows that IPO presentations with a high ratio of financial content price consistently better than those with relatively few slides in the financial section. In our survey of the informational content of 107 IPO presentations, the top performing IPOs also mention growth in the investment highlights more frequently than those that price poorly.

If investors are unable to recall the story's core or do not believe its defining feature, the presentation is a failure. If it does not test well during pre-marketing, it must be refined until it does test well. Once the presentation is shown to the first investor on the Roadshow, it is too late to change.

The Narrative

The presence of narrative -- a storyline -- is what separates great presentations from others. Narrative structures have been shown to greatly enhance understanding and connection with an audience. The human mind is built to think in terms of narratives with an internal logic and dynamic that appears as a unified whole.[8] The IPO presentation boils down to a story that tends to share the same formulaic structure as other IPOs regardless of size or industry.

Narrative reduces the tendency investors have to look at a sequence of facts from the prospectus to support or invent an explanation based on a preconception based on a recent news item or other vague or unrelated opinion they have formed about the deal. Narrative is effective because it focuses the attention away from the broader stock market or anything else investors may be thinking about.[9] Management must define the frame of reference and the relationships between the most salient facts and suggest how the firm's qualities should be best interpreted and prioritized.

Outlining the IPO story is the first step to establishing management's narrative. Let's take a brief look at the two primary storytellers. Chapter three offers more information about other actors that participate in the Roadshow.

The Role of the CEO

As the firm's leader, the Chief Executive naturally plays the most important role in setting the tone of the story and establishing its key inflection points. The CEO summarizes the firm by covering the investment highlights, outlining the firm's growth strategies and convincing the audience of his team's ability to execute without surprises.

Authenticity is always important, so the CEO must have a clear and focused mind going into key one-on-ones and large group meetings.

The Role of the CFO

The CFO is essential to a credible narrative, and brings it to life through the world's only truly global language: numbers. By providing hard facts portrayed through audited financials and associated ratios, the details of the firm's story become reified and concrete. Abstractions such as the firm's predictability of cash flow or other inputs related to valuation take on new meaning when viewed against the backdrop of the CEO's growth story and market opportunity.

Outlining the Presentation

Three main components are 'book-ended' by a slide titled "Investment Highlights." The investment highlights allow investors to determine what the firm's key competitive strengths, opportunities and growth strategies are at a glance.

As figure 10 on the next page shows, the first component of the IPO story is an overview of the firm's industry and operations. A discussion of the firm's growth strategies and financial review follows.

Figure 10: The Structure of an IPO Story

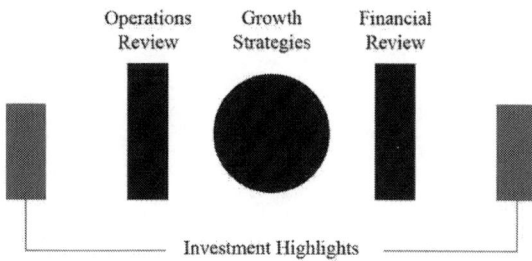

Operations Review · Growth Strategies · Financial Review · Investment Highlights

Immediately after the first investment highlights slide is the first section that discusses the strengths of the firm and its operations. It explains how the company is positioned within its industry and in what markets or segments it competes and excels in.

The second main section -- growth strategies -- hones in on the company's growth strategies and states exactly how the firm plans to achieve growth. There are usually at least as many slides related to growth strategies as there are for operations review.

The third and final section is the financial review. The CFO covers this section and provides salient financial highlights and a discussion of steps the company is taking to improve performance. This section typically utilizes several bar and line graphs to show improving historical financial data. Graphs that show increasing compound annual growth (CAGR) and other thematic concepts and ratios should establish the firm as equal or better than competitors. Well-performing IPOs have a high ratio of financial slides relative to the number of slides used to introduce the business potential.

Most IPO presentations consist of three sections totaling twenty-three slides, not including up to seven so-called "fluff" slides.

These fluff slides (also known as "filler" or "boilerplate" slides) are: the cover slide (also known as the "logo" or "opening" slide); "Safe Harbor/ Disclaimer/Forward-Looking Statements" slide; "Offering Summary"; and two or three "name" (or "title" slides) used to signal a new section delivered by a different presenter). The final "investment highlights" slide is sometimes also a fluff slide because it often repeats the exact same slide the CEO opened with. It is not optimal to repeat the investment highlights verbatim the second time, but many firms choose to do so.

Figure 11: Holding or "Fluff" Slides as seen in Twitter's IPO.

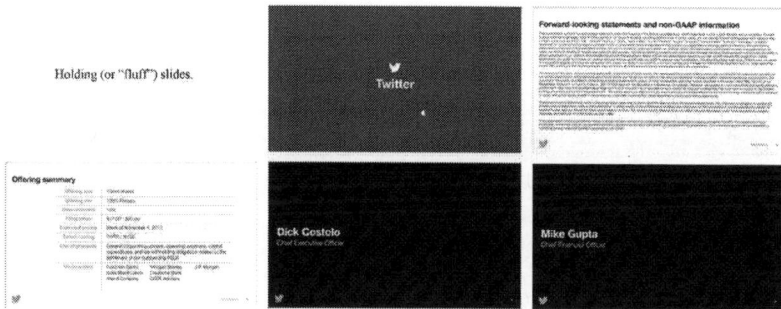

More on the Three Major Components

The majority of successful IPO presentations use a well-recognized and familiar structure. There are three defined segments of the presentation, the detail and strategy behind each investment highlight are often tracked in the order in which they appear on this opening slide.

Section 1: The Business and its potential -- investors want to know immediately what size the firm is and how large its current and untapped opportunities are. The firm's industry, markets and relevance within its markets are the first priority when outlining an IPO presentation. A broad picture of the firm's operations, products and services is helpful to educate investors who likely know little or nothing about its business or competitive strengths and advantages. Concrete data should support the firm's desired positioning and opportunities.

Educate investors about the company's key performance drivers and the dynamics of the industry using just two or three slides. Emphasize areas that support the investment thesis. Do this by demonstrating how your the firm's strengths enable it to capitalize on high growth or increasingly profitable situations. Don't spend too much time reviewing the business itself; investors are more interested in growth strategies and how firms plan to exploit their competitive advantages to the fullest extent possible.

Section 2: Growth Strategies -- This section is the most important as it is the heart of the equity story. It involves a discussion of the tactics and rationale behind the firm's growth strategies. Be clear about why each strategy is geared to creating "shareholder value", a common reference to the increase in shareholder's equity that occurs when the firm's share price increases. Discuss both short and medium-term strategies (present time to one year out). Cover the correlated tactics and desired results, as measured by the impact on various financial metrics. Support the firm's current strengths and advantages with strategies. Longer-term growth strategies (3+ quarters ahead) may also be considered.

Section 3: Financial -- The CFO wraps up by demonstrating long-term visibility, stable/predictable revenue/operating model, fiscal prudence, attractive historical operating performance and other metrics that suggest a future return on investment. Illustrate concepts such as operating leverage, low cost producer, scalability, and productivity. Demonstrate risk management and control. Soft forecasts can be identified as "target financial model" or "target operating model"; securities law prohibits financial forecasts in the US. Communicating that IPO proceeds are sufficient to enable the firm to achieve its growth objectives without a secondary ("follow-on") issue. Pro-forma capitalization and use of proceeds are also often covered.

Slide by Slide: Section One -- The Introduction

The first section consists of five slides that introduce the firm, its management team and the investment highlights:

Slide 1: (Title slide) This is the very first slide of the presentation (almost always produced in PowerPoint). In group meetings, this slide is displayed on the TV monitors or projection screen as people walk into the room. In one-on-one meetings, this slide serves as the cover of the flip-books. It determines the first impression made with investors about the company's style, apart from the impression formed while management entered the room. The graphics are usually understated and most often use a common font like arial or helvetica. The words "IPO Presentation" or "Initial Public Offering" is often dark blue to convey credibility. One or two images depicting the firm's products or global reach may be used to emphasize its revenue opportunity in a way that feels positive.

Slide 2: (Forward-Looking Statements): the second slide is chock full of legal text no one really cares about except the SEC, which is why it is required by law. You never know if a janitor (or pilot) will buy stock in an IPO based on a deck he found in a trash bin or behind a seat. If the firm's investor relations officer is in the room, she should read the disclaimer aloud. If not the CFO should simply say, "Before we begin I ask you to refer to the cautionary statements and risks of this offering as explained by the disclaimers in our S-1 and IPO deck". Because the presentation occurs in someone else's boardroom, you can expect to be recorded. If you take issue with this, you must say so before the meeting begins

Slide 3. (Summary of The Offering): this slide has roughly fifteen statistics about the transaction, including the trading symbol, price range, closing date, share structure, offering size and use of proceeds. At large group meetings the lead banker will talk to this slide. At one-on-one meetings, the CEO hits just a few points: deal size, price range and percentage of secondary shares because investors can read the slides for themselves. The ratio of secondary shares offered is perhaps the most interesting data point because it indicates how aggressively existing shareholders (insiders) are cashing out. Investors generally prefer to see no secondary shares for sale, as the proceeds go directly into the pocket of existing insiders at the IPO firm.

Slide 4. ('Management Team' or 'Senior Management'). This slide includes the names and titles of the speaker team. It can also include career highlights, prior industry experience and post-IPO holdings. Some choose to display the age and education of managers if they are short of experience. In such cases it is recommended to delete the slide entirely because it only highlights that the management team must be so inexperienced that they resorted to using age as a barometer for quality. Investors will rapidly judge management's experience for themselves regardless of how old senior management is.

Slide 5. (Investment Highlights). One of the most important slides in the deck. The CEO starts and finishes with this slide. At one-on-ones, the CEO should direct people to flip right to it, ignoring all disclaimers before it as they have already been disclosed in the prospectus. Before jumping into the Investment Highlights, the best CEOs preface with a fifteen second overview to highlight the collective experience of the Roadshow team and management's personal commitment to creating shareholder value. CEOs that retain high ownership stakes after the lockup expiration should say so.

The investment highlights is best delivered when the presenter does not look at the slide. The first investment highlight must convey the fundamental reason why the firm's new equity security is worthy of consideration as an investment. The four or five highlights that follow should provide concrete evidence to support the main thesis.

The investment highlights is the framework for the entire story, so it is imperative that investors agree with the logic and assumptions of each of statement. Addressing a well known, serious risk factor up front is a good way to frame perceived threats and manage the development of key issues.

Section One: Business Review

In the first act of section one, the firm explains its market, opportunities, and competitive strengths. By the beginning of the next section, investors should have a firm grasp on the firm's appeal. After hooking investors on the premise of the equity story, part two begins to explain the details behind the firm's future equity returns.

Part 2. (Industry Overview) 1-2 slides. Dimension the market size and the most salient opportunities by geography or revenue or whatever metric looks best. The bottom line is that investors need to understand how large the total market is and what segments offer the highest reward with low levels of risks. Do not bother covering more than three; this will only dilute what is truly important.

Part 3. (Operations Review) 2-6 slides. Discuss the company's operations and products and why they are compelling or better than other competitors.

Section Two: Growth Strategies

Part 1. Growth Strategies (3 slides). These slides define the short and long-term possibilities the company plans to achieve and how it plans to do it. The growth story is at the heart of every new equity issue. Investors want to hear about sustainable growth -- and lots of it. Begin with the current in-progress growth strategies that are already underway or are already accretive. Conclude with the far-off (1-2 year) growth initiatives after discussing the near-term aspects of growth.

Section Three: Financial Review

Part 1. Financial Review (5 slides). The CFO reviews key financial data for a minimum of two slides and then turns to the story of how the growth strategies and operational improvements are (or are expected to) translate directly into improved financial performance.

The Final Slide

Unless appendix slides exist (such as GAAP reconciliation) the *Final Slide* is again the Investment Highlights (1 slide). The CEO returns to provide some wrap up remarks. Unlike the first time, the CEO does not review every point on the slide but rather gives a concise summary.

Some firms show "Question Period (Q&A)" as the final slide, which remains on screen for thirty minutes. It is better if something substantive is on the slide -- such as ancillary data that support answers to key questions. It is a good idea to have backup data to flip to on screen that may not necessarily be included in the final bound presentation.

Let us now review each of the three major components in more detail.

Elements of Section 1: Business Potential

IPOs that price well require about eleven slides to convey the information investors need to know about the company's business, markets, opportunities, and long-term potential. Transactions that price poorly add 40% more content (an additional 15 slides for a total of 45 slides, including the "fluff" slides) to cover the same material, even though the majority of these firms are not necessarily as large or complex as better-performing transactions.

This 45% differential indicates that the longer it takes for management to articulate the potential of its firm, the less convincing the effort is. Relatively lengthy introductions seem to be a reliable indicator of inexperience.

The following headlines appeared as part of the "business potential" section from recent IPO presentations that priced well:

21st century technology
A well-established global leader
Addressing the widest spectrum - TV
Attractive growing footprint
Authentic lifestyle brand
Best in class specialty retailer
Broad, integrated product portfolio
Compelling industry dynamics
Content is key to teacher loyalty
Core operating principles
Dynamic multichannel distribution model
Established category leader with the premier brand
Established track record of success
Exclusive access with high barriers to entry
Family of products using a single platform
Global infrastructure developed over two decades
Global market opportunity
High profit distribution model
Home office culture of excellence

Innovative platform investments

Integrated product development

Interactive whiteboards drive tangible education benefits

Key differentiators

Key drivers for broadband video and data markets

Large and fast-growing interactive whiteboard market

Largest installed base of America's largest 401(k) plans

Leading global brand creates strategic relationships

Leading position in our markets

Leading specialty retailer

Long history of successful innovation and IP development

Long-standing customer relationships

We are more important today than ever before

Our core CMOS RF Technology platform

Our leadership position

Our mission

Our opportunity

Our strength in design

Our strong results

Our team

Our value proposition

Our vision

Outstanding product design

Platform for broader market opportunity

Platform to support a large, entrepreneurial sales force

Powerful trends driving growth

Predictable and controllable drivers of production

Product breadth & accessibility

Product strategy

Proprietary DSP-enhanced radio architecture

Proven community bank model with local accountability

Proven track record of driving profitability

Rapid execution

Relentless innovation

Sales drive recruiting: recruits drive sales

Scalable technology delivers high quality at low cost

Significant technology lead

Solving an age-old problem

Stable base of deposits

Stable performance through a turbulent environment

Strong management team

Top-tier customers

Unique market position

Universal appeal

Unparalleled scale of face-to-face distribution

Vast opportunity in the middle market

We are leading a transformation

We own our distribution network

We start with the consumer

Who we are

Elements of Section 2: Growth Strategies

The growth strategies must be convincing so they are often difficult to write.

Marketers must distill the firm's strategies for growth into three broad and

distinct opportunities to leverage the firm's competitive advantages and create solid or achievable opportunities over the long-term. Cite no more than four growth strategies; more than four will convey that the firm is not focused.

Well-priced IPOs identified 3.5 growth strategies, on average, compared to just 1.3 from IPOs that priced poorly (below the range or postponed). Firms must be cognizant of the emphasis that investors place on clearly defined growth strategies. These growth strategies demonstrate that a dollar invested today will be worth more in the future. They are the basis behind calculating the majority of valuation multiples and every effort must be made to prove they are a legitimate means to generating sustainable future cash flows.

Each growth strategy should directly address how the firm plans to expand its current markets or enter new ones. Investors want to understand how the firm expects to generate more revenue and improve overall financial performance -- by segment, geography, consumer or product line.

The content of the growth strategies section must provide the answers to several fundamental questions: how will the company grow its revenue base? How will it attract new customers? What is the implied growth opportunity? How achievable is it? How long will it take? Is the firm well defended against competitors executing a similar strategy? Where will the growth come from: organic growth or acquisition? Will the firm penetrate new or existing markets? What stage is the company at with executing its plans for growth? Is the growth just starting or is it already underway? Are there any results to substantiate progress if any has been made?

Here are some examples of headlines appearing in the "growth strategies" section of successful IPOs:

Built-in growth

Business and government markets in early stages

Capture additional technology spend in the classroom

Developing markets

Expand and enhance our product offerings

Expand in under-penetrated markets

Experienced and invested management team

Follow the baby boomers at work and through retirement

Growing the direct channel

Growing the indirect channel

Growth framework

Highly achievable growth plan

Leverage leadership in interactive touch technologies

Member acquisition strategy

New market opportunities

Our compounding growth strategy

Paid membership growth

Service provider acquisition strategy

Service provider growth

Significant opportunity for whiteboard growth in education

Tangible benefits drive growth in business and government

Three sources of growth

Specific discussion about each major growth strategy should incorporate simple language to clearly answer how the company intends to grow its revenue base and by how much. It is up to the investor to make an educated guess to predict how long it will take for strategy to impact financial performance.

IPOs that were effective at defining their growth strategies used words such as these:

Angie's List ($114 million): Grow and retain members, grow and retain service providers. More households per market; more verticals per household, more products per vertical.

Nielsen Holdings ($1.9 billion): Revenue contribution from higher growth businesses in developing markets ~1/3; steady growth businesses with multi-year subscription revenues delivering predictable results ~2/3; "These are solid, solid growth opportunities"; Tuck-in acquisitions, revenue share opportunities...numerous growth opportunities.

Vera Bradley ($176 million): Expand and enhance our product offerings, expand in under-penetrated markets, Grow the indirect channel, grow the direct channel.

Mattress Firm Holdings ($106 million): Add new stores in established markets; expand franchisee footprint; enter smaller markets with less competition; add 100 new stores per year in a market that can support 2500 new stores; Double-size over 5 years without entering competition rich areas. Grow without taking on complex growth projects.

Elements of Section 3: Financial

Many writers prefer to start developing the financial section first so that the information and concepts investors are most interested in aren't left until the end of the process. The first slides that are circulated receive the most attention, regardless of their absolute importance.

A useful starting point is to identify all graphs and data that demonstrate growth in areas integral to various valuation calculations. Content directly related to inputs into valuation models is the most important.

The financial section typically includes data related to revenue, compound annual growth (CAGR) of sales, net income, operating income, EBITDA, cash flow, free cash flow, leverage (debt to equity) and other valuation inputs and common performance measures.

Consider data related to segmented information, operating margins, capital expenditures, operating efficiencies, operating costs and other metrics if they accomplish the goal of conveying the firm's most attractive financial attributes.

Private companies are not subject to the standards and conventions of GAAP accounting; if the SEC has approved the presentation of financial data as it appears in the prospectus the firm is free to re-purpose it as long as reconciling the numbers is possible.

Consider the 2010 IPO filing of Groupon, which attempted to use a nonstandard (e.g. non-GAAP) financial measurement for operating income called "adjusted consolidated segment operating income", or CSOI, to exclude the firm's massive marketing costs. On a GAAP basis, Q1 2011 operating income would show a $98 million loss, but using CSOI the same period shows a $81.6 million *profit*. Obviously, this is a big difference from GAAP. Institutional investors are much more likely than retail investors to monitor the performance of the various discretionary components included in non-GAAP adjusted numbers.

Determine what period looks best for each type of graph. Show progress by quarter instead of yearly, for example. Not every company can show five consecutive years of growth. Those that can, do.

Produce as many graphs -- one per page -- in a single PowerPoint document. Be sure to include the referenced data from the prospectus so the graphs can be re-formatted easily. The idea is to produce an inventory of possibilities that can be used to shape the financial story.

It is advantageous to be clear about permanent, visible, or persistent earnings. Permanent earnings are considered to be high quality compared to transitory cash flows that are prone to unexpected or sudden declines due to changes in consumer consumption or cyclical factors that can be very hard to predict.

Any text that accompanies a graph or other visual display of financial information must be conscientiously conservative, devoid of superlatives or promotional language. If investors get the sense that the CFO is not a true "numbers" person, much is lost. A CEO is allowed a wider margin of personal expression relative to the CFO, who has close to none. For this reason, it is advisable to use language to describe financial performance that is very similar to the language used in the prospectus.

Financial information is usually presented as a bar or line graph, or a table. Financial data that trends upward (ramps up from left to right) is best suited for bar and line graphs because investors much prefer to see numbers trending sequentially upward. Use a table to present numbers that do not visually demonstrate increasingly improved performance if they must be included. It is unusual to include a graph that does not show a strong trend upwards. Often, the scale of the graph is manipulated to enhance trends that otherwise would appear modest. The X axis (left-hand side of a graph) is where dollar amounts ($ millions) are shown to scale, with the time series (by fiscal year or quarter) forms the bottom ("Y") axis.

Graphs that are presented in a non-traditional format will attract unwanted attention because it may seem as if the firm is trying to hide something. For this reason, it is not advisable to switch axes (e.g. show the time scale on the left side rather than the bottom) or veer in some major way from the traditional presentation of financial information. Investors will take the time to interpret the reasons why management would choose a non-standard approach and will likely conclude something negative about the approach.

To help investors or analysts recall information, studies show that memory is improved if the conditions at retrieval closely match the conditions present when the memory was first encoded. In effect, decision makers often receive and encode information arranged in one format, and then later try to recall it in a different format. For this reason, try to keep the information as it appears in the presentation consistent with the prospectus.[10]

Here are titles of slides in the financial overview section of recent IPOs that priced at the top of the range or above:

Adjusted net income is an important metric

Attractive funding mix

Balanced, low risk investment portfolio

Buy and watch revenue performance

Capital efficiency drives ROI Capitalization

Compelling financial model

Conservative approach to capital management

Conservative investment portfolio

Consistent growth across key top line metrics Consolidated net revenue growth

Consolidated operating income performance CRE and construction loan portfolios

Diversified loan mix

Driving increasing profitability

Flexible, scalable operations

Foundation for growth

FY 2011 year to date results

Growth has accelerated

Growth has been global

Growth in powertrain business

High revenue visibility

Highly attractive new store economic model

Historical key financials

Historical key ratios

Investing in growth

Investment and savings provide earnings diversification

Key business metrics

Liquidity

Long-term financial goals

Long-term financial targets

Long-term loan and deposit growth

Long-term objectives

Long-term operating model

Long-term performance targets

Low capex supports strong cash generation

Non-performing loans

Our expositions segment

Outstanding record of growth at scale and strong margins

Predictable revenue model

Proactive balance sheet management

Pro-forma balance sheet

Pro-forma capital structure

Pro-forma capitalization

Pro-forma financial profile

Pro-forma capital position

Projected cost reduction roadmap/revenue opportunity

Proven ability to improve gross margin

Recent developments

Recurring, predictable revenue growth

Revenue from multiple product categories

Selected peer comparison

Significant capital leverage

Significant competitive advantage

Significant sales momentum

Solid AUM growth in unsteady markets

Strong financial performance

Strong gross margins and operating leverage

Strong margins and net interest income growth

Strong profitability trends

Strong revenue growth

Superior credit quality

Target financial model

Target store economics

Term life growth profile enhanced through reinsurance

Transaction sources and uses

Specific language related to the most commonly cited metrics are as follows:

Revenue: CAGR over x sequential years/quarters, consistent/stable/ predictable/constant revenue/currency growth, revenue by segment/ product line/market, historical vs. pro forma, revenue mix, sales momentum, x consecutive months of positive comparable-store sales, predictable revenue model (monetization, drivers); high revenue visibility (deferred revenue, contract backlog, renewal rates);

Recurring revenue: high renewal rates, x% recurring revenue

Operating leverage: sustainable operating efficiencies, EBITDA margin increases from x% to y% (q-o-q or y-o-y).

De-leveraging: strong free cash flow generation, favorable tax attributes, disciplined capital spending, declining leverage from x% to y% (q-o-q or y-o-y), sustainable low cash tax rate, modest financial leverage.

EBITDA: Adjusted EBITDA margin CAGR over x sequential years/ quarters, Increasing adjusted EBITDA and margins.

Financial targets/goals: revenue growth: mid single digit, adjusted EBITDA growth: ~1.2x revenue growth, developing market growth: double digit, Adjusted net income growth: ~2.3x EBITDA growth, deleveraging: ~0.5x per year; Annual EPS growth: ~25%; annual comparable-sales growth: 2.5%-5%; cash on cash return; payback period; Annual net income growth: high teens; Operating income margin expansion: ~30bps/year.

Miscellaneous: working capital dynamics: cash conversion cycle; Strong margins and cash flows; earning diversification; capital strength.

Broad Themes

A 1996 study of annual reports revealed that six themes were prevalent in the President's Letter to Shareholders: business environment, growth, operating philosophy, markets and products, unfavorable financial reference and favorable financial reference.

The same can be said of IPO presentations, with the exception of "business environment" and "unfavorable financial reference". Issuers of new equity always avoid including anything negative in the IPO presentation, especially unattractive financial trends. This is acceptable because all negative information has already been fully disclosed in the prospectus, including evidence of a deteriorating financial condition, opportunistically-greedy selling shareholders or a seriously damaging competitive threat.

The various themes mentioned above contain information found to be useful in predicting changes in sales, return on equity, price to earnings and dividend changes at least one year ahead.[11] Many investors that attend the one-on-one meetings make note of management's initial disclosures, whether they buy or not at the time of the IPO. Some only decide to become shareholders at a future point when the stock is trading and the company triggers a metric monitored by the investor established during the Roadshow.

The First Thirty Seconds

Audiences tend to project their own emotions into a story at key intervals when it seems reasonable to do so and expect the presenter to demonstrate a similar and authentic mode of expression when talking about such content. Presenters that do not appear to be aligned with the audience's notion of a consistent reaction will suffer a significant impairment to credibility.

Avoid the standard opening line "I'm happy to be here today" and its permutations. Instead, begin the presentation with a forceful statement that stirs genuine emotion in the presenter and audience:

"When I started with the company eighteen years ago, I never could have imagined we would be as successful as we are now. But we are. And because of our success I'm proud to invite you to join me as a shareholder"; or

"Five years ago we decided if we wanted to be the best we'd have to focus. We'd have to change our mix to markets that required less capital. To do this, we needed to re-structure, borrow money and take on some risk. But those decisions were the right ones. Now, five years later, we are the leaders in our

category -- a category that is growing. The same team that was with me then is still with me today and I speak for everyone when I say we will work hard for you. If you like what you hear today, please join us as a stockowner"; or

"I have 14 years of CEO experience at much larger companies. Both of those firms were like this one: at the pre-clinical phase. I was successful at guiding both portfolios to economically attractive commercialization. So I am absolutely confident in what we're doing here...and I can tell you that this opportunity right now -- this is the best opportunity in our market right now. There isn't another that comes close."[12]

The most effective opening statements are personal without sounding trite. When the CEO takes the microphone, it is up to the CEO to take control. Failing that, the CEO must avoid sounding cliché. If a hint of a cliché is detected, the deal will immediately be classified as mediocre. To an audience of experienced ears, there are few things more unpleasant than listening to a CEO who sounds forced or unnatural.

For this reason, avoid "I know how busy you are" or "I'll quickly run through the slides". Instead, try "We're going to take about ten minutes each to walk you through what we believe is a good story for a few good reasons".

Or: "Thanks for your attention today, I'm going to tell you about why we are market leaders and why we expect to be successful. We hope you find our story compelling. Now let me tell you why…"

Mitigate Risks and Threats

Your presentation should negate any major threat by weaving each of them into different contexts. For example: "the firm enjoys excellent relationships with long-term customers in very large markets with a significant barrier to entry because adoption of new products is risky for consumers and could take years to implement". Or, "the firm's design patents cover specific equipment consumers have become familiar with, making adoption of an alternative design for the same purpose very difficult". Or, "the firm has a new product it expects to introduce next year that will be produced at a lower cost and higher margin".

Avoid Ambiguity

The results are not optimal when investors are forced to figure out for themselves why they should risk capital in a story that is unclear. Weak pricing and anemic liquidity in the secondary market are two common side effects that pose difficult, long-term ramifications that are vexingly difficult for a new company to confront.

The key to a successful IPO presentation is to be absolutely clear with establishing the firm's differentiation. Information is devalued if it is described incompletely relative to information that is fully described.[13]

Do not mince words or dilute key messages by introducing other concepts that will confuse investors that are time and attention-starved. Capture the audience's attention from the very beginning and hold their attention by feeding them packets of the story that underscore the firm's growth prospects.

Open and Close with Investment Highlights

No more than ninety seconds is required to open and close the presentation. The CEO will deliver her opening salvo while investors stare at a slide with the headline: "Investment Highlights". The best prepared CEOs walk the audience through this critical introduction without glancing at notes; the only objective is to make the point using her own natural language to do so. When the slide turns, everyone in the room has sized her up and made a judgment call about the quality of the firm and its potential.

Considerations of Preparation

Ninety percent of Roadshow meetings are in a "one-on-one" format. These meetings engage prospective investors face to face. Management walks through each slide of the IPO presentation and then takes questions. One hour is allotted for each meeting; thirty minutes for the formal presentation and thirty minutes for Q&A. This format of "give and take" helps to alleviate the tendency of passive audiences to automatically discount information more often relative to those that are engaged. Presenters who are able to "connect" with their audience enjoy better outcomes because higher value information is exchanged and is less likely to be degraded or distorted.

The speaker team must rehearse together several times and simulate as closely as possible both the one-on-one and group meeting presentation formats. Simulations accomplish the important objective of exposing the obvious kinks and disconnects in a story prior to the planned launch. The flow of the story, the resonance of important concepts and whether key objections are countered successfully must be ferreted out in private before they are revealed to a wider audience.

This allows management and its bankers to make the adjustments necessary to ensure the emphasis and supporting evidence is convincing. Once the Roadshow begins, investors will be looking for every tiny hole in the story. Every obvious weakness and inconsistency will be exposed on investor websites and perhaps the front page of USA Today, so preparation is integral to success.

It takes time and practice to bring a thirty page PowerPoint presentation to life. Only diligent and repeated rehearsal will reveal the best story. Slides will go through a long process of being re-written, re-ordered, deleted, and strengthened. Any management team that does not rehearse together before the Roadshow is at a severe disadvantage.

It is not the best idea to use the same presentation for both the one-on-one and group meetings.

One audience handles a paper document eighteen inches in front of them while another sits eighteen feet away with a plate of food in front of them. You would not expect to see the front page of the newspaper on the local news, so be mindful of transferring PowerPoint slides to the screen. What looks good on paper may not be optimal for projection.

The vast majority of meetings use "flip" or "color" books. The only other type of meeting format is the group presentation. Group presentations do not use flip books. This is because all color books *must be* collected at the end of the meeting. This is too onerous of a risk for anyone to accept because some investors may be tempted to absent-mindedly pocket the document in a zipped up briefcase.

For those firms conducting multiple tranches or simultaneous offerings (such as a concurrent debt issue of convertible debentures or senior notes), it is worthwhile to note that only one presentation is required for the Roadshow. Slides related to any concurrent transactions marketed by the firm can be included in the Appendix. By law, every investor at every meeting must receive a prospectus. Sending them by courier ahead of time is a good approach in some cities with a high concentration of investors. Otherwise, a box must be lugged around and checked through security at each location.

At group meetings, instead of printed slides, an LCD projector or other large screen is used. Because text displayed on a screen or projected surface can be much harder to read than on paper, format a different version of the presentation so it is legible to the audience. This "screen" version will use bigger fonts, bolder subtitles and text, and larger, simplified graphs.

Audiences must be able to read all text that appears on screen, so test the presentation for legibility before the Roadshow launches. If an investor is unable to read what is on screen, her ability to comprehend the slide is obviously limited and may compromise anything she hears as she squints in an effort to decipher the presenter's spoken word. This is due to a phenomenon known as "attentional blink" which occurs when observers search for two or more targets at the same time. Processing the first target temporarily prevents adequate processing of the second, so the second target is impaired when the second target lags the first.[14]

Humans process one piece of information at a time. If the acquisition of a second or even third piece of information is occurring simultaneously, attentional blink causes all of the information to decay until it becomes so impaired that all of the information may be completely discarded. Investors still trying to make sense of what appears on screen after management has already moved on to discuss the next item will be frustrated and any information that follows will be compromised whether the investor is aware of being confused or not.

When deciding whether to reveal content all at one time or build it click by click, consider the process known as cue competition. Cue competition occurs when salient cues vie for attention, with the brain automatically determining what cue is more dominant because of color, size, or volume. Predictably, stronger cues weaken the effects of less salient ones, and the presence of irrelevant cues will cause an audience to use relevant cues and base rates. As humans are limited in their ability to process information, they tend to use information in the form they see it rather than modifying it appropriately.[15] The upshot is that it may be necessary to give important messages enough time or support so they truly "sink in" before moving to the next piece of less important content.

The Presentation Drafting Process

Pulling together the firm's four of five investment highlights and assembling the content to support the fundamentals of the story is straightforward. Prioritizing the order and sequence of messages and facts is a lot more difficult. Producing the precise wording of each statement and ensuring each is as powerful as possible is the most demanding task.

Generally, there are several investment bankers working on the transaction who will have varied opinions about the presentation's structure and emphasis. For this reason, it is advisable to work up the deck until only the slide headlines and financial section are complete, and then hold a presentation review by conference call to receive comments and suggestions from senior bankers only. This will save an enormous amount of time and is effective insurance to ensure the flow and substance of the story is correct, as early as possible.

Analysts and their senior counterparts will often have theories or knowledge of dynamics of your operations they may consider important even if management does not. The biases and opinions about what is highlighted or downplayed -- will persist throughout the numerous drafting sessions.

When the time comes to craft the presentation, two bankers generally emerge as the most knowledgeable about the process. One of them is usually from ECM (equity capital markets), the other an industry head from investment banking.

Drafting sessions are much more efficient when a PowerPoint operator revises slides in real-time, incorporating comments as they are submitted.

In this way, the working group can step through multiple revisions and get an important and immediate sense of how the presentation is taking shape. Without a PowerPoint operator, revisions are left to an investment banking analyst who works all night on changes submitted by as many as fifteen people on a conference call. This is not the best way to go. It is much preferable to turn the deck quickly and get it back into circulation. Otherwise it invites the opportunity for a very senior banker who hasn't seen the presentation to unceremoniously rip it apart after dozens of drafts have been made by others with less experience.

As the launch date of the IPO nears, the deck will receive greater scrutiny. Bankers and lawyers who have not participated directly will enter the picture and ask for various changes, such as additional material or re-ordering of certain slides.

At this point in the process, it is best to appoint one person who is responsible for the master slide deck. It is suicide to have two or three editable copies of the deck in circulation -- only one version at a time is allowed to run in the wild. Keep one master deck only and hold regular conference calls to review the presentation and make changes to it. Every page should include a timestamp, filename and current page number of the total number of pages (e.g. page 6/30).

As stated previously, various parties must not have their own version of the PowerPoint presentation to edit freely. Use PDFs at all times when circulating versions. If necessary, set security permissions using Acrobat's security function to limit emailing and printing. Distributing files that anyone can modify will amputate the process, as it becomes unnecessarily onerous to track and integrate the changes and comments made by various stakeholders to slides on different versions of the deck. Without disciplined change management procedures, old versions tend to suddenly appear back in circulation.

Managing Revisions

Tracking changes is an important element of managing the IPO Presentation. At a certain point you need to focus on honing language, instead of entertaining questions related to "where's my change?"

Once the content for the presentation is finalized, a printed version for use in the one-on-ones and a screen version for the group meetings are produced.

The printed version, termed "the flip book" is a color book that consists of all of the slides in your presentation, one per page, and bound. It may have tabs separating the three or four main sections (Operations, Growth Strategies, Financial Review, Appendix).

Presentation Creep

In an attempt to satisfy everyone, it is common to see extra content added in the late stages -- material that may not be completely on point. This phenomenon is known as "presentation creep".[16] Presentation creep arises from the perceived need to incorporate the answer to every possible question in the slides themselves. When this starts to happen, the team should focus on adhering to communications protocol and limit the presentation to 25 slides that are presented in 25 minutes. This is more difficult than it sounds because as the presentation continues to develop, one-off comments are inevitably incorporated. Slides will begin to swell with information. In the late stages it is important to keep unnecessary material out of the deck.

Presentation creep affects not only the PowerPoint file itself, but the speaking points as well. Remarks such as "just add that concept in there" or "maybe we can work that in somewhere", generally signal that presentation creep is about to occur or is already underway. Similarly, "let's answer the question here so investors aren't sitting there thinking about it" or "can we just throw it in here somewhere and drive on" are other telltale signs of the phenomena.

And with these words, the deck grows. And grows. Twenty minutes is now pushing thirty-five minutes. Somehow, the importance of fully explaining that new line of products scheduled for release in Kuala Lampur has been added.

PowerPoint files grow much faster than they shrink, just as stocks tend to fall faster than they rise. When it comes time to cut, scour the deck slide by slide and identify content that is not closely or directly related to the investment highlights. Then ask whether it must stay -- will it really be missed? If not, cut it. The more content that is added after the messaging framework has been built, the greater the potential for dilution. And you don't want to introduce unnecessary risk unless it is really worth the reward.

Regardless of the type of Roadshow meeting (group or one-on-one), IPO presentations rely on investors to process information using both verbal and visual inputs. As management talks to a set of printed or projected slides, investors listen as they continually review the slides -- and the presenters -- in front of them.

Research on the topic of selective attention suggests that it takes between one half to one and a half seconds to switch from processing a visual to verbal input. This is a consideration if the last point made is still being processed and the presenter says "as you can see from this slide", forcing the audience to abandon whatever is currently in the mind of the audience. It is better to preface any switch with "in a few seconds I'll show you how this has a positive effect on our results by asking you to refer to page 34." This not only prepares the viewer by framing the upcoming content positively, but provides fair warning that any current thinking should stay in memory.

Another relevant study found that people are better able to remember and recall information when it is provided in the same format it was first seen at the time of recall. In one study a spreadsheet with two years of financial ratios and ratings was given to two separate groups. The spreadsheet of the second group reversed the ratio/rating names and years (using columns in stead of rows). Comparisons between the groups showed that memory improved as the match between encoding and retrieval conditions increase -- the first group was better able to recall the information when the formatting was the same for both encoding and retrieval.[17]

Design Considerations

Investors sit though a great many number of presentations. In the same way a doctor looks at both numbers and pictures to reach a diagnosis, so does an investor when assessing an IPO presentation. Through their depth of experience and familiarity with specialized content, investors have acquired preferences about formatting and structure. They know what "success" looks like.

Effective presentations are those that employ images and graphics conservatively. Extra graphics or images should only be included at times when it is necessary to emphasize elements of the story that would require too many words. The power and economy of graphics is best preserved for times when it is most required, or to be consistent with how certain data appears in the prospectus.

The largest, most successful companies often use simple, basic graphics.

They do not sacrifice readability with clutter or color-coded navigation schemes. Avoid any unnecessary elements to remain crisp, clear and sharp. Embrace this approach.

The majority of the CFO's financial review will consist of bar, pie, or line graphs to convey the underlying intent of financial trends (growth, reduced expenses, expanding margins) more easily than words or numbers in a table ever could.

Investors will deduct credibility points to those who submit to the urge to fill up all available white space with photography or other design flourishes. Investors appreciate white space. It demonstrates restraint and discipline. It allows the written word to be easily digested, free from the noise and attention demanded by extemporaneous graphics. Adding images of the company's products and the happy family pretending to use them must be considered with extreme prejudice. Most investors could care less if an IPO presentation has photography or polished graphics, unless the firm's future revenue stream depends on its branded products. Attempts to establish a metaphorical relationship between largely symbolic graphics (picture of the latest Porsche) and adjacent text ("Powerful engine for future growth") signals inexperience.

The most serious investor presentations are those prepared for rating agency meetings (Moody's, S&P). These presentations utilize no graphics whatsoever beyond the sober depiction of numerical data seen in bar, line and pie charts. Three-dimensional (3-D) pie graphs are rarely seen, as it sends a signal that extra and unnecessary resources were expended when a straightforward 2-D approach would have worked just as well, if not better.

Companies with established brand guidelines should incorporate a realistic means by which typographic conventions and style sheets are used within the context of PowerPoint. Many designers use typefaces that are too small or colors that are not consistent with investor preferences. It can be frustrating to spend months crafting the perfect presentation only to see it "tweaked" by a designer who makes it difficult to read.

It is imperative that investors are able to read every word of every footnote. If an investor at the back of the room is unable read a footnote on the screen, a bigger screen -- or more of them -- is required.

Given the choice, investors would choose a semi-amateurish but highly legible presentation over one that may win a graphic design award but is difficult to read. The vast majority of investor presentations use Arial as a typeface. It is the industry standard for IPO design and those that try and impose their own typefaces risk looking like amateurs. There are a lot of billion dollar deals that have been done with arial.

The IPOs of Vera Bradley and Potbelly are two notable exceptions. As a designer of interior decorating products, Vera Bradley used overly-fancy graphics which sometimes sacrificed readability. But the transaction performed well because it was brief enough to survive an unconventional approach.[18] Potbelly Corporation was successful because of the CEOs former experience with Sears -- an organization more than *one hundred times the size* of his new challenge: a neighborhood sandwich shop with 280 locations.[19]

There is a risk to making a presentation look "too good". Be cautious with 'overdoing' a presentation in an attempt to burnish credibility. The end result will likely be the opposite of what was intended. Especially in circumstances where required information is lacking or not provided, the inference will likely be that the firm sacrificed substance for sizzle.

Bankers do not like to see text flying around or any other type of animation. This includes slides that "build" (when one bullet point comes on and then fades to a lighter color after the next bullet is revealed). The financial community prefers to see the content of an entire slide revealed at once, at the same time.

The Electric Wiener

The "electric wiener" is slang for a graphics box that contains text at the bottom of a slide.[20] Designers often like to use curved corners instead of square edges for boxes, which makes the box look like an *Oscar Meyer* wiener.

Inside this wiener-shaped box is a summary of the entire slide, which serves the purpose of a second main headline. Many IPO presentations use this summary text box as it provides a convenient way for the presenter to sum up an entire slide after reviewing its contents with the audience. Text inside a box also appears larger than it really is, providing a useful way to emphasize important text while maintaining consistency.

LinkedIn is just one of many IPOs that used the electric wiener to sum up each slide. LinkedIn's first wiener reads "Fundamentally changing the way the world works" which at first seems like an epic overstatement. But further examination reveals that the unconventional grammar (is it a dangling participle?) is on purpose, as "the world works" is not a philosophical reference to how the world actually works, but a statement meant to relay the firm's key competitive strength as a website where people around the world can find employment.

Using rounded text boxes to sum up slides is absolutely fine (even if they do resemble wieners), but other non-traditional approaches can backfire. LinkedIn employed a "trendy" design style throughout its presentation. One example was its inclusion of two *Polaroid* pictures separated by a "+" sign to suggest a formula that was displayed in a handwritten font. To some, this signaled that the company's culture might not be as finance-oriented as others with similar valuations. These concerns eventually disappeared as the company demonstrated the advantages of scale and positive cash flow, proving to investors that the firm was a solid investment.

Google made a similar mistake when they took a non-traditional approach to their 2004 IPO presentation. Because of the post-IPO success of Google, many forget that transaction was forced to lower both the pricing range and number of shares offered halfway through the Roadshow.[21] Many institutions were skeptical after seeing Google's PowerPoint slides that consisted of a series of cartoons, presumably intended to support the firm's assertion that it is "not a conventional company" that believes in "Don't be evil".[22]

Figure 12: LinkedIn's Electric Weiner

In the short-term, Google's remarkably non-traditional approach left a lot of money on the table, as demand for IPO shares exceeded the supply by a multiple of twenty-five times (or, in Wall Street terms, the transaction was twenty-five times oversubscribed). The highly profitable internet firm paid a steep price for pursuing an auction approach even though the firm's financials were far superior to its peers. Within six months Google's stock price doubled, and the firm fell in line with other public companies by adopting a traditional approach to communicating with investors.

Headlines appearing at the top of each slide should stand out. A large typeface that is easy to read in a different color than the rest of the slide is a proven and common approach. Many presentations that are professionally designed for screen viewing utilize large yellow or white text "reversed out" of a black, dark blue or green background for headlines. Yellow over black is the easiest color combination to read, but is too "edgy" for most firms to be a practical solution unless the colors exist in the corporate palette.

Those that believe extra graphics are required to "spice up" the PowerPoint presentation should tend to this as the final step, just before the lawyers sign off on the final deck with all footnotes, disclaimers and graphics in place.

Two Versions for Two Different Meetings

Produce two versions of the final presentation once it is signed off. The one-on-one meetings require a printed hardcopy version while the group meetings require a version that is projected on one or several screens around the room.

The one-on-one meetings use a printed slide deck (always in landscape format) with dark text over a white background. This is the best scheme because people are still used to reading black type on a white page.

The version used at group meetings should generally utilize a dark background with reversed or "knocked out" type over a dark background. This can be easier to read although modern design and technical equipment makes dark type over a white background more popular. However, in a small group meeting it can be hard on the eyes to look at a blazing white screen for sixty minutes.

IPO presentations reference many numbers from the prospectus. Research shows that people are more likely to recall specific numbers than those presented as ranges (e.g. "between ten and twenty") or with words that are subjective or ambiguous.[23] For example, investors are more likely to remember "$11 dollars per share at the midpoint" instead of "between $10 and $12 per share" or a "$2.1 billion market opportunity" instead of a "very large", or "massive" market opportunity.

The "Retail Shout-Down"

Investment banks such as Morgan Stanley and UBS have large retail operations that listen to a four-minute version of the presentation that is broadcast to their stock brokers. Management teams should check ahead of time whether they are required to deliver this highly abridged version that follows the salesforce presentation.

If so, start with the investment highlights (skipping the management team highlight, if present) and sum up each of the three sections in the remaining few minutes. Start with the size of the markets and why the firm is currently well positioned in them through its products or whatever strengths are applicable. Then, review the most attractive growth strategy, making specific reference to the exact size of the opportunity ahead. The idea is to make the listening brokers understand the "upside" potential using precise numbers they can relay to their clients. For example, "*Our firm has developed a drug that is the leading candidate for FDA approval in a market that, by the most conservative estimates, is $1.2 billion in North America alone. We're not even talking about China where we plan to go next. China is an even larger opportunity. Again, conservatively, China is a $2.1 billion market. These* *are solid growth opportunities and we're close to making them happen in markets that account for $3.3 billion in existing sales."*

Creating the Presentation

1. As you write each slide, ask yourself why anyone would care about the slide. Is the content on the slide as succinct and direct as possible? Is it a logical step used in the construction of a solid story?

2. Use 3x5" index cards to quickly re-order the story when drafting headlines. It's easier to storyboard the flow of the presentation on paper instead of on screen. Read them aloud when you play with the order. You can make cards by printing the slides off at 25% directly from PowerPoint.

3. Keep the PowerPoint presentation in black and white for as long as possible. This will ensure early comments stay focused on content. This will also make handwritten edits much easier as dark backgrounds confound those who prefer to work with paper. Drafts of the presentation are usually printed using black & white laser printers that do not reproduce color well. Until the final version, use patterned bars instead of colors or shades of gray to differentiate graphs. Wait until the deck is almost finalized before adding

necessary photos, design details and color to charts and graphs.

4. Eliminate 'bullet points' (•). They are redundant and take up space, especially when they precede every single sentence. Removing the bullets will allow more room for a larger typeface. It can be very frustrating for an investor to attend a group meeting only to discover she is unable to read the slides from the back of the room.

Chapter Ten

PR and the IPO

Publicity has a profound impact on how an IPO is received. For this reason, public relations (PR or "media relations") activities are essential when planning the launch of a major IPO ($250+ million). Even modest media relations efforts or those executed with mixed results can positively influence the pricing of a transaction and enhance liquidity. Media coverage has been shown to influence the outcome of pricing and be a pivotal factor in whether an IPO prices low or high.

Not long ago, PR was considered optional. Lawyers and underwriters were of the opinion that the consequences of violating quiet period rules and the unintended consequences of promoting an IPO by possibly inexperienced non-financial marketers were risks not worth taking. This is no longer the case.

Now, with fewer new equity offerings raising more capital under constantly volatile conditions, institutional investors view media coverage of an IPO as a critical feature to a profitable exit. News coverage conveys important signals about how soon an exit can be made after trading begins. For some institutional investors, the mother of all shortcuts is the amount of media attention an IPO receives before an S-1 is filed.

Many private companies thrive without publicity. Public companies cannot. Research shows that stocks need attention to succeed.[1] PR and the publicity it generates is a reliable proxy for demand. Since the financial crisis in 2008, launching a high-profile IPO without PR is like flying a plane without a fuel gauge: the threat of an unscheduled landing looms until touchdown. Never mind the fact that two thirds of IPOs cite "reputation factors" as a reason to go public.[2]

Mediocre stories that gain media attention prior to an IPO will fare better than good stories that receive none. One study found that a firm's valuation is a function of the prior levels of investor interest it has attracted.[3] Publicity is also positively and significantly correlated with Nasdaq returns.[4] This is because publicity brings sentiment investors (retail investors) into the market for an IPO. Investment bankers then incorporate information related to changes in demand in subsequent offer price revisions.

A new breed of IPO analyst exists online, with many maintaining popular blogs aimed at institutional investors. They can be quick to point out any obvious flaws in a pending transaction for the world to see. It is common to see headlines such as "hint of desperation", "overpriced", "low margins" or "too much debt" introduce deals that are set to launch. Sites such as *StockTwits. com, SeekingAlpha.com* and *Twitter.com* are all popular destinations where investors visit to get the inside scoop on transactions in the pipeline.

Firms that retain lesser-known underwriters to lead their IPO must focus on ways to generate coverage using their own resources, as smaller investment banks ("boutiques") generally do not have the capacity or experience to assist with PR.

List All Possible Future News Headlines

The first step to generating coverage is to list all possible news releases (both financial and otherwise) that the firm can draw from during the pre-marketing, quiet period and post-IPO phases. This ensures that enough content will be available to establish ongoing contact with investors and the media during each phase. Any opportunity to create news through ancillary means other than a press release should also be included. Examples include speaking engagements at industry conferences, company-sponsored events, and informative podcasts and webcasts featuring senior management.

Create a separate list of relevant investor and industry websites to monitor. Websites, blogs and twitter users that focus on the IPO market can prove to be valuable sources to gain or disseminate information.

The goal of any Roadshow is to convey the value of the firm to institutional investors that analyze Initial Public Offerings for a living. The overwhelming majority of institutional meetings occur face-to-face in boardrooms on the investor's home turf, wherever that may be. These smaller meetings dominate the majority of time scheduled over the course of the Roadshow because institutional investors are allocated -- and have the ability to buy -- the majority of the offering.

Media relations activities can benefit even a $100 million IPO. Common concerns related to liquidity, ongoing awareness, the presentation (or "framing") of key issues, volatile market conditions, credibility of management, and crisis control are all threats addressed through defensive PR tactics.

Defensive PR is focused on articulating features centered around risk control and mitigation. Describing the business as "stable" or "relatively immune" to volatility can help offset concerns related to turbulent markets. Retaining external "ghost" bloggers to characterize management as "solid" or "highly experienced" with details related to management's past performance and success at previous organizations can also be helpful as long as it is true.

Media relations campaigns are most effective when the marketer has an existing relationship with the journalist or media outlet targeted as a potential source for news coverage. These relationships can be formed in the months leading up to the first S-1 filing.

PR is a necessity, and can be extremely useful through its ability to inform, highlight, and portray qualities about a company going public. But it can also produce unintended consequences as the media presents market participants with information that affects how impressions about the firm are formed and the legitimation of firms.[5] Misrepresenting financial data or performance will damage the credibility of any firm and its managers, so great care must be taken not to adopt an over-promotional tone.

Most PR firms are not familiar with the dynamics of transaction marketing. Only recently have US investment bankers become more comfortable with media relations activities. In contrast, Chinese IPOs have always viewed public relations as a necessary cornerstone to marketing new equity listings.

The shift to a more PR-centric strategic communications approach occurred in 2008 when PR came to the rescue after other methods failed to restore confidence in many of America's best known stocks. Even investor relations (IR), the traditional communications discipline favored by Wall Street, failed to assuage the mounting concerns of the financial community. Audited balance sheets and objective performance data became meaningless until confidence in the system itself failed, leaving no other alternative but government intervention. PR firms were forced to take a crash course in finance jargon to understand why clients were suddenly demanding talking points around 'price to tangible book' and 'third party CDO exposure risk'. It was clear that traditional press releases were no longer enough.

Some firms were finally able to crack the code to a problem many others in the industry were also trying to solve: how could the functions of PR and IR be combined without making any disastrous errors along the way? Hindsight shows how these two fundamentally different disciplines were successful at working together to produce results far better than if each worked in isolation.

Typically, IR practitioners view PR as an inferior, less complex field best used for promoting non-financial aspects of a company, such as those related to HR (human relations) and community-based issues. This is because IR typically has much more ongoing contact with the most senior members of management at successful public firms.

Taken together, the head of IR and PR coordinating with each other on their individual goals and plans will create value while keeping both disciplines looped in.

Objectives: Pre S-1 Filing

The objective of any Roadshow is to attract a high percentage of institutional investors. IPOs with larger institutional shareholdings tend to subsequently earn significantly higher long-run returns than those with small institutional holdings.[6] One proven method to accomplish this goal is to generate media coverage.

One study analyzed the affect of the Wall Street Journal's "Abreast of the Market" column. It found that either the media reports investor sentiment before the sentiment is fully incorporated into market prices or the media directly influence investors' attitudes toward securities.[7] Another study found that retail investors are more likely to purchase attention-grabbing stocks.[8] This is due partly to the fact that people generally assign a level of importance to events that is proportional to the frequency they are mentioned.[9] Taken together, there is ample evidence to suggest that firms must consider ways to establish themselves in the media while they are still private.

Media Properties and Contacts

Consider a range of media properties and contacts when communicating to potential investors and others before filing an S-1. This will maximize the audience size and potential exposure of news disseminated by the company.

Relevant properties to consider are: the firm's website, industry websites and conferences, investor websites, magazines, newspapers, the firm's official blog, radio, downloadable transcripts, podcasts, TWITTER, TUMBLR, the firm's FACEBOOK page, employee newsletters, LINKEDIN executive profiles, SCRIBD, FLICKR, GOOGLE+, YOUTUBE, broadcast television media and associated online counterparts.

The firm's website should include 'follow' buttons related to an ever-growing number of social media properties. New attempts to tap into investor audiences include *PassFail.com* and the massively popular picture-sharing app INSTAGRAM.

The Communications Audit

To understand what potential investors are going to read about the firm when it files its S-1, simply google the firm's name and its senior executives and check out the top twenty search results. Or, better yet, search for mentions about the company using a paid search service such as highbeam.com. If numerous articles or opinions appear that are not particularly favorable or accurate, flag them as potential threats to the firm.

Another worthwhile method is to use E-TRADE or other online trading platform to download research reports on the firm's peers to discover what analysts are saying about industry issues.

Members of the financial community may even seek information about the firm from the firm's employees, including those who are not top ranking officers or directors of the firm. For this reason, it is prudent to disseminate and receive confirmation of receipt from all employees -- regardless of tenure or position -- of the following disclosure standards before the company submits its initial filing with the SEC:

To: All Employees

Re: Any and All Requests for Company Information

From: VP, IR

cc: Top executives

Please reply to this email by entering YES after you have read it and understand it. If you require any clarification whatsoever, please contact me at any time. Our company is entering a new phase that will make the media or investors curious about us. Please refer any and all requests for information about the company or our initial public offering (IPO) to the Investor Relations department. This does not affect the normal contact you have with customers and suppliers. Providing information to others outside the company may violate securities laws and will result in immediate dismissal. Again, should you require clarification or have any questions about the above please notify the sender immediately. Thank you for your prompt reply.

Follow up quickly with those who have not responded and create a signed off document once everyone has complied with the request. When dealing with media requests for information beyond the prospectus, it is a good idea to preface the conversation with "we are in the quiet period so I cannot disclose to you anything we haven't told everyone else, so I respectfully refer you to the prospectus. I will forward a copy to you now. But we are happy to listen to your questions and to try and answer any questions to the best of our ability".

Behavioral Tendencies

Several rules of thumb are good to keep in mind when preparing to launch an investor marketing campaign. Intangible features such as management's credibility are embedded in disclosure signals, such as the tone and complexity of press releases. Profitable firms issue less verbally complex earnings releases and shorter press releases. Ritualistic disclosure behaviors also send clear signals even if they are passive and repetitive procedures.[10] Price-to-earnings (P/E) or Earnings-per-share (EPS) is by far the most popular metric the business media relies on when assessing a firm's value. Earnings are more important than other aspects such as cash flow and accrual numbers, even though cash flow and accruals may be better indicators of the true contributing factors to earnings per share.[11]

IPO price revisions are positively correlated with promotional efforts: when pre-offer publicity is greater, the valuation based on an IPO's final offering price tends to be higher for firms with higher media coverage relative to other comparable firms. The average size of initial trades is negatively correlated with pre-offer publicity and initial returns are positively correlated with pre-offer publicity. Generating news flow must be approached with caution as negative publicity can be a disaster, because investors believe others will behave pessimistically about bad news 80% more than they actually do, creating an artificially negative force that can be dangerous if it does emerge.[12]

When planning Pre-IPO publicity, marketers should consider the fact that institutional investors consider a tight set of metrics when determining the valuation of an IPO. Reference to these metrics -- or comparative multiples that demonstrate their growth characteristics (e.g. 2x or 200% compared to last year) include: pre-IPO sales, pre-IPO income or EBITDA, pre-IPO sales growth, insider selling (% of secondary shares offered in any pre-IPO transaction), tenure of senior management and number of years in the industry, and the age of the firm.

Once the prospectus is available, these and other metrics will be factored into the valuation.[13] The profitability of the firm and the various inputs that contribute to the discounted cash flow calculation (e.g., net cash provided by operations) and the IPO's market timing are heavily weighted considerations.

Post-IPO

A picture commonly seen in the business newspaper after a high-profile IPO is launched is that of the exuberant CEO ringing the opening bell at NYSE or Nasdaq. After all, the ceremony is a well-choreographed event marking the end of a brutal rite of passage that coincides with the exact moment the firm becomes publicly-traded. There are abundant cameras and recording devices wielded by experienced journalists. The firm's executives should consciously refrain from participating altogether because the downside risk is simply not worth it. On Twitter's opening day on NYSE, the Roadshow team stood aside and elected instead to have a few celebrities ring the bell for them (Patrick Stewart of Star Trek was one such personality in front of Twitter's logo), a wise move.

New CEOs are cautioned against ringing the opening bell or appearing jubilant or otherwise exultant during the stock's first day of trading. If the stock goes up and management is jumping for joy, it looks bad. If the stock goes down and management is jumping for joy, it looks worse. It is better to avoid the bell ringing altogether as one never knows with any certainty how the "tape is going to trade", a trader's term for the ubiquitous uncertainty that cloaks the future of all stocks.

Consider the example of the IPO of SkullCandy, a $188 million transaction that beat expectations and priced above the range in July 2011. The Wall Street Journal noted the transaction reflected "strong demand for the deal".[14] So far so good. Until the CEO made an off-the-cuff remark that betrayed how thrilled he really was, leaving investors feeling that perhaps the firm didn't deserve such a warm reception after all.

During SkullCandy's first few hours of trading, an obviously exuberant CEO told reporters "We are stoked to reach this important milestone for our company".[15] If this tone was indicative of management's speaking style during the Roadshow, it is a safe bet that major investors knew exactly how the IPO would perform once it was listed. As it turns out, SkullCandy opened at 17% above the offering price of $20, but erased the gain by the first day of trading. In the months that followed, SkullCandy shares fell well below its IPO price.

The poor trading performance of the trendy headphone company may also be partially explained by the tendency for investors to retrieve the most recent memory of a person when more than one representation exists. Famous last words, as the saying goes.[16]

Like many other firms that have faced this same situation, SkullCandy was left to contend with very low trading volumes which became virtually guaranteed after it issued guidance for the full year that was below analyst's estimates -- only one month after its IPO.[17]

On a regular basis, firms should release information about the firm's progress since the IPO regarding new business initiatives, products or world-view. Investors are hungry for any new information about new stocks as the shares they hold may have risen (or declined) in value since they purchased them and they are looking for sell signals. Investors reward management teams that take a proactive approach to communicating with them immediately after going public and establish a desire to go beyond the mandated quarterly calls.

Announcing the date of the firm's first "Investor Day" or non-deal Roadshow will solidify credibility and may persuade some institutions to hold the stock and wait until after the annual voluntary event to make changes to their holdings.

Although firms should avoid excessive self-promotion, the reality is they must stay in the public eye and provide sufficient financial information to ensure access to capital markets.[18] Investors are much more likely to be net buyers of stocks that are in the news than those that are not. At large retail brokerages, the buy-sell imbalance is −1.8% for stocks out of the news and 16.2% for those in the news.[19]

PR and the Quiet Period

The intent of quiet period laws is to prevent any inadvertent promotion of the company's IPO in the media. Interviews with senior management or news articles published during the quiet period are highly discouraged and may be punished with impunity by the authorities and, ultimately, investors.

Firms must make their own news and signals or the market will do it for them. When traditional differentiators of firm quality are lacking, markets turn to secondary sources.[20] Framing the message using a tone that is positive may cause retail investors to think about the results in terms of increases relative to reference points. The impact of tone on market reaction also relates to the notion that a reinforced statement is "a stronger argument for a particular conclusion than the non-reinforced version".[21] People seek evidence to support their conclusions, so marketers are wise to provide investors with the facts necessary to confirm that a recent purchase was the right move.

Tactics

One way to approach the subjective concept of tone is to think about how to best manufacture search results. This is also called "covering up." You want to control the top twenty results produced by Google or Bing. You will need to issue several press releases and find out who the top bloggers are mentioning stocks in your industry. A search on SeekingAlpha or StockTwits for the symbols of your peers (e.g. $GE) will be very informative about who is shaping opinion in specific sectors. Make contact with them by sending information to them directly or by attending industry conferences, trade shows and providing strategically value information about your firm on the firm's website and through social media.

The top investment banks spend a lot of time discussing PR strategy. The content an IPO firm communicates before and during its debut contribute to media risk and create perceptions that will surface through the media. Perceptions that are established may take root and pose significant problems. This is why altering a sub-optimal point of view that has already been established is the hallmark of top-tier investment banks. The so-called "bulge-bracket" investment banking firms are generally very effective at limiting negative media coverage. The primary reason for this is that they discuss sensitivities early through pragmatic debate.

Scrutiny of large transactions is on the rise, especially at times when deal flow is weak or when the expectation is that marketing will start soon. It is common for the lead bank to communicate a fake timeline so that any expected and perhaps even inevitable negative comments or leaks do not prove disastrous.

Facebook is a case in point. The timing of this historic IPO was anyone's guess. But three months before the IPO, there was widespread speculation that the IPO was "perhaps a year away". The reality was, however, Facebook knew its Roadshow was just around the corner.

Credibility is integral to the success of any IPO. There are several means to instill and build credibility such as including pictures of members of the Roadshow team on the firm's website, in the presentation, and in the prospectus. Headshots have been shown to enhance credibility; even if people do not recognize management. One study found that credibility ratings were significantly higher simply for faces people saw repeatedly, regardless of whether they were remembered. Female faces were rated more credible than male faces.[22] Just one minimal prior encounter is sufficient to increase later-rated credibility for several weeks.

Negative Media Scrutiny

Do not underestimate the possible consequences of undesirable media attention. Negative news is powerful enough to sink almost any deal. Should the media start speculating about certain aspects of an IPO, the firm must be very cautious -- and confident -- about how to respond, if at all. There is no one size fits all solution; every situation is different and must be evaluated on its own. What the media speculates about one IPO does not necessarily affect another although a surprisingly poor opening day (Facebook) will cause other IPOs to be hyper-vigilant. It remains unclear exactly what happened with Facebook although the firm blamed Nasdaq for a technological glitch. Others believe the exchange trading system operated as expected.

Knowing what to do when you catch the unmistakable whiff of negative sentiment is critical. Consider this scenario: what if Andrew Ross Sorkin of the NEW YORK TIMES publishes something negative about your IPO in *Dealbook*?[23] Would you attempt to cover it up by blanketing Twitter with "hash-tagged" (e.g. #IPO) references about your firm, hoping someone at a major news channel will re-tweet the material? Would you send Sorkin a quotable source who disagrees with his analysis for good reason? Or, would you send your employees a confidential memo castigating the quiet period restrictions while refuting the opinions of The Times' respected columnists? Or, would you simply ignore the negative news coverage and chalk it up to life as a public company?

With the exception of ignoring the negative coverage, every response is considered -- officially -- to be "off limits". For starters, there is no such thing as a confidential memo addressed to all employees once you apply to become a public company. Secondly, because quiet period rules limit communications once the SEC has received an S-1, the advice of any corporate securities lawyer would likely be to not engage the media shortly before the S-1 is filed and never while the firm is "in registration".

In circumstances where the media does print a story even though the firm is in the quiet period, it can be brutal for an issuer to sit idly by and watch speculation run rampant without the ability to comment. In this situation when a response is absolutely necessary, adhere exactly to the language derived from the prospectus, or an amendment must be filed that can be quoted verbatim. No employee in any part of the organization can be publicly quoted with information that runs counter to the prospectus or opens dialog in areas not fit for exploration. The standard procedure is to send the prospectus to the media with relevant passages highlighted, but not to talk to them after the S-1 is filed.

Flag any major issues that could be raised by the media before the IPO and detail the responses to each potential issue. Avoid surprises during the quiet period at all costs, especially concerning material not contained in the prospectus. The time to bring up anything new is long over.

The stock market has been called a "game of expectations".[24] It is true that firms that perform well are also skilled at setting expectations with investors and then managing those expectations. Successful firms issue a series of media releases before the initial IPO filing and then again following the stock listing.

All media releases must not contain any content or information that differs substantially or materially from what appears in the prospectus. Should a material change occur (e.g. an investor increases their holdings beyond 10% or a major lawsuit is filed naming the firm as a defendant), an addendum to the prospectus must be filed. This may stall the IPO but is strictly necessary.

Both Groupon and Google put their IPOs at risk while they were in registration. In a famous example, Playboy published an interview with a Google co-founder during Google's IPO Roadshow. Fortunately for Google, the interview was recorded several months prior to its quiet period so the firm was allowed to proceed. Three lesser-known companies were not so lucky. Webvan, Wired Ventures, and GoDaddy canceled their IPOs after violating quiet period rules. Webvan's deal was halted on the last day of the Roadshow -- the pricing day -- by the SEC. The WALL STREET JOURNAL wrote:

"The SEC is concerned that Webvan executives have made themselves available to the media despite that required silence...The SEC is also concerned that Webvan has been sharing information in its road-show presentation that it did not provide in its prospectus."

If your IPO is expected to face serious challenges such as valuation, legal battles, reputation or rumor risk, detail a plan to deal with them before the quiet period as the last thing you need is for these threats to "run wild" and potentially derail your IPO. PR can be used with great effect if planned and executed properly ahead of an S-1 filing as it gives firms an opportunity to re-cast perceptions that exist about the firm and frame other material information related to the IPO.

It is common to see feature articles, interviews and news briefs on companies months before they file to go public. Upon closer inspection, you may recognize that the articles are attempting to address weaknesses or threats, such as the credibility of management, the scope or breadth of a company's operating units, or valuation.

The odds of getting an article published are better when it is sent to weeklies and twice-weeklies than when sent to dailies. When approaching a news organization, it is a good idea to ignore past events or suggest "feature" articles. News releases that sound too "institutional" will probably also be unsuccessful as editors are not receptive to these kinds of articles.[25]

Case Study

Facebook executed a PR plan ahead of its IPO filing. Throughout the quiet period, Bloomberg and other prominent financial news outlets published strategically beneficial tidbits related to the social media firm's valuation, such as:

"Facebook revealed in a conference today that the users of its popular Farmville application outnumber Twitter users by a factor of 100"[26]; and, the private equity site GSV Capital which invests in pre-IPO internet companies announced "an additional investment in Facebook...Facebook's most recent valuation according to SharesPost, was $66.6 billion"[27]

The approach used by Facebook was designed to prime the market for a massive valuation number once the firm filed to go public. As a private company, Facebook was selective about its public financial disclosures but understood that key pieces of information furthered its goal of overcoming future valuation hurdles as long as its revenue model remained opaque. Twitter was sued for $124 million by two firms that claimed Twitter had fraudulently organized a private sale of its shares to "stoke investor interest for an initial public offering" and then canceled the private pre-IPO share offering.[28]

Facebook wanted certain numbers out in the public domain so that journalists and analysts had verifiable benchmarks several months ahead of the firm's Roadshow. The strategy worked, as these sources were then quoted as in the example above which ran in daily newspapers across North America.

Pre-IPO PR moves are also designed to elicit a reaction to certain information so that an IPO communications plan can be built that will actually work once the quiet period goes into effect. Media outlets are hesitant to cover stories that have already been reported, so many are likely to pass on reporting the same story if they feel audiences heard enough the first time.

Some interesting research from 1991 found that the presence of negative biases stemming from any number of sources -- such as negative media coverage, a discouraging analyst opinion or miscreant rumor -- will reduce the probability that presented facts are learned. This reinforces the notion that Roadshow teams must monitor and control media channels (investor blogs and websites) early in the process to the extent that they are able -- before the initial S-1 filing.

Preparing for a Crisis

A major execution risk to any IPO is the possibility that unfavorable discussion about the firm or its management team appears in a prominent financial publication such as the Wall Street Journal or The New York Times' Dealbook.com while the Roadshow is underway.

Negative news is a serious problem because once the firm has entered the quiet period there is often not much a firm can say to adequately defend itself -- and certainly nothing outside the bounds of what is already said in the prospectus. Such a situation is exacerbated when opinions and discussion play out and evolve in the press, inviting further scrutiny and highlighting issues at a time that couldn't be worse. The Roadshow meetings are dominated by defensive maneuvers in an attempt to address the headlines articles and dispel bad impressions and misconceptions. When the Roadshow becomes spoiled like this, it is a bona fide crisis.

Those who expect disastrous news during the Roadshow must explore all available options thoroughly -- there are few -- and put a plan in place to deal with an eventual crisis. The first step in formulating an action plan is to identify the one critical threat that a journalist or blogger is likely to exploit during the Roadshow.

Formulate detailed talking points that address the full range of considerations that will help alleviate the pressure of a direct attack. Raise other issues, for example, that the media has not considered. No response is often worse than a poorly-articulated or incomplete one. Always use as much language sourced directly from the prospectus as possible and include commentary gleaned from prior press coverage and published interviews with the management team or industry allies. If there are details that do not appear in the S-1 for whatever reason, an amendment may be required to include them. Then, prepare a boilerplate formal statement that addresses the topic directly. For example:

"The Company has formally entered the quiet period and will not discuss any matters beyond the content that appears in our S-1 filing. This filing, once final, represents a complete and truthful account of all material information relating to any and all issues related to the Company including articles and other media coverage beyond the Company's control."

If an attack article is published that contains rumor or speculation, state that the company does not comment on rumors and speculation but that the underlying facts are as follows: (list the facts as presented in the prospectus).

"We believe the article published today is irresponsible. It contains rumors and speculation that are contrary to legally established facts. Your organization should issue a correction immediately or we will pursue corrective legal action."

Aside from issuing a threat letter, another solution is to connect at least one industry expert to the offending journalist. An ally who is sympathetic and supportive of your situation should also have the credentials and experience to comment on specifics about the issue. Allies can be valuable assets. They may be clients, vendors, friends of board members, or recognized industry experts. Anyone interfacing with the press on your behalf will require a candid briefing to become familiar with specific references and content sourced from the prospectus.

Provide allies with a list of talking points and direct them to stick to the talking points only. A list of what to say and what not to say should also be provided with the precise wording of sensitive statements or issues. Cite the fact that the quiet period is in effect time and again, as it is considered unethical to attack management during a time when it is common knowledge they are defenseless. Posing the question "Why are you choosing to attack us now? This isn't new information" is generally enough to remind the reporter that the charge can wait until after the transaction has closed and the firm has received its proceeds.

There are several proven methods to re-direct difficult questions but an experienced journalist can spot an evasive answer with ease. Re-frame original questions and re-cast issues with caution as they might raise red flags. Specific statements that trigger dubiousness include: "well, that's not really the issue, the issue is this..." or "I wouldn't put it that way. I prefer to view the issue this way...".

Prepare a "hot list" of emergency personal contact phone numbers and e-mail addresses and circulate them ahead of time in a face-to-face internal briefing. This list can be presented to the media if the firm's strategy is to get the last word.

What Not to Do

No firm should flaunt its success, either through lavish company events or a parking lot full of Ferraris. Success can be fleeting, creating a nasty mess if the media exposes scandalous levels of greed.

Loudeye, a highly unprofitable streaming media concern, made the mistake of throwing a Goldfinger-themed party to celebrate newfound riches after their $72 million IPO tripled on its first day of trading in 2000. The press had a field day with the firm's avarice, causing consternation among shareholders who stampeded out of the stock during a downward death spiral that saw the stock fall from $445 to $3. Angry shareholders filed class action lawsuits against the company seeking $30 billion in compensatory damages. Further reputation damage was caused when a bizarre pre-IPO video was leaked on YouTube showing interviews with Loudeye employees. Filmed by a consultant, the content demonstrated such egregiously poor judgment that no reasonable investor would ever purchase shares in the organization again after seeing clips such as: question: "How much do you estimate you stand to profit as a result of the IPO?" Answer: "Millions and millions. Too much").[29] Nokia bought the fledgling company in 2006 for $4.50/share.

Chapter Eleven
The Quiet Period

A firm declares its official intent to go public the moment it files an initial registration statement (also known as the "S-1" or "preliminary prospectus") with the Securities and Exchange Commission (SEC). At the same time, the firm also enters "the quiet period". True to its name, the quiet period essentially restricts information the firm can release to the public from the time it declares its intent to list to the time it gains a listing.

Although securities laws do not define the length of the "quiet period", it can terminate on the same day as the transaction prices or up to a month afterwards. A common misconception is that the quiet period ends after 25 days of listing, which is simply not true.

Officially, the quiet period concludes when the SEC declares the registration statement "effective". Many firms are declared effective the night before the stock starts to trade for the first time, so those with an urgent requirement to disseminate investor-oriented communications have the means to coordinate with the SEC to ensure a swift declaration of effectiveness.

Information that is restricted under quiet period rules is the same kind of information that many firms would find helpful during the IPO marketing period. For example, some firms would find it advantageous to indiscriminately broadcast certain metrics or competitive strengths. But the quiet period is also intended to protect issuers from media inquiries. Given the ubiquitous presence of social media and investor websites, some question how effective the rules are.

The JOBS Act, which was signed into law on April 5, 2012, affords several key provisions to companies going public, including relief from certain regulatory and disclosure requirements and the ability to "crowd fund" private placements.[1]

Still, within the constraints of the quiet period, not all information is prohibited from being disclosed. Firms are still allowed to publish "factual business information that is regularly released and intended for use by persons other than in their capacity as investors or potential investors".[2]

The JOBS Act relaxes the restrictions for the marketing of private placements significantly. However, the quiet period remains a dutiful consideration for those firms that have yet to enter into it. Depending on market conditions or investor sentiment, it can last a very long time. The inability to release information to an audience that might be considered as "potential investors" (such as employees, or industry participants), might seem like an eternity to some.

In turbulent markets, an IPO may suffer several false starts because of overall conditions, and could be delayed until bankers find another "window". This is potentially problematic during the quiet period because the only "talking" a firm can do is through filing revisions to its prospectus. Waiting in registration can be tedious. It can also be very frustrating because the only response a firm has to news and opinions generated by a community of stock-bloggers and investor websites that continually feed off S-1 amendments is to make changes to private documents, such as the investor presentation.

Companies already in registration must obey the restrictions imposed by the "quiet period". It is advisable for these firms to adopt a defense-only posture; they cannot publish opinions or facts beyond what appears in the prospectus. Do not post content on any website that could be construed as promoting the offering. The regulators are very sensitive to such infractions and respond immediately when such violations occur. The result can cause expensive delays -- or worse -- intense scrutiny by the SEC of all of the firm's marketing activities going forward. In the event the firm must correct or clarify clearly erroneous information, it is appropriate to cut and paste sections of language as it exists in the prospectus if the SEC has blessed the material (e.g. the information being quoted is not currently being revised or seeking further comment). Pasting "just a little bit more" by citing various passages from the S-1 is acceptable as long as there is no evidence of a desire to promote the offering.

During the quiet period, marketing activities are confidential. The development of the IPO presentation, Q&A and presentation coaching, IR website development, and other aspects related to producing investor meeting materials (signage, set and other environmental branding) takes place behind the scenes.

Liquidity is a subject that must be carefully considered during the quiet period. Liquidity is the primary concern for newly-listed stocks as liquidity levels determine whether there will be enough buyers for the inevitable sellers. Will there be a sufficient number of daily trades to ensure the price is stable and has adequate support through a base of new shareholders?

Trading technology is so widespread that automated trading platforms, electronic communication networks (ECNs), and mathematical optimization algorithms can trigger high volumes of selling in an instant. Preprogrammed trading signals based on a wide variety of market and stock-based signals have ultimately created shorter holding periods, which substantially impacts liquidity.[3]

The "Terms Set" Press Release

Just prior to the launch of the Roadshow, the firm or its underwriters will announce the "terms" of the new equity offering via a press release. This signals that the Roadshow will be launching imminently, generally the very next day. The release specifies the number of shares being offered and the price range the shares will be offered to investors. It may also specify the underwriters and various facts about the company as they appear verbatim in the prospectus. No new material facts can enter into this announcement or any other new disclosure because the firm remains in the quiet period.

It is advantageous to issue the "Terms Set" news release on a Thursday or Friday so that weekend publications and investor websites have time to pick up the news and attract interest in time for the Roadshow. Monday is generally a busy day for mergers and other financial news so gaining attention is more challenging.

The following example is from E2Open, a cloud-based provider of transaction software provider, which issued its "terms set" release on Friday, July 13, 2012:

E2open sees IPO priced at $15-17 a share

(Reuters) Cloud-based software maker E2open Inc said it expects its initial public offering of 4.7 million shares to be priced at $15 to $17 each. At the midpoint of the expected price range, the company expects to raise $75 million from the IPO, E2open said in an amended filing with the U.S. Securities and Exchange Commission. The company, which makes supply chain software and has clients such as Boeing Co., Cisco Systems, Dell Inc. and IBM, had filed to raise up to $86 million in February...E2open said it expects to use the net proceeds from the IPO to repay outstanding debt and fund capital expenditure. The company expects to list on the Nasdaq under the symbol "EOPN".

Bank of America Merrill Lynch will be the lead underwriter to the offering.

Marketers should seek to capitalize on the high levels of attention that already exist once the firm goes public as awareness levels will be at their highest on the day the listing is achieved. Plan to attend high-profile industry events shortly after the listing day and gain keynote or featured presentation slots at industry conferences. This requires advance planning and coordination, so reach out to conference organizers early.

25-day Working Group Quiet Period

The SEC mandates a twenty-five day quiet period for analyst reports. No underwriter or insider that worked on the IPO are allowed to issue research reports or earnings estimates for the company because of SEC regulations. Following the end of this 25-day hold on research reports, brokerages that served as underwriters on the stock may begin initiating coverage on the security.

Material Changes and Developments

New developments considered to be "material" must be announced through a press release if they occur before the first conference call. Integrate any new announcements into the firm's first earnings report. Examples of material developments include the formation or expansion of strategic partnerships, progress in geographic territories or markets, and the reduction (or introduction) of certain risks due to new factors. Firms often do not have new developments; those that do often have made plans in advance to keep some powder dry.

The "terms set" release outlines the number of shares offered, the pricing range at which they expect the shares to be sold and the participating underwriters, although not all information is required or appropriate for all firms. In many circumstances, firms maintain a high degree of secrecy regarding key details such as the number of shares, price range, or lead manager (underwriter) until it is absolutely necessary to disclose them. This strategy provides future flexibility as the IPO community will draw inferences from any voluntarily disclosed data and will immediately judge any changes to the disclosure.

The number of shares offered provides a very accurate clue related to valuation, as a combination of high and low earnings or sales multiples from competitors is easily applied to produce a plausible result. Analysts can (and will) compile an inventory of various sensitivities that will impact aspects of the valuation.

Chapter Twelve

Guidance and Disclosure

Guidance and disclosure are essential to every successful public company. Together, they provide the transparency necessary to set and manage the ongoing expectations of investors. Outperforming companies -- those firms that command the highest valuations and multiples -- consistently exceed expectations, quarter after quarter.

Firms that file to go public confront the fundamental issue of disclosure immediately: what is to be said about the future? Exactly how much information and how much detail is to be disclosed?

The informational requirements of an investment banking analyst varies widely from that of a research analyst. By law, an information firewall known as a "Chinese wall" must exist between the investment banking and research departments. Confidential information known to investment bankers must not be shared or come into contact with research analysts. However, this will not stop a research analyst from attempting to gain information that has yet to be disclosed from other sources. Investment bankers routinely sign privileged confidentiality agreements, while research departments do not.

For this reason, it is critical that management be familiar with what level of disclosure is acceptable and be resolute in their denial to repeated requests for information that is not explicitly stated in the prospectus. New management teams undertaking smaller transactions may fall prey to the tactics of skilled information predators.

Experienced investor relations (IR) professionals develop and then strictly adhere to a "disclosure policy" document which exists in the domain of corporate governance. From a legal standpoint, disclosure policies are required to ensure that information about the firm complies with all securities laws, including Regulation Fair Disclosure ("Reg FD"). Disclosure policies stipulate that when the firm publicly discloses guidance regarding future financial performance, it will also include a description of any associated material risks, uncertainties and challenges.

The disclosure policy also specifies the individuals or titles at the firm (e.g. Vice President of Investor Relations) that are allowed to talk to whom about what. Take this abridged example from a utility company's website:

"Other officers or employees of PG&E Corporation and its subsidiaries may, in some instances, interact with Securities Markets Participants for reasons other than a potential investment in securities of PG&E Corporation or its subsidiaries. The Vice President of Investor Relations must be notified of the context and content of these interactions in advance if possible, or immediately after any unplanned interaction. During these interactions, only non-confidential information that relates to general industry, technical, trade or similar matters may be disclosed, provided that such information does not constitute material non-public information. A member of the investor relations department is not required to participate in such interactions.[1]

Although disclosure policies like this one protect the firm to some extent, when a disaster strikes the policy may not necessarily improve the situation. But it may prevent it from getting worse.

Consider any public company that had a major PR disaster in the last decade. Toyota's suspicious series of faulty braking incidents during the US automotive meltdown in 2009 and BP's disastrous oil spill in the Gulf come to mind. In July 2013, a rail car disaster in Quebec claimed 47 lives, sending a ripple throughout the entire rolling stock and oil industry.[2] The company's private Canadian operations were quickly bankrupted.

Although major events like these trigger the crisis component of a disclosure policy, force majeure and other crisis situations that could cause any stock to implode should always be specifically addressed. The practice of commenting on rumors or events taking place at other companies is another aspect covered in this policy.

Guidance

The importance of guidance cannot be understated. Guidance refers to information released by the firm regarding its expectations for future performance. Stated differently, guidance is the practice of providing forecasts for certain operating metrics and other non-financial aspects of a company. Guidance is provided for each metric, such as revenue, by giving a range relating to the lowest and highest amount you expect to achieve. For example:

"Juniper Networks, Inc. (NASDAQ: JNPR) has issued preliminary guidance for the quarter ended March 31, 2009. The networking company said that the revenue range is going to be between $760 million to $765 million. *This is below the prior guidance of $800 million to $830 million and under the First Call estimate of $794.3 million.*[3]

88% of public companies provide guidance in some form. Firms choose between two types: quarterly or annual guidance. An annual estimate updated every quarter is the most popular form of guidance.[4] Quarterly guidance refers to the practice of releasing information four times a year for targets reported in each fiscal quarter. Annual guidance is given only once a year – typically before the first quarter of a new fiscal year begins -- and establishes the expectations for the full fiscal year ahead. Annual guidance is usually reiterated (or updated) every quarter.

The decision to adopt one type of guidance over the other is predicated on the guidance practices of other companies in the sector. Annual guidance is the most popular not only because it is less onerous from a reporting standpoint, but also provides "wiggle room" if conditions take a turn for the worse. In some sectors, quarterly guidance is expected, so those who choose to guide annually instead will likely by punished for not conforming.

Disclosure and Liquidity

For public companies, guidance and disclosure are the most important features within their control. The best performing companies have mastered the black art of purposely guiding low and hitting high. This art is what executives at newly public companies should also seek to master, as they will quickly discover that the financial community scrutinizes every detail looking for any sign of weakness across a full range of metrics (revenues, cash flow, net income, operating margin).

For new members of the capital markets, guidance is like a trap hidden in the snow, ready to ensnare the unprepared. Those already familiar with the well-worn trail may have been caught before and have no desire to repeat the experience again.

Companies that consistently miss their own guidance targets are often left for dead as this signals something is wrong at the firm, not the least of which is a troubling disconnect between finance and operations.

Firms must consider their financial reporting systems and how quickly accurate data is available before an estimate can be released comfortably. Many learn the hard way that guiding close to what they actually thought would happen isn't a good strategy because even a small miss on earnings per share caused serious damage to the stock price. The street takes guidance and the company's forward-looking estimates very seriously, so firms are advised to aggressively guide low and hit high.

It has been shown that better disclosure leads investors to demand shares at higher prices and to provide a greater degree of liquidity.[5] Better disclosure addresses two major challenges of running a public company: how to generate higher share prices and create additional liquidity.

According to a 2010 study from The National Investor Relations Institute (NIRI), the most common financial performance measurements are earnings, earnings per share (EPS), revenue, and cash flow. The most popular financial guidance is revenue, capital expenditures, tax rate, and earnings. Firms said they provide guidance to increase transparency (82%) and to ensure sell-side consensus and market expectations are reasonable (78%).

The most common method for providing guidance is to state the expectations for each metric as a "range". For example: "the company expects annual revenues to increase 3% to 5% resulting in $350 million to $500 million of revenues". Earnings per share (EPS), net income, return on equity (ROE), operating margin, and so on are stated the same way. Although providing a fundamental metric negates the necessity to conjugate the associated ratios, unless there are one-time charges or non-GAAP items that are expected to impact results.

To traders and institutional investors, a calendar year consists of four reliable opportunities to profit: the release of earnings each quarter. Those who are confident that a given company will "miss its numbers" (e.g. fail to meet its guidance targets) often take a short position in the weeks or days leading up to the release (or "posting") of the firm's official quarterly results, or sell ahead of earnings altogether. Substantial returns can be generated for those that bet correctly.

During the week of October 17-21 (2012), for instance, 100 companies of the S&P 500 index reported earnings, representing 33% of the total market capitalization of the index. With so many companies reporting at once, the firm that misses can expect to get hammered.

The punishment can be so brutal that a stock that misses its numbers may not recover for a very long time. In 2005, a neuroeconomics research paper suggested that the tendency to punish stocks that fail is a hard-wired condition. Our brains are sensitive to change, which explains why violations of expectations trigger powerful emotional responses.[6]

US firms are not permitted to furnish earnings forecasts in the S-1 (prospectus).[7] Instead, newly-listed stocks generally announce guidance through a press release after the quiet period ends but before the first quarterly earnings conference call. This usually occurs within one two months after the IPO. The details about the call (dial-in, passcode) are usually included in the same release. During the Roadshow, guidance can be articulated on a slide titled "target operating model".

Managing Expectations

It is management's responsibility to set expectations about its quarterly performance and then manage those expectations in perpetuity. How closely actual results differ from guidance is a major factor that determines if the stock is bought, held or sold once actual results are posted. The importance of "hitting the numbers" is critically important for all stocks, particularly IPOs that are reporting for the first time.

Some industries are exposed to rapid changes in consumer demand that make forecasting notoriously difficult. Others face cyclical conditions so challenging that disappointing results are inevitable. These situations cause some firms to shift from quarterly guidance to annual instead. Others abandon the practice altogether. But even those that do not provide guidance are not immunized against the fixation investors have on guidance.

Instead, the financial community will establish expectations for the company using its own methods. Targets for most companies are established through consensus, and may be derived without any cooperation or participation from the company. Expectations established by consensus vary more widely, resulting in broader ranges than those issued by the firm itself. Targets set by consensus are also less accurate than those established with management's participation.

Guidance and Punishment

Firms have a major incentive to meet forecasted numbers -- missing on just a single key metric can punish the stock with impunity.

It happened to Dreamworks Animation SKG (Nasdaq:DWA). Only nine months after their $933 million IPO, the entertainment company's estimate of DVD sales in Germany fell far short of actual results. Soon after the disappointing results were announced, the stock plunged 40%, prompting several shareholder lawsuits alleging the company had misled investors. To make matters worse, several analysts downgraded the stock and the SEC announced it had opened an informal inquiry into the company's stock trades.[8]

To anyone looking at DWA's stock chart for the period starting from the end of its fiscal quarter to the day when it announced these results, it appeared that a sell-off had indeed occurred before the information was made public. Just days before the end of the firm's fiscal quarter, the stock traded at $38.55 and declined steadily for two months although no 'official' disclosures were made during the period. It seemed that only insiders of the company could have known about the disappointing results before they were released. On the date of the earnings announcement, July 11, 2005, the stock closed at $23.27.

It took more than four years for the shares to hit $38.55 again.

A new public company will never escape the inspection of analysts, so firms must learn to work with them, not against them. Firms must spend time guiding investors and analysts through basic questions and assumptions. No analyst should receive information others do not have. Data must always be directly sourced from the prospectus. Do not provide an analyst with information that has not been disclosed or published unless there is a non-disclosure agreement in force.

Authoring the Guidance and Disclosure Policy

Usually at least two pages, the "Guidance & Disclosure Policy" document details each element of the firm's plan to disclose its future expectations over a range of metrics and related targets. Include background information discussing why the approach is appropriate.

The board of directors is responsible for the scope of the guidance and disclosure document. This document is subject to change due to legal regulations.[9] The key aspects are:

1) The frequency of disclosure: what period of time will guidance cover? Yearly, biannually, or quarterly? How often will it be reiterated or updated?

2) Guidance metrics: What data is to be disclosed and within what parameters? Are the metrics the same or different than the firm's peers?

(e.g. what level of detail is to be disclosed about separate business units that are being combined only because segmented data would likely assist competitors?);

3) What are the appropriate ranges for establishing future expectations about various metrics? How much "cushion" (margin of error) should the firm build in?

Guidance During the Roadshow

The expectations management sets with initial investors during the IPO will be echoed by research reports published by some of the analysts employed by the syndicate of investment banks involved with the IPO. Although rarely seen, a slide titled "target financial model" provides a basis for communicating future growth expectations. These initial research reports are typically produced immediately after the preliminary prospectus is issued and faxed to clients.[10] Research suggests that analysts tend to trust earnings forecasts until the forecasts turn out to be surprisingly different from what analysts have been led to expect.[11]

It is not common for investment bankers working with new equity issuers to encourage an optimistic posture when firms seek advice from the bankers about guidance. Aggressive forecasts directly influence valuation multiples and play a large role in how an issue ultimately prices and performs. To a large extent, valuation is based on future cash flows, so higher sales and other growth multiples imply higher future cash flows.

It is important to rein in optimism when describing future expectations during the Roadshow meetings. When there are more than three presenters, the tendency is for one to take an overly optimistic stance, using passionate language to characterize future performance or operating goals. It can be very tempting to emphasize upside potential but the future is unknown. To avoid the perception that members of the speaker team disagree or are not consistent, it is worthwhile to conduct Q&A and presentation coaching in the early stages of the quiet period. Firms that violate Regulation FD (Reg FD) are required to issue a press release within 24 hours and make the material non-public information public.

More on Reg FD

During the Roadshow, no one from the company must be quoted in the media about the IPO or any other topic that might alter material information contained in the prospectus.

Providing disclosure to one party and not another contravenes Regulation FD. This legislation is intended to ensure every investor has equal access to information.

As a rule, never provide the exact timing of a forecasted number during an IPO presentation (i.e. "by Q3 we will hit $100 million in revenue"). You may articulate one but never the other ("we expect that sometime in the next 12 to 18 months to hit $100 million in revenue" or "by Q3 we expect to generate $75 to $125 million in revenue").

To circumvent management's scripted remarks, analysts rely on what is known as "mosaic" theory. This theory states that different and distinct analysts work together to figure out the total picture even if one has a piece the other does not have. The ability of analysts to connect disparate pieces of information should not be underestimated. Selective disclosures can sink an IPO so each and every investor should receive the same information during the IPO presentation and Q&A period.

It is inevitable that someone will ask "what can we expect for revenue growth in the first year?". The popular response is "we would not think it unreasonable to expect rates of growth comparable to prior years", if this is indeed true. Another acceptable way to answer the question of forecasts is to say "obviously I can't provide you guidance at this time as it is not published in the prospectus but I would point you to our historical growth rates and the new markets we are entering and suggest that perhaps a sensible approach would be to calculate a blended rate of growth based on these items".

Draft Analyst Reports

During an IPO, an analyst may produce a copy of a report they are working on for the CFO to review. The analyst is placing the CFO in a very difficult situation, so any discussion should occur face-to-face and not be recorded.

Reviewing a draft report to correct factual errors is acceptable but commenting on the analyst's financial model and projections poses a risk of revealing information that go beyond the disclosures provided to the market regarding content that might be material. The safer course is to decline to comment at all on the analyst's prospective models.[12]

The Consensus Number

The financial community has been conditioned to rely on quarterly earnings results to such an extent that the expectations about management's own expectations has produced yet another, even more important set of guidance numbers known as the "consensus results" or "Street Estimates". These consensus results are compiled by *FirstCall* and can be accessed for free at *data.cnbc.com* or *finance.yahoo.com*.

These consensus targets are an example of reflexivity in action, as they are calculated based on the weighted average of analyst forecasts that incorporate management's historical pattern of guidance behavior. Consensus estimates rein in those companies that try to "rig" the system by consistently guiding low even though they know actual results will exceed guidance by a considerable margin.

The firm that consistently and methodically guides low and inevitably "beats the street" (Apple became America's most widely held stock this way), is a firm that under-promises and over delivers.[13] As simple as that sounds, this strategy often pays off handsomely as equities that beat are likely to trade at a considerable premium to peers. Investors reward stocks that are reliably predictable four times a year. Newly-listed IPOs should view the first-ever quarterly earnings call as a solid opportunity to establish an early pattern of guidance behavior.

The Guidance Fixation

Shareholders want as much information about the companies they own, regardless of whether the content informs for the near or long-term. Newcomers to the capital markets may not realize the extent that guidance practices play in determining how a stock trades. Constrained by time and the lack of alternative opinions, some firms simply follow the advice of their banker when formulating guidance and so they must also simply accept the consequences. It is the company that must live with the forecasts it provides, not the banker who vanishes the moment the IPO starts to trade.

It is important to recognize that the investing public is focused on short-term performance. Guidance provides good, reliable data for traders and institutional investors but it is a sharp double-edged sword: exceeding targets attracts new shareholders, but missing targets can punish a stock immediately and with more force than the firm that didn't provide as much guidance, or gave it less frequently.

The ability to achieve or surpass guidance targets at the very first opportunity is an important step to forming an initial base of credibility. The professionals that follow and own a stock may not be interested in anything a firm has to say, but everyone seems to be listening when a company announces a change to previously issued guidance.

During the quiet period, examine the guidance and disclosure practices of the firm's peer group to understand the specific informational requirements of investors and how often this information is updated. The firm that goes public halfway through a fiscal year is better off than one that must report results for the full fiscal year. Although both companies will be expected to give guidance, the firm with only two quarters remaining is statistically less likely to miss than the firm that provides guidance covering four quarters.

Managing Earnings to Hit Targets

Investors and analysts are keen to learn if management is likely to rely on some form of "earnings management" to meet guidance. This practice of adjusting certain numbers to meet targets is widespread. According to *The*

Economist "companies that make up the Nasdaq 100 index together reported $19.1 billion of profits in pro-forma earnings for the first three quarters [of 2002] also reported to the Securities and Exchange Commission (SEC) a total loss for the same period of $82.3 billion".[14]

One research study suggests that conceding to certain uncertainties and providing less precise forecasts strengthens credibility.[15] It is unclear whether the gains in credibility offset the probable negative impact less precise guidance triggers at the company with an established guidance coda in place. Analysts and institutional investors easily identify accruals and recognize earnings management to meet forecasts and conceal variability of earnings. Total accruals is the difference between net income and cash flow from operations.

Other methods to manage earnings include artificially reducing pension plans by deliberately assuming a low rate of expected compensation growth or a higher expected return on plan assets. Both methods ultimately lower reported pension expense and increase net income. Firms can also make subjective adjustments to calculate depreciation, including overestimating the salvage value of an asset, allocating an asset's cost over a longer duration of its artificially extended useful life, or allocating funds reserved from good earnings years for bad, effectively padding the numbers.

Timing of Disclosure

Guidance is generally provided during the firm's first conference call as a public company. Within two weeks or no more than four hours before the call, the firm should issue a press release announcing that guidance will be updated or provided on the quarterly call. Guidance must then be posted on the firm's website and as a slide in the quarterly earnings presentation, usually at the end of the presentation.

Missing the Numbers

The length of time it takes for a firm to release earnings after the quarter has ended is a reliable signal of performance. Apparently good news travels fast and bad news slowly. 88% of the top fifty companies reported earnings within two months of the fiscal period, while 60% of the bottom fifty companies waited longer than 2 months.

Traders understand the value of information and how to make money with applied psychology. Their ability to predict what effect the public release of information will have on the price of a given stock is a positive function of the precision of that information.[16] Since bad news takes more time to be released they prepare their trading strategies accordingly. As many traders follow the same rules, the aggregate effect on a heavily-traded stock on a watch list (e.g. on the fence if the outlook turns negative) can be disproportionately heavy-handed. All new public companies should plan on reporting within two months of the fiscal period.

Experienced companies know to re-adjust guidance promptly if conditions change, as they often do. There is little sense in being punished twice.

One research paper suggests that "companies that provide earnings guidance and pre-announce their earnings surprises realize superior stock price returns. Companies that did not provide guidance were punished far more severely for missing the analyst consensus estimate than companies that did give guidance. Pre-announcing a guidance surprise, whether positive or negative, resulted in stronger stock price returns versus not pre-announcing. Contrary to conventional wisdom, companies that pre-announced a downside miss were not "punished" twice. They actually experienced better returns than companies that did not pre-announce.[17]

Chapter Thirteen
Preparing for Q&A

There are several activities involved with preparing for the Roadshow. Among them, preparing for Q&A is a key priority. The management team that is prepared for the question and answer period (Q&A) is well positioned to generate lead orders, early.

The importance of Q&A cannot be understated; it constitutes half of the time spent at every one-on-one meeting. It is the reason why the formal portion of the investor presentation must be thirty minutes or less. Investors rely on the considerable advantage afforded by the ability to ask questions, face-to-face, as many investors never get the chance to attend private Q&A. During the session, investors will continually try to determine why the firm's future performance might decline and what might prevent the firm's performance from improving.[1]

Personality Traits

There are five qualities (the "Big Five") about a person that have been identified as traits that strangers use when assessing each other at their first meeting: extroversion, agreeableness, conscientiousness, emotional stability

and intellect. These are useful to keep in mind when building personal rapport

in meetings or establishing a public personae through marketing materials.[2]

Figure 13: Q&A Follows the Formal Speeches

One study showed that audiences make judgments related to the dimensions

of extroversion and conscientiousness when watching someone recite a short

piece of text while walking around a table for ninety seconds. "Thin slices

of expressive behavior" such as clothing, gait, posture, and jewelry provided

useful information to making a judgement.[3] Plugging parking meters

religiously and being on time are also signals related to conscientiousness.[4]

Intuition is a personality trait present in eighty percent of portfolio managers and twenty-five percent of analysts.[5] One team of researchers demonstrated that investors are only overconfident about private information signals. This reflects the notion that an investor's self-esteem is tied to his own ability to acquire useful information. This explains why personal contact with top management is so highly valued by the investment community.[6]

The popular television shows *Dragon's Den* and *Shark Tank* are representative of the format of a typical investor meeting: the first half of the meeting is allocated to management's formal presentation with the remainder assigned to peppering management with specific questions about the business, opportunities and risks. As with these TV shows, the decision to pass or subscribe to the offering is often made during Q&A.

Any institutional investor that subscribes to a new equity offering is an investor willing to accept considerable risk. Investors that place big bets on certain transactions do so for good reason. Exposure to a poorly performing IPO can harm the performance of a portfolio and the reputation of the manager that made an overweight investment. The Q&A period is the time when decisions related to discretionary risk are carefully considered and often concluded.

Q&A might be the only reason the investor agreed to a meeting in the first place. If given the choice, many investors would prefer to spend the entire hour asking questions, dispensing with management's presentation altogether. Many will have already seen management on *NetRoadshow.com* or *RetailRoadshow.com*

Q&A allows investors to interact with management and get a read on exactly what the firm's challenges are. In an attempt to truly understand the company -- and its managers -- investors ask a barrage of questions about any topic they want. Some investors spend the entire thirty minutes focused on questions regarding a single topic to explore its intricacies. Some questions are elicited simply to witness management's response.

Investors want to understand the risks inherent in a business and the transaction itself. They know the obvious risks -- the ones listed under risk factors in the prospectus -- but they are much more interested in the factors that could transpire to *trigger* those risks. Are there signs that something is *already* underway that could negatively impact future financial performance?

After the stock market meltdown in late 2007, one study determined that "the identification of future risk is now much better understood which has led to some pronounced effects on the IPO market. This risk-based reality means firms going public must be vigilant in their preparation and explicitly conscious of specific performance signals they send during IPO marketing".[7]

Q&A provides investors the opportunity to witness the signals management emits first-hand, regardless of whether management is aware of the signals they are sending. This is especially important because research shows that institutions are able to outperform more frequently when there is higher information asymmetry about the IPO firm, namely younger IPOs and IPOs underwritten by less reputable investment banks.[8] Q&A is the best opportunity for some investors to reduce high levels of information asymmetry.

The investor requires hard evidence of management's conviction that the firm's business plan will work and persuasive evidence that the firm's financial performance will improve. If the investor doesn't feel a palpable sense of conviction on both counts, they may simply pass on the IPO or buy it in the secondary market because they know many others will also lack confidence. Tepid institutional interest will cause the stock to perform poorly during the first two weeks of trading, making the long-term goal of creating shareholder value more difficult at a time when there are no shortages of challenges.

Preparing diligently for Q&A is essential. Investors judge Roadshow teams incessantly. They can't help it. They judge the clothes they wear, how they express themselves, how confident they appear, how they make eye contact, how they recover from a mistake and how they articulate answers to difficult multi-part questions. All of these are criteria used by investors to evaluate new management teams.

Some investors that participate in the latest IPO are simply making an educated bet. Apart from analyzing the prospectus, they want a reasonable degree of comfort with the CEO and her track record. Investors don't necessarily want to "connect" with management, but if management is successful with efforts to connect with an investor, the odds of increasing the size of an order also increase.

To "connect" with an investor audience is to make them believers. It takes confidence, forthrightness, interpersonal skills, experience, and the ability to trigger innate feelings that management -- and the business -- has the right stuff.

Connections do not happen easily. Some investors will try to purposely throw you off track by using overly aggressive tactics in meetings. Such tactics include asking innocuous or patently ridiculous questions just to see management's reaction. A real-life example is when an analyst at a small money manager asked "on page 181 of the prospectus in the sixteenth note to the financial statements there is a mention of a foreign tax credit that was incorrectly reported five years ago. Can you explain how this could have happened?"

An experienced CFO would reply "our accounting standards and procedures have changed a lot since then. We don't expect any material issues with our reporting going forward although if our own audit committee or our external auditors don't catch a mistake, which is unlikely, it is a risk. It is to any public company".

But the CFO in this example was new. He took the bait. He and his IRO went into a frenzy, furiously flipping pages to find the offending footnote. After two minutes, the only response he could give was "we'll have to get back to you on this".

Preparation is Essential

It is imperative that management dedicates sufficient time to prepare for Q&A, which consists of simulations, dry runs, and education about recognizing patterns to questions. This is supported with feedback and actual video-based examples.

Q&A is where executives stand out -- either because they excel at it or lack the expected skills. Those who do not excel at Q&A are not considered to be proficient and are therefore classified as such.

Large institutional investors have seen so many management teams that they have become naturally attuned to signals conveyed by body language and speech patterns. Just a single, needlessly errant response can ensure an investor will not subscribe to the transaction. With the right materials on hand, the time commitment to prepare adequately for investor Q&A is not terribly onerous. Four sessions spanning two weeks is usually sufficient.

Investors are well aware of the techniques that enable them to assess management while gaining valuable insight about the future of the firm. They have a distinct advantage over management because investors have been on the receiving end of hundreds of presentations. They know exactly what to look for and the best ways to find what they seek. One study found that people are reasonably good at predicting the actions of their partners in a prisoner's dilemma game after observing one another for thirty minutes prior to making their decisions.[9] Q&A feels like such a game.

Management will be much better equipped to negotiate the subtleties of investor Q&A if it is already familiar with the methods and techniques investors employ regularly. Thorough preparation is essential to any team that wants to be perceived as a high quality candidate ready for the capital markets. Issuers have an incentive to misrepresent themselves to potential investors as being higher quality than they actually are so investors will do their best to decide the quality of management for themselves.[10]

A Grave Warning About Selective Disclosure

No discussion about preparing for Q&A would be complete without issuing an explicit warning against providing selective disclosure. Securities law prohibits the activity of providing one investor with information that has not been disclosed to all investors. Selective disclosure is the equivalent of shoplifting; there may be plenty of opportunities to steal but the legal penalties and social cost to the offender prevent most people from doing it. The same can be said of selective disclosure: private company executives must be absolutely familiar with the strict limits of disclosure or face potentially crippling consequences.

At all times during the Roadshow it is unlawful for a firm to disclose or provide any information beyond what is published in the prospectus. When a hedge fund probes management for specific information related to the composition of margins for a component of revenue that is presented on an aggregated basis in the prospectus, management must always defer to the figure as it is published or as it could be reasonably worked out. It is perfectly acceptable to provide references and direction to publicly available information and methods of calculation to guide the investor with helpful clues or hints as long as the means of guidance has already been established.

For example, consider the question: *"in terms of your plastics business which is not presented on a segmented basis, do you expect that segment to grow faster than your durable goods business or what kind of growth can we expect from plastics?"* An acceptable response is "if what I'm hearing is correct, what you are really asking is if we expect our plastics business to grow faster than the industry average. Since most of our demand is from China -- which is currently out pacing the industry -- I would expect that, yes, we expect to grow at least as fast as the industry average." Not exactly what the investor asked, but necessarily legal. The key here is to re-frame the question so it fits within the boundaries of what has been disclosed in the prospectus. If the response frustrates the investor, that's too bad. Laws are laws. A well-prepared Roadshow team would then add one or two facts about consumer dynamics in China and their insatiable appetite for similar products.

Another appropriate response is "of course I can't give you the exact figure for that specific product line, but since the margin for the entire segment is 17% it might be worthwhile to look at the mix to better understand what products have been out there for a while versus others that are relatively new". To this, an investor might follow up with "so would it be safe to assume that you expect the margins of newer products to be better, like we saw when your competitor introduced polyresinthol to Japan?" This is an altogether different question, and one that management can more easily satisfy by talking about demand drivers and consumption patterns as they are discussed in the prospectus.

Anecdotes are often effective in these situations to illustrate how customers and their purchase decisions were influenced by various industry dynamics or firm qualities. Real stories are effective and completely legal as they maintain enough ambiguity to be considered as "non-material". No prospectus ever published has ever contained dozens of anecdotal stories only because they skirt around concrete and material content.

High-Performance Techniques

1. Take command of every meeting. At group meetings it is especially important to set one ground rule before starting Q&A: one question per guest (it is prudent to remind the audience that they are guests instead of people or investors). You can always allow more than one question if you decide to later.

2. Know who is answering what questions. Investors prefer specificity so if possible let the CFO answer questions that could be answered by either the CEO or CFO.

3. Silence is powerful. In the same way a white page in a magazine full of ads has impact through startling contrast, pausing can also have

powerful effect. Start your presentation with silence. Let people look you over and start only when you are absolutely ready.

4. Know the *one thing* you want your audience to remember at the end of the meeting. State it early and state it often, revealing the subject from different perspectives. If you have one point of clear differentiation, one compelling feature that no else has -- hammer away at it.

5. Answer the question you were asked. Figure out what kind of question is really being asked.

6. Don't be hesitant or slow to respond. Keep the length of answers consistent. Be succinct. Avoid the tendency of two or three managers to take turns answering the same question when only one is required.

7. Don't appear emotional. A serious, bland or monotone response is generally appropriate. Bear down when you are being deadly serious: "if there's one thing that really gives us an advantage it's this…" Use your eyes and hands to get people focused on what you're about to say.

8. Never be flippant or casual. Investors may want to lull you into a trap that starts with being friendly, but stay strong and maintain your ground.

9. Be a listener. Actively engage using eye contact and react responsively

(nod, uh huh, yes). Consciously seeking out eye contact and listening closely will drastically reduce boredom and considerably increase your ability to read people.

10. Do no try to be funny. Ever.

11. Discuss problems directly. Start with the one you're most comfortable with and get off to a strong start. This will create a favorable impression.

12. Be specific. Information that is not made specific is often neglected even when it can be readily accessed.[11] You can also boost the credibility of disclosure by increasing its precision.[12]

13. Don't pre-empt a response with information that might sound defensive.

14. A few actual examples are helpful, as are anecdotes and brief case studies. It is fortunate to get a question that will allow you to use an actual example based on real experiences with customers.

15. When the questions stop, ask your own by leading investors to topics and messages you want them to hear by asking the rhetorical question "a question we often get is..."

16. Once you've answered a question, stop talking. Inexperienced managers tend to carry on. When you need to stall for time, try: "this is a complex

question that involves some pretty interesting issues. But we've taken some steps to address some of these types of challenges." or "that's a tough problem for anyone to solve, but here is how we are managing it".

17. If you don't know the answer to something, just say so: "I actually do not know the answer to that. I can tell you that my best guess would be _____ but it's just a guess". Private company CFOs are often concerned about not knowing the answers to questions, but rarely do they find themselves at a loss for answers by the time the Roadshow is underway.

18. Audiences remember what you told them last, so do a good job wrapping up. Don't run for the exits. End Q&A with "I just want to leave you with one more thought..." and insert your friendly key message.

19. Look for an opportunity to transition between the answer and what you really want to say.

20. Q&A isn't a contest, so don't try to win. Just answer the question.

21. Steer clear of responding with "that was a good question". This remark is often interpreted as being condescending and patronizing. The investor will think, "of course it's a good question, that's why I asked it" and

instantly become less engaged.

22. In a group meeting, be sure to repeat the question so everyone in the room can hear it. You are the person with the microphone so it is your responsibility to make sure your guests are on the same page.

23. Maintain your own personal copy of the color pitch book. Update your handwritten notes regularly. Make your notes legible so you can read them. You will learn your presentation inside and out by the third or fourth day. These notes are a great way to ensure you stay on message while helping you to memorize your speaking points.

24. Content is more important than skillful presenting so don't get anxious about performance. There are dozens of examples of transactions that performed spectacularly by CEOs who knew the material well and didn't oversell.

25. Read people and their expressions. There will likely never be another opportunity to study people in a completely acceptable manner as during your Roadshow. It will alleviate the intense boredom that can emerge from sitting silently while someone else speaks, because you are not allowed to check your email or respond to texts (never use your mobile

device in a meeting). It is also helpful to your co-presenters if you nod subtly in agreement at various times during their presentations. This silent action will assist them with their efforts to persuade the audience.

26. Don't sit directly facing people. Angle your chair a bit so that one of your shoulders is closer to the person you're talking to than the other. It puts people more at ease.

27. You don't want to get caught staring intently at people, so break your gaze once in a while just in case your mind wanders off and you forget you're actually locked into someone's eyes across from you.

28. Don't sit or stand with your arms crossed.

29. Cross your legs and tilt your head slightly to one side when you stand. It's less aggressive.

Managing Nervousness

For those managers that get the jitters: overcome anxiety by speaking your name and title and then give two or three sentences describing the highlights of your career. Videotape the exercise and watch every attempt with the sound off until you like what you see. When you give your first presentation, remember the tape and what you looked like. And just start talking. Say exactly the same things looking straight ahead at no one in particular: introduce yourself to the audience just as you practiced and give the highlights.

Don't bother being self-conscious. Remember lots and lots of people who aren't as smart as you have done the same thing. If you're still nervous, just look down at your slides and scrape by. Look up when the slide changes. Just get it done. By the third day of the Roadshow, you'll be a pro and no one will remember you once flailed. The other alternative is for your doctor to prescribe propanol, a pill that reduces stage fright. But be careful: it was the cause of Michael Jackson's death.

Combat Skills: Preparing for Confrontation

Management should expect to deal with confrontational investors from time-to-time. Investors that pose questions in an aggressive, probing and generally unfriendly manner can affect the performance of some managers who are upset by such behavior. It is imperative that the Roadshow team remain composed and cooperative. Simulations are particularly helpful with overcoming the natural instinct to blanche or appear flushed when an investor becomes overtly combative.

Admittedly not for everyone, the fastest and most effective method to prepare for a combative investor is a technique known as the "ambush".

The ambush works like it sounds. The speaker team arrives to the boardroom expecting the facilitator or presentation coach to take them through what they believe will be the usual, calm module of training and video playback. Instead, the coach appears incredibly irritated and fires a series of unnecessarily harsh questions, interrupting answers and generally brow-beating the Roadshow team.

There comes a point when the managers have had enough; either the attack becomes so ridiculous that it becomes obvious the exercise is a ruse or the coach halts it to save himself (or a manager) from prolonged embarrassment. It is valuable to videotape the sessions and then delete them later.

Investor meetings take place in environments beyond the Roadshow team's control, so being prepared is essential.

Investors use combat techniques to catch managers off guard which can lead people to say and do things they would normally never say or do. Information has a way of becoming dislodged when people are off kilter.

Investors have sophisticated financial models and identifying one particular number may solve a nice little mystery that exists at your firm or others ("is the high end of the market crumbling?").

People generally agree with persons they like, so maintaining a good "bedside manner" throughout the long schedule of meetings is advantageous.[13] This requires a strict code of conduct during all meetings and constant self-monitoring to ensure investors do not perceive any degree of defensiveness or irritation resulting from combative tactics during Q&A.

Management teams should be polite, but not inauthentic. It is always a good idea to ensure all initial contact with investors is confident and without any sign of discomfort. During meetings, maintain an outwardly calm and pleasant disposition and always interact with colleagues and investors in a friendly manner.

When handling a question that is confrontational or otherwise provocative, keep cool and recognize that provocation is a test. Questions related to compensation are often aggressive but can be answered simply with "the details of my compensation and other members of the management team are disclosed in the prospectus and there isn't any other color I can add to what's already in there". It is not necessary to say anything else.

Pointing investors back to the prospectus is a useful technique for questions that are clearly antagonistic. But be cautioned against referring investors to the prospectus more than once -- it could be perceived that you are ducking questions.

Models of Questioning

There are several models of questioning the financial community uses to acquire information. Recognizing the type of question being asked is helpful towards providing the best answer. Listen for certain phrases to identify the type of questions being asked:

i) *People are talking about this...* Usage: "A lot of investors are talking about new capacity coming online from your competitor. What are your thoughts on this?"

This line of questioning is a passive means to acquire the presenter's true thoughts about an issue without having to ask a direct question about the issue itself. With this line of passive questioning, the investor seeks to understand 'why did she answer the question this way and not another way?'.

Institutional investors often form a hypothesis about an issue that can contribute to an overtly biased judgment if they believe there is evidence to support their intuition.[14] This line of questioning is a way to ask multiple questions about the same topic at once, thereby saving time because the answer reveals more about what you are trying to avoid rather than the content of the answer itself.

Re-phrase this question and take ownership away from the questioner -- who has foisted it on a hypothetical person. Ask the question on your own terms: "I like to think of the new capacity in a few ways. First, we're bringing our own additional capacity on because of the growth in the market and our timing is ahead of what you've identified. Second, we have five year contracts in place and we expect new capacity to vend into those contracts. Next question?"

The best way to handle this kind of question is to strip it down to the bare essentials: what's the question really about? Eroding margins? Sluggish sales? Under-performing assets? Re-phrase the question in your own terms by saying "I wouldn't look at it in that exact way, but the way I think about our sales is this…"

ii) *Pick either yes or no...* The ability to recognize whether a question can be answered with simply a "Yes or No" is critical to solid Q&A performance. Management is never limited to only yes or no.

However, when the questioner demands that the question be answered *only* one way or another, this is usually a sign to explore the question more fully. Or, that the answer "both yes and no" or "either" or "neither" is appropriate. Then provide the particulars for why the answer could be any of those responses.

However, it can also be prudent to respond quickly with yes or no to questions that are not complicated and then follow up succinctly with the reason why.

If a simple yes or no is not accurate, try "it's a little more complicated than yes or no. It is 'maybe' because there are factors that have yet to be determined. We really have to see how things play out before saying unequivocally we would or would not do such a thing". In order for 'maybe' to make sense, investors need to hear the qualifier.

iii) *If you were to choose between A or B, which one would you choose?* This is a lesser of two evils question. Remember, don't allow anyone to limit your choices. Generally speaking, a reasonable answer is "I really don't like either solution, which is why we're doing this..." Usage: If you had to choose between eliminating the dividend, cutting the workforce or slashing R&D, which one would you choose?" Answer: "That is totally hypothetical because if such a decision had to be made, it would probably require action not captured in the three alternatives you mentioned. So before doing anything as drastic as cutting the dividend, we'd certainly take a good hard look at every alternative before changing the dividend."

iv) *What if...* *"revenues keep declining and you fail to gain traction in the UK market?"*. This is a forward-looking question, so it is hypothetical. A good answer for this is: "it isn't possible to know with certainty what will happen in the future but it won't take long before we know whether we need to make adjustments to our marketing spend or perhaps accelerate our plans to penetrate other markets. We are prepared and equipped to deal with a worst-case scenario like the one you've suggested. But the reason we chose that market in the first place is that customers want it and there is very little competition..." Stick to the talking points and main messages that support the investment highlights.

v) *The droning question...* This type of question arises at group meetings when an inebriated stockbroker wants to perform in front of a live audience. Relatively uninformed investors ask long-winded, confrontational questions. It may start innocently enough, but after thirty seconds of personal opinions and inaccurate statements have been linked together, the questioner demands a response. Do not ask to hear the question again.

This type of question is best handled systematically:

"That's a lot or material to cover. But I believe I understand your question. I'll try to address it. First, with respect to..." Then, address the easiest portion of the multi-part question first, or whatever part of the question the manager is best prepared to answer. A lengthy response focused on just one of the issues raised by the droner can be concluded with "to be fair others who also have questions, we're going to stick with our rule of one question per guest, please. Thank you". Then take another question from somewhere else in the room. Management should not engage the hostile individual but should take the time to review at least one part of the question.

vi) *On a scale of one to ten...* These questions always include some sort of scale. Don't be inclined to answer ten or any other number -- it's probably a trap. Issues are subtle and change over time. Management doesn't want to be misquoted in the future or taken out of context.

A good response to scale questions is: "Although I'd love to be able to give you a number, I would be reducing a rather complex issue to something that can't be simply boiled down to a number. Instead I'd say we are actively making improvements such as _____ to achieve a better level of performance. We'll get there".

vi) *Random questions...* From time to time, management will get a question that makes no sense. The best way to handle this situation is to tell the questioner that you'll try and answer the question later, after the meeting. Don't seek clarification or circle back to the questioner again. Don't act confused or embarrassed or criticize the question.

Common Mistakes

There are several common mistakes people make during Q&A. The most common is when a presenter appears to stall or be evasive -- either consciously or not. This creates an environment of distrust. This is because when someone does not voluntarily disclose information that can be independently verified, he will be treated with extreme skepticism because he did not reveal what the audience knows he knows.[15] Even infants as young as nine months old react impatiently when an actor appears unwilling to perform an action, but not when the actor appears unable to do so, indicating an understanding of intentions even when the outcomes are held constant.[16]

Another mistake to avoid is the tendency to answer simple questions with answers that eat up two or three valuable minutes, raising more issues and questions in the process. When the answer to a question is straightforward, avoid opening other possible avenues for investigation. Just answer the question and aim for brevity. Use the extra time to plant some of your own questions.

Related to the issue of unnecessarily lengthy responses is the inclination for some speaker teams to perpetually extend the answer given by a colleague by tacking on yet another answer to one already provided. One member of the speaker team should answer a question, not two or three. Several responses from different people indicates disorganization and a lack of preparation.

The Fortune-Telling Trap

Be very careful with questions related to the timing or amounts of performance data "when do you think your acetate complex will generate break-even revenue?" or "will your current run-rate be enough to cover your expenses by Q3?". If you have not previously disclosed this and mistakenly answer a question like this, you may be written off completely. It demonstrates a level of experience not consistent with being at the helm of a credible public company. There are lots of examples of companies and executives that took the bait and paid the price dearly. If it's not in the prospectus, don't say it.

How to Prepare

Becoming proficient at Q&A requires six hours split between three sessions, a list of approximately twenty questions and the "right" answers, and a video camera with some means to play back portions of the footage.

I prefer a system that allows multiple cameras and immediate playback. It is worthwhile to have a technical operator working both the camera and playback machine so that management isn't waiting for clips to load. The instantaneous feedback is important so that adjustments can be made on the fly, which accelerates learning. The same equipment is used for presentation skills training.

Each session adheres to the same format: a ten minute review of the curriculum followed by guided written materials. The third part of the module is comprised of actual video-based examples from other Roadshow teams and an open discussion. There are both one-on-one and group meetings. Once each person is comfortable with the approach, there are usually several questions about the right answers to certain questions. Avoid singling out or criticizing the performance of a manager, even if they explicitly state they want to be openly criticized.

Simulated Q&A begins after the theory, research findings, and actual examples of Roadshow presentations have been reviewed.

Simulations are videotaped and then circulated with notes tailored for each manager several hours after the session is over. They can read the notes and watch footage of themselves at their leisure. Use camera angles that consist of extreme close-ups and wider angles so the participants can see themselves as investors see them. Stand behind the camera so the presenter has someone to look at; most people are not comfortable with looking into the black lens of a camera.

The module that executives seem to think is the most interesting relates to micro-expressions. If you've seen the TV show *Lie to Me* or any number of other series that feature FBI profilers, you may already be familiar with what a micro-gesture is. For five or more hours a day for two weeks, the Roadshow team will sit across a table from a variety of sharp and experienced investors. From a mere four feet away, investors will pick up on the smallest change in facial and body expressions. Some may record your presentation for future analysis.

At all times, managers must be aware of any changes in body language. Over the course of a one hour meeting, any single presenter will speak for up to a total of roughly thirty minutes. The remainder of the time is spent idle or reacting. When presenters aren't presenting, what they are doing is reacting -- to the investor in front of them and their co-presenting colleagues. An investor can discern more about the answer to a question by looking at the expressions on the faces of those who did not answer the question. It is these expressions -- micro-expressions -- that involuntarily betray concerns with what is being presented as straightforward fact.

A gallery of micro-gestures is included with complete descriptions later in this chapter.

The Modules

Each of the three modules is covered in a two hour session. Together, the modules cover a range of Q&A techniques, including response classification, question modeling, investor orientation and motives related to line of questioning. Proprietary education and research using peer-reviewed materials and actual examples are applied through simulations. Individual performance is guided by real-time and written feedback supported by video-based evidence recorded in an individual and group setting.

The first module focuses entirely on the opening thirty seconds: how to introduce yourself and your colleagues. A brief introduction to delivering the investment highlights during Q&A is also covered as are effective closing remarks: "I want you to join me as a shareholder. I hope we have convinced you today that our firm has true merit as an investment and will work heard to meet your expectations."

After completing the first module, participants usually perform at a level that far exceeds their initial expectations of personal performance. Results are achieved quickly when participants watch their take-home recordings and self-critique their own performances.

The second module covers material related to handling objections and negative questions. Examples are provided to demonstrate techniques to ensure managers are perceived as direct and unapologetic when discussing objections.

Module Two

Participants are coached until they are comfortable with re-phrasing a question, a skill developed through considerable practice. It is better not to re-phrase a question unless it is absolutely necessary. Investors quickly become annoyed if innocent questions are being re-phrased for the sake of it, so save the technique for a sensitive issue or a question that has no desirable alternative. But be prepared for follow-up questions that are even more direct than the original question.

The other way to handle a difficult question is to assist the questioner to see the big picture by stepping back and introducing a new frame of reference, one step at a time. This approach can be effective when the question is rephrased in a delicate and deliberately sensitive way that retains the flavor and intent of the original question. When performing surgery to a question that can't be answered directly, a patient and deliberate reliance on visual language can be useful to moving away from a stubborn frame of reference: "If you picture a roadmap in front of you with the final destination being free cash flow growth in the mid-teen range, the stops we see along the way are _____ and _____."

Five Techniques to Respond Effectively

1. Every IPO can expect investors to express concerns about some aspect of the firm's business. Concerns arise from investors' own private information

or experience about the firm's industry or its belief in management's ability. Do not raise old issues that have already been covered or answer questions that have already been answered. You'll needlessly raise concerns. To reduce doubts, be open to discuss specific topics but avoid over-stressing information, as this tends to increase doubts about the veracity of the argument.

2. An effective way to deal with investor concerns is to present the contentious issue as a pure problem-with-a-solution combination. With this approach, management summarizes what investors perceive to be the problem and then provide a solution. This can minimize the perceived risk of the issue:

"Look, the problem we're facing now is the economy. Our consumers are having a harder time justifying the purchase of cedar fencing when a composite exists for half the price. So our solution -- which is happening right now -- is to ramp up our marketing spend with an in-store promotion so we can cycle through existing inventories to better reflect the change in demand mix. The marketing highlights the importance of natural beauty with age. Our fences simply look a lot better after a few years."

3. Another method of answering questions is to identify the consumer need

at the heart of the issue. If one does exist, start with the need and then explain how the product's benefits meet the need. For example: "enterprise customers all need the same thing -- security. And security is what we're best at".

4. People remember what was last said. So don't end with negatives about a point you're making. Always start with the disadvantages first and then finish with the advantages.

5. Don't be tentative. Be definitive: "I think you'll agree that"...

Off Script Attempts

Management must be aware of the techniques used by investors and analysts to put them "on the spot" in an effort to take them off-script. Questions that irk executives can be particularly valuable as they reveal true thought patterns rather than window dressing communication.[17] Language of the eye, tone of voice, and face of the speaker (especially the mouth and movement of the hands) is particularly revealing.[18]

Becoming adept at evaluating responses does not take long. With just two days of training, parole officers improved their ability to detect deception accurately three out of four times.[19] Should management outwardly express irritation, discomfort, surprise, or overconfidence this can be interpreted as a sign that something is afoot. In Malcolm Gladwell's book "Blink", he describes a study where people viewed several physicians on videotape, including one doctor who was ultimately sued for malpractice. The majority of respondents could spot the guilty doctor within forty seconds of watching the tape.[20] This example underscores the importance of management to be aware of their own behavioral traits and tendencies when answering questions.

Common signs that tell audiences that a question might merit further exploration are those that produce changes in "baseline behavior". This refers to how an executive reacts when he is comfortable; his posture, speech rate and tone are a few examples. For this reason, investors may first throw a few 'softballs' to establish a baseline. Then, when it comes time to put the speaker team on the spot with a question designed to uncover what's really going on about a particular issue, they know immediately if a further line of questioning is warranted.

About Trust

Several clues are commonly known to signal discomfort or uneasiness: a lack of hand or eye movement, slower blink and extended pause rates, slow speech rate, vague descriptions, repeated details, and emotional 'leakage' in the face.[21] As there are abundant opportunities to unintentionally communicate signals that may come across as deceptive -- especially if the questioner is predisposed or 'on a mission' to find them -- it is in management's best interests to stick as closely to their normal pattern of behavior whenever possible. If, halfway through an answer, the CEO finds himself emotionally charged up, waving his hands around while talking loudly, he should change course immediately to keep himself in check.

Credibility is eroded when managers preface answers with "you know" " I think" "I guess" "uhm" "so…" or "ahh". They must also show a willingness to make themselves vulnerable through benevolent, cooperative, non-hindering actions. Any failure to display these actions precludes progress to the next level of trust. Audiences tend to ascribe misalignments to traits (for example, the person is "insincere" or "dishonest") rather than to another version of the situation or circumstances that motivated the behavior.[22]

People are more likely to trust each other if they communicate freely before they make a choice. This is why Q&A can be very helpful, as the decision to subscribe to an equity offering is available until the final day of the Roadshow. Interestingly enough, the introduction of a disliked third person increases the tendency to make trusting choices.[23] Employing the services of a fastidious Roadshow coordinator who is instructed to interrupt management while a one-on-one meeting is in progress and then continues to pester the team at regular two minute intervals is one technique that may increase empathy on behalf of the investor if management appears to be put off by the interruption.

One study determined that managers of dominant companies sometimes become overconfident, overestimating their control of the environment and underestimating the role of chance.[24] After enough practice, a manager will be aware of her behavioral response to various stimuli before an audience and will catch herself before fully committing to a reaction that could be interpreted as something other than what is optimal.

Behavioral Cues

The executive who establishes a pattern of answering every question immediately and then pauses before a difficult one signals to the questioner that he is on to something. Much like a poker player with a good hand checks early and often to neutralize perceptions, so should the manager have an inventory of responses to control difficult questions.

The give and take of information that occurs during Q&A is an integral part of every one-on-one meeting. Management should look forward to taking questions and actively engaging investors. One study concluded that participants invest more money in trustworthy-looking partners that reciprocate frequently and the least amount in trustworthy partners that reciprocate infrequently.[25]

It can be difficult to read people who are extremely polite, but it can also be very annoying if the person is just pretending to be courteous. When used as a stalling tactic, however, prefacing a question with an over-courteous remark can buy enough time so that an intelligent response can be assembled and produced.

CFO Hot Buttons

Investors expect the CFO to identify key trends and relationships in the numbers.[26] Investors expect to gather information on which to base their own forecasts, including more information about operating opportunities and risks. CFOs should expect to talk about any number in the prospectus, no matter how insignificant. CFOs are also expected to cite key data and ratios without searching for them.

Since the key challenge for investors is to reduce information asymmetry between managers and themselves, one of the most reliable means to do so is to monitor a company's message for signs of internal contradiction by asking questions that elicit information.[27] Through these and other information strategies, investors are able to better anticipate the consequences of changing performance metrics that can make the difference between realizing a loss and making a profit.

Investors look for ways to establish relationships and connections between various financial metrics so they can refine their forecasts. For example, how does revenue growth impact operating leverage? How should these variables be weighed and combined? Investors seek to look deep into the numbers to try and solve difficult problems by breaking them down into more manageable chunks.[28] This results in several

scenarios which they seek to simplify through the answers and 'color' management provides to very specific questions.

This example is from Gogo's first ever conference call as a public company.[29] It illustrates the level of probing that managers face in a one-on-one meeting:

Operator:

Your first question comes from the line of Simon Flannery with Morgan Stanley.

Simon Flannery - Morgan Stanley

Thanks very much. Nice quarter. Could we – Michael, could we start up on the international side - you talked about the FAA Iridium testing and the Delta contract. When do you think we can start to see the Delta fleet coming online...is it early part of next year? And then if you could just provide a bit more color about your conversations with the international airlines you talked about a two year time-frame where there will be a lot of decisions made, where are we now and then when do you expect to be able to sign some new contracts there? Thanks.

Michael Small - President and Chief Executive Officer

Okay. Thanks, Simon. We - our two objectives internationally are to start flying commercial satellite aircraft and our first objective is FAA approval of Iridium installations as it is becoming increasingly obvious the FDA has increased its scrutiny - they see that virtually all aircraft in the world will be getting large scale Iridium's as connectivity proliferates and rightfully they should be very concerned about the safety of flight. So, we're working with them. We're targeting install this fourth quarter. We indicate that in our quarter but there still are final concerns to make sure we wrap up with the FAA. We think it's in our interest that we do this safely. It's in shareholders' interest so we're working in close partnership with the FAA. On the second question, international expansion, we're talking to the world's leading airlines. We've got lots of proposals out there. We'll announce them as soon as they come through. I'm not prepared to say anymore than that at this time.

Simon Flannery - Morgan Stanley

Okay. Thank you.

Operator

Your next question comes from the line of Phil Cusick with JPMorgan.

Phil Cusick - JPMorgan

Thanks. I wonder of course you can talk about the ATG-4 upgrade. Can you talk about what the CapEx split there is for the upgrade with carriers? And what have you seen in terms of change in usage and uptick on flights that have been upgraded?

Michael Small - President and Chief Executive Officer

So first on the CapEx we did describe during the Roadshow that some of our earlier contracts we owe the carriers upgrades on some of their fleets - not necessarily all their fleets - and all the situations that carriers are paying for the upgrade we have not broken out our percentages on that yet but it is driving a fair amount of our CapEx currently and into next year doing the ATG-4 upgrades...we probably have to wait another quarter before we really come out on answering the customer behavior but from a technical point of view we are very confident in the performance of ATG-4.

Operator

Your next question comes from the line of John Hodulik with UBS

John Hodulik - UBS

Two questions. First one follow-up to Phil's question on the Business Aviation. You talked about layering in the talk and test in 2013. Could you talk a little bit about what that's going to provide your customers and whether we are going to see any sort of change and maybe ARPU in the numbers if that gets rolled out and then in the Commercial Aviation side you had a strong quarter of installs I think I remember seeing in the prospectus that you expected to install about a 170 by the end of the year from second quarter on I don't know if that's the right number but are you going to see somewhat of a slow down in the second half of new planes in the North American side?

Michael Small - President and Chief Executive Officer

Yes as currently scheduled that will be a significant reduction in the number of installs in the second half of the year versus the first half of the year we completed the U.S airways fleet and we are at an elevated level doing that. So you are right to expect a material decline in the number of installs in the second half of the year.

John Hodulik - UBS

So that 170 number still holds I think it.

Michael Small - President and Chief Executive Officer

I'm not sure where you got the 170 number.

Norm Smagley - Executive Vice President and Chief Financial Officer

The 170 is good well we likely come in a little better than that.

Michael Small - President and Chief Executive Officer

Yeah so and John Business Aviation we expect to during the remainder of this year to announce several new products and services. One of well I guess two of which we referred to in the scripts, text and talk as well as the smartphone but there will be more we think that will be helpful not only to increase the average revenue for customer aircraft it will be helpful on a crafting additional operator aircraft owners to come to our service.

Norm Smagley - Executive Vice President and Chief Financial Officer

I would expect since those come later in the year we expect to bigger financial bump to have in 2014 versus 2013.

Accounting Treatments

Investors want to know what the real risks are that drive asset prices and expected returns.[30] They are also keen to understand certain accounting treatments that may indicate financial engineering. There are a number of potential red flags that the CFO should expect to get grilled on if there is sufficient evidence that indicates further exploration is warranted. Clues may exist in the following numbers:

1. *Capitalized costs* that should have been expensed and vice-versa (e.g., when already outdated software development costs are capitalized it may falsely inflate earnings or when new product-generating R&D costs are expensed it may falsely deflate earnings);

2. *Income booked from doubtful receivables* (e.g., the company that sold time-sharing condominiums books all its income as 100 percent financed consumer debt -- but what happens when those consumers don't pay?);

3. *Last-in-first-out/first-in-first-out* (LIFO/FIFO) cost of goods sold issues (the valuation of inventories by the last-in-first-out or the first-in-first-out methods can disturb margin analysis, especially in a time of inflation);

4. Timing differences (e.g., delayed and quickened shipments) and tax deferrals (their cause and resolution);

5. *Net operating losses* and tax credits;

6. *Non-recurring profits* and losses and tax credits;

7. Changing accounting methods and reporting periods.

8. In a post-IPO context, reported earnings differ from cash flows by accounting adjustments known as accruals.[31] These accruals, and especially discretionary accruals, are abnormally high at the time of IPO equity issues. If investors have a pre-conceived notion or theory regarding accruals, they will look for confirmation.

Evaluating Liabilities

Investors may look closely at specific aspects related to the firm's liabilities, including:

1. Debt structure and principal repayment schedules

2. Loan covenant restrictions and possible penalties

3. Off-balance-sheet and contingent liabilities

4. Guarantees of third-party and related-party debt (e.g. debts of executives and owners)

5. Long-term leases and supply contracts (at above or below market cost)

6. Underfunded or over-funded pension plans and medical retiree obligations

Evaluating Equities

Other questions that are likely to arise relate to the consequences of share issuance in a multi-tranche transaction, such as convertible equity:

1. Dividends and covenants on preferred stock;

2. Dilutions through convertible debt, preferred stock, and warrants (possibly enormous in smaller companies);

3. Contingent dilutions (such as stock used for acquisitions and dependent on future market price and/or operational performance).

You Are Ready for the Roadshow When...

Management is ready for the Roadshow when it is able to consistently respond to a series of difficult, random question by flipping instantly to the right page and taking the questioner through the data while weaving together key messages with the facts in front of them. Managers who are ready are also able to "read" an investor to determine if it is necessary to clarify or expand on a point without the investor asking him to do so.

Chapter Fourteen

Speeches and Speaker's Notes

Although the style and objectives of investors vary, all expect management to tell a good story and tell it well. Formal speeches and speaker's notes are two script formats that are essential to keep management crisp and on message.

Goals

The goal of a speech is to provide investors with the information they require to make a well-informed decision about becoming owners in the firm at the time of the IPO. The case has to be made that strategy, leadership, momentum, visibility, and new capital drive growth. Do not mention the markets or make predictions about how the stock will price or trade. No one -- including the underwriter -- can predict such things. References to where the firm stands relative to peers in the current industry cycle can be advantageous.

Speeches should anticipate and answer any major objections investors might have with the firm's valuation. Integrate the various arguments supporting management's valuation directly into the story: the size of the market and future opportunity; the growth strategies that exist to capture the opportunities; trends or other evidence of the firm's financial performance that credibly support aspects of the valuation; and finally, the comparable valuation table (or "comp" table). At the large group meetings in New York and Boston, the lead banker usually covers off the firm's valuation relative to others based on key financial ratios. At the one-on-ones, the CEO or CFO will review the comparable valuation.

Audiences constantly gauge the probability and fidelity of a manager's narrative.[1] Convincing presentations are highly coherent. The speeches of high-performance companies are easier to listen to and more forceful than those of lesser performing firms. The narrative of better performing firms is also more direct and reflect a higher level of understanding derived from the same set of facts that exist in the prospectus.

They are also delivered in a language investors expect. This expectation has been formed through thousands of impressions made by some of the most experienced and seasoned executives in the capital markets.

A true genre in its own right, investor presentations occupy a category of unique discourse. They are comprised of language and content found in speeches and visuals that are based on a convention that has formed over half a century and which satisfies a stylistic set of criteria. For this reason, an IPO presentation would not be effective or perhaps even understood by any other audience except investors. The flip side to this is that an investor will not understand an IPO presentation if it does not conform to the genre. Put another way, if the firm presents a story that is outside the boundaries of what is expected, it will fail.

It is critical that the vernacular of institutional investors be used to ensure nothing is misunderstood. Confusion has disastrous consequences, so get to the point and remain concise. This is crucially important at the start of the presentation when the audience is in pattern-matching mode: will this transaction be any good? It is best to avoid language or inferences that sound boastful and to eliminate complicated words and concepts.[2]

Those who are successful communicate directly: if a CEO has built the company from nothing and is retaining a substantial stake, she should say so. If she made difficult choices that have positioned the firm better than ever, let audiences know in plain language what decisions led to today. If the transaction is important because it provides the capital and credibility necessary to execute the firm's business plan, state it as a matter of fact. If the firm believes it is at the bottom of an industry cycle and asset prices have never been more attractive, don't beat around the bush. If you've seen a transformation in your industry and the firm is better positioned than others to leverage its strengths, make certain that investors understand.

Effective IPO presentations include "key posts" or "major moments" that serve as the obvious highlights of the investment story. These highlights must be evident not only through the content of the messages themselves but by the emotion expressed by the presenter. This is when simulations, dry runs and applied coaching pay dividends. Demonstrate credibility and power at the most important parts of the presentation through the right combination of words and legitimate expression. Finding the right words and delivering the associated expressive gestures takes practice.

Introduce three key themes during the investment highlights. Reveal the first through the firm's operational review. Describe unassailable competitive strengths that lend credence to the firm's positioning in its markets.

The second major theme should relate to the firm's growth strategies.

If the firm is successful at impressing investors with the most desirable characteristics embedded in its plans for growth, the Roadshow team has made a significant step towards the goal of establishing full valuation.

The third and final highlight of the story emerges during the financial review. Financial data and associated concepts underscore the firm's viability as an investment because the future looks promising based on established data and compelling trends.

For example, demonstrating that top line revenue will grow while expenses will remain the same or decrease is one example of convincing evidence that a business has operating leverage -- a compelling financial attribute of any growth story.

Anecdotes and true stories of customer success that highlight the firm's competitive advantage can be a memorable way to instill messages. Describing how a well-known client of a competitor switched to the firm's high-margin product after realizing cost savings is often more effective than simply saying the product delivers key advantages to customers.

Begin and End Strong

Daniel Kahneman and Charles Schreiber invented the term "utility peak end" to describe the tendency for people to remember the main highlight and the last thing they remembered about an experience. Although there may be other emotions present, everything else is relatively meaningless when it comes time to making future judgments about an experience. For this reason, a strong start that defines the highlights followed by a presentation of the main highlight is advisable. Contrasting content on the slide with graphics or sound is one approach that can ensure the material stands out and stays in memory.

To be credible, it is important to begin and end an IPO presentation empirically. People tend to remember the first and last thing they hear. So, instead of "I'm excited to be here today", tell investors exactly why the time has come to take the company public now. The beginning of a speech is the only time to establish credibility and trust early, so a good set of opening remarks can be enough to cinch an order.

During opening remarks, presenters should avoid glancing down at scripts or stumbling at any time during the first thirty seconds. Appearing to be overconfident or arrogant is a bad move because someone will attempt to take you down through an uncomfortable and perhaps inappropriate question when it comes time for Q&A.

Script Formats

Every Roadshow consists of two distinct meeting formats: "one-one-one" and "group" meetings. One-on-one meetings are known as "management presentations" while group meetings are often referred to as "formal presentations". Some managers, short on experience, make the mistake of delivering speeches at one-on-ones.

The two classes of meetings are distinct because of each varies by audience size and uses different method to display the investor presentation. For these reasons, each format requires a different type of oral presentation. Both meeting formats accomplish the same goal of conveying a story through a series of key points and major moments that traverse a beginning, middle and end.

For the dozens of small meetings -- the 1x1's -- each presenter relies on speaker's notes. These notes accompany the color 'flip book' -- another term for the printed slide presentation reviewed with investors. The speaker's notes are included in each presenter's personal flip book. This eliminates the risks associated of reciting a thirty minute presentation purely from memory on day one of the Roadshow.

Formal Speeches

For group presentations, a formal speech is almost always used. A group meeting can consist of an audience that ranges in size from twelve to four hundred people. At these large meetings, the formal speech is read from a script while standing at a podium or lectern (depending where you're from). The speech is synchronized to slides that contain text and images that the audience views on one or several screens around the meeting room. The speech should include markups and other notations to indicate to the presenter when it is time to pause, emphasize, or gesture at certain times throughout the oral presentation. For example, the bold italicized reference in square brackets [e.g. *point at CAGR slide*] will ensure your audience gets the point while the text formatting will prevent even a nervous presenter from reading it aloud.

Speaker's notes are usually written first -- before the formal presentation is scripted -- and continually evolve until the slides are finalized. These notes serve as talking points while formal speeches provide management with a personal resource that includes the precise language, content and remarks for each and every slide. A formal speech is particularly valuable because it ensures that group presentations stay on message and do not run longer than planned.

Speaker's Notes for One-on-One Meetings

Speaker's notes consist of a series of talking points (or "bullets") that serve as reminders for content found on each page of the flip book. These books are distributed to each investor at every one-on-one meeting.

Speaker's notes are highly personal. Typically, there are only two copies produced -- one that is used by the presenter and a spare. It is not unusual for a manager to misplace or mistakenly leave behind their personal copy of the color book in a meeting, plane or car. For this reason, keep a backup version in a colleague's briefcase. This is a good idea -- particularly during the first few days of the Roadshow -- when items are most likely to be left behind or misplaced.

Speaker's notes do not repeat verbatim what already appears on a slide. Instead, they provide personal remarks and annotations that are helpful (or essential) reminders of what to say to increase the audience's understanding of a particular slide or topic.

Speaker's notes are constantly referred to, so they may be handwritten as notes that appear in the margins of the color flip-book or on and above each slide. They can be used throughout the duration of the sixty minutes while the speaker team is seated at the same boardroom table as the investor.

The color book is a coil bound document with thirty to forty color pages that are printed full page from PowerPoint in landscape format (11" x 8.5" wide). A clear acetate cover and plastic backing is included to protect the pages. When each page is flipped, vertically, two pages can be seen: the bottom page contains the current slide but the top page is the back of the preceding slide and is white. The coil binding separates the top and bottom pages. Some people call this the "pitch" book, but this term should not be used in the presence of investors and should generally be avoided entirely.

From the investor's vantage point across the table, he may notice that management is referring to additional notes that he does not have, but this is completely acceptable.

Figure 15: Color Presentation Flip-Book

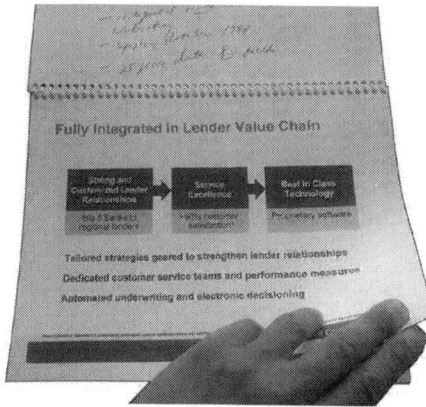

The one-on-one book: For maximum convenience, Speaker's notes are often printed or written on the top of the page -- on the back of the preceding slide.

Personal preferences determine how notes will be formatted for each speaker team member. The size of text, highlight color, use of underlines or handwritten annotations varies by individual. Those with less than 20/20 vision may prefer very large fonts, while others just want to see four or five words that trigger material committed to memory. It is also common to see notes that resemble a formal script, filling up the entire space on the adjacent page.

Writing Speaker's Notes

The easiest way to produce speaker's notes is to simulate and record a one-on-one presentation. Then, transcribe and refine the language from the best portions of the recording. Additional notes and other edits can be made to cut or further strengthen the material, slide by slide.

Another method is to use an outline or current draft of the PowerPoint and review each slide with the banking team on a conference call. When the team is stuck on a slide, ask aloud: "what are we trying to accomplish with this slide? What are we really trying to say here?" If there are no responses, delete the slide.

This creates a valuable collection of comments and arguments that can be tightened to reflect the key concepts and information on each slide. Record the "dry runs" so that all comments are captured, as it can be difficult to track every change and note.

Formal Speeches for Group Meetings

Scripts are used for large meetings or group presentations. When delivered verbatim, scripts are a necessary means to ensure management's presentation is on message and on time. A well-rehearsed manager will become familiar enough with his speech to deliver it with only a minimal need to look down at the prepared text.

Speeches ensure that every important fact, concept and detail is covered in a timely and efficient manner. Presenters who read or refer to a speech in front of them are less inclined to stray off topic or wander off on an unexpected tangent as those without speeches tend to do. Securities law prohibits managers from providing one investor with information others do not have, so a speech provides solid insurance to prevent such violations which are usually caused by a spontaneous remark or reaction to a question still in memory from a prior meeting.

Speaker's notes are usually authored before the formal script is complete, and are often used as the basis for the formal speech itself. For this reason, formal speeches are often written once the presentation is nearly finalized.

A script ensures the presentation doesn't exceed twenty-five minutes.

Good speeches incorporate an individual's natural speech pattern, language and style. Speeches are best when they incorporate language that is direct and sounds natural; the audience should feel like the presenter is using a conversational tone, in her own words. Audiences can sense when a presenter is delivering a speech she is not familiar with. Stumbling over words or making mistakes while reading an awkwardly worded sentence is a reliable signal that a presenter may not be as seasoned or comfortable with public speaking, or has not familiarized herself enough with the speech to prevent production errors.

The benefit of scripting a speech is that worthy ad-libs during rehearsal can be captured and incorporated into the script.[3] For this reason, it is a good idea to say the words out loud as you write them, as you would if you were actually reading the speech. Stand tall when you read off the page, and speak as loudly as you would to a room full of people. As you progress through your speech, eliminate difficult words and make other necessary edits to make your presentation powerful, concise and confident. Do not put your hands in your pockets. Instead, hold on to the sides of the podium.

Nail the First Thirty Seconds

It is often easy to predict how a Roadshow will perform by watching the first sixty seconds as it appears on *RetailRoadshow.com*. If it looks as if the CEO isn't adequately prepared -- he talks too fast, he's not wearing a tie, his presentation exceeds thirty minutes -- in all likelihood the transaction will price at the midpoint or below.

The CEO who does a solid job from the outset increases the transaction's likelihood of success. In a study of annual reports, half of the top-return reports stated their main point within 200 words. 21% stated the main point in the first sentence, whereas only 9% of the mixed-return reports did so.[4] Similarly, of fifty-four narratives taken from annual reports, forty-nine of the cases were correctly classified on the basis of the thematic content of the first sentence alone.[5]

The first thirty seconds must arouse interest, establish credibility and prepare the audience for the remainder of the story. Presenters should practice until they can speak the first few sentences without hesitating or referring to a script. In the first few sentences, the audience should learn what to expect. Use concrete, specific language and avoid any form of ambiguity. Good presenters make their point and move on without lingering. Emphasize key points and review them using hand gestures, which can be powerful when used sparingly.

Roadshow teams must inform the audience of why the firm is well positioned for the future, and what led to the decision to pursue a listing.

Own the Presentation

The use of first-person pronouns ("I", "we", "our") has a dramatic impact on the credibility of a speech.[6] In fact, the lack of language that indicates ownership of the material constitutes a red flag.[7] It is management's presentation, so managers must take ownership of the story.

Combine first-person pronouns with emphatics to effectively promote the image of a determined and confident executive. Using "I", "our", or "we" can play a significant affective role by making it easier for investors to believe the story by emphasizing the CEO's personal disposition or sensibilities.[8]

Personal pronouns convey a sense of ownership and strengthen the speaker's presence by including him in the material and viewpoints he is expressing. Statements such as "I know from my experience...", "I am sure that our company...", and "I believe strongly that our people..." overtly accept personal responsibility and explicitly attempt to build a personal ethos of competence and authority.

Compare the following two statements and judge which one you would be more inclined to believe:

1) "Our performance was solid last quarter. During our last earnings call I told you our plan to enter hyperplastics made sense for several reasons, so I am encouraged by the progress we are making in this new market." Or...

2) "The company generated solid operating results last quarter. Hyperplastics is a new market that contributed to these results, exceeding previously stated expectations."

The first treatment is far preferable.

Presenters are more likely to produce the optional word "that" when they are experiencing difficulty speaking "off script" or answering off the cuff. To the trained ear, using unnecessary words, talking slowly, the presence of a preceding pause, or initial disfluency are signs that could erode credibility.[9]

Signals

Subliminal messaging actually works. Even though an audience member may be unaware that they are being subtly manipulated, certain phrases provide enough of a reason to make believers out of some who might not otherwise be so inclined.

For example, sentences that start with "few would believe" or "everybody knows" or "you often hear about..." are biased phrases. They carry with them clues that attempt to instill a history or degree of credibility in a statement where no such direct evidence exists. But, such biased introductions may provide enough circumstantial evidence to give the listener a basis for becoming invested in the veracity of the statement, especially if it is true.

When assessing statements that begin with "it is well known that..." or "many people believe that..." or "it is often said that..." the presenter's personalization and natural characterization of the entire statement is a major contributing factor in the truthful evaluation of what is being sold.[10]

This is why Roadshow teams must personalize their speeches and practice them until all difficult words are removed while ensuring certain favorable expressions or content the presenter actually likes to talk about are included. The facts are the facts, and they are derived from the prospectus, so introducing a few biased phrases can accelerate the uptake of credibility and understanding.

The language used by management when delivering a formal speech to a large audience of investors at a group lunch in New York must be consistent with the style and format of the transaction. A multi-billion dollar transaction looks and feels like one, and management's presentation is expected to be consistent with the size of the transaction. Staging techniques are almost always an effective solution for improving the aura surrounding a transaction. See chapter 16 for a discussion on creative production and staging.

It is also helpful to provide listeners with signals that an important concept or destination is close at hand. This allows them to re-focus their attention and be alert to something important. Terms such as "as I draw to a close…" or "next slide I'll show you how our operating leverage is improving" ensure that key messages have the best chance of being delivered.

The Introduction

The first two sentences are the most important. Don't burn the opportunity (especially by starting a speech with "we're excited to be here", especially at a recorded salesforce meeting. Even if it is true, you are wasting a precious opportunity to actually say something that will resonate. Similarly, "thanks for coming" is also weak. There's a good chance the audience is being paid to listen; using a hackneyed expression will make them less interested in listening.

You want people to like you from the beginning. And people actually want to like you. So don't divide the attention in the very beginning between you and your slide. Show nothing on the screen except for your name and title and then take over.

Try being provocative from the start. Contrast another company, market or opportunity but make sure the comparison works. By being convincing from the start, you'll make the rest of what you say easier to learn because your audience is more apt to believe you. Don't ask people to raise their hands or participate; these are not self-help meetings.

A provocative statement at the beginning of a speech often works well, considering it doesn't sound corny. If an opening remark sounds too rehearsed -- like you've said it a hundred times -- it will rub the audience the wrong way. Try using an intriguing number or a recent news item to make your point. Any discussion about markets or future opportunities should use precise numbers.

If you are quoting an article or other content from a periodical such as *The Wall Street Journal*, cite it. But be cautious with quoting material that's not in the prospectus; anything that's in the public domain is fine. Remember that articles in newspapers are often slanted to reflect one point of view (the one you agree with) but the audience may be on the other side of the argument, if only because they can.

When introducing a colleague, it is best to refer to the individual first by title and then by first name ("Our CFO, Mary, will now take you through our financials"). If appropriate, the briefest of biographies can be helpful towards building confidence in the upcoming speaker ("she spent 12 years as the CFO of GE's international energy unit"). Referring to the title and first name enhances the connection and engagement all presenters have with the audience.

When introducing yourself, refer to your full name and title and, if appropriate, how long you have served in your current role. If you have one notably exceptional career highlight, bring it to the audience's attention in a confident but clearly humble voice.

Anecdotes

Anecdotes can be an effective way to talk about a particular subject in an engaging and convincing way. Demonstrating the success of a newly introduced product with a large customer is an appropriate time to use an anecdote (e.g. "Cisco's VP of sales told me last week our product was responsible for winning a major government contract"). Be prepared for investors to call the customer to check on the veracity of your claim.

The Drafting Process

The first step to writing a speech is to outline the presentation using headlines only. The most efficient means to draft an outline is to determine the investment highlights. The highlights provide you with the direction necessary for a clear story, as they provide the pivot points for the narrative.

A proven approach is to use index (or "recipe") cards, or PowerPoint slides with just the title in large letters. Adhere to the standard logical flow used for new equity issue presentations (i.e. the market opportunity, competitive strengths, growth strategies, and appealing financials). The investment highlights should encapsulate each important aspect of each of these four sections.

Section by section, tackle the key posts using facts from the prospectus to write the story. Flush out the language of the most important slides to ensure they are top priority. A major moment in the presentation is often introduced by two or three slides leading up to the key slide, which is almost always an investment highlight or convincing evidence of the highlight.

After reviewing different story scenarios by sorting and adjusting headlines, review the finished outline with bankers and management. Make notes on the feedback given about each slide, as well as the global comments about the flow and emphasis of the story itself. Pay particular attention to comments that start with "we'll speak to that".

Develop the speaker's notes in tandem with the presentation. It is better to wait to write speeches until the presentation is largely complete. Focus attention on the presentation first, then the notes, and then the speeches.

The logical flow of the story is much easier to establish by working with discrete content such as slides. The investment banking community is most comfortable working with slides and will not find a typewritten script useful.

In a deck with thirty slides, the duration of each slide is approximately one minute. If a slide takes longer than one minute to review, either change the slide by moving content onto another slide or pare down the commentary. Keep only what is necessary to convey and develop the story. Incorporate only the most important facts and supporting details as other content will eventually seep in as part of a natural process known as 'presentation creep'.

Formatting Speeches

Set the typeface of speeches in double-spaced, twenty-four point text or larger. Large text is easier to read when standing at the podium, although it requires more page flipping. Some executives prefer a sans-serif typeface (Arial or Helvetica) over a serif typeface (such as Times New Roman or Garamond). Use a typeface the speaker can read comfortably from 18" away. Make sure the presenter is not reading from her script for the first time at the salesforce meeting.

The time, date, page number and revision of the speech should appear on each and every page as there may be thirty or more drafts of the document before it reaches the final version. Tracking changes and managing the revision process can be a major undertaking, so be disciplined with file naming conventions when saving versions (*CFO_Speech_rev034_16_Feb_2015_002* is far preferable to *Fred's Speech_final*).

The final text of the speech should track the presentation closely -- line by line -- with every headline and subheading appearing in the text of the speech itself so the presenter is oriented. Some executives prefer to format text that is not actually read out loud so that it is justified flush right, to differentiate it from the flush left (or center) text that is meant to be read aloud.

Other formatting conventions:

1. Number the pages and include the optional 'out of Y pages' where Y is the total number of pages.

2. Only print on one side of the page.

3. Mark pauses in the speech with a large white gap on the page that is visible from two feet away.

Avoid Jargon

Delete all slang, acronyms and jargon from the speech. Eliminate meaningless statements such as "we are dynamic", "passionate", or "innovative". These words do not mean anything to anyone. If what is being said is not measurable or in some way quantifiable, do not include it. For example, unless "passion" can be expressed through customer satisfaction awards and industry recognition, investors will not be interested in hearing about it. They prefer concrete numbers and fact-based evidence.

The author of *Presentation Magic!*, Nick Fitzherbert, advises not to use the following words in a speech:

So to speak

And so on

Indeed

Actually

Which means to say

Of course

More or less

I think

At the end of the day

I find

In my opinion

As they say

As you can imagine

As I said earlier

I'm convinced

Use the Present Tense -- Always

Writing a speech can be a stressful exercise because it often needs to be turned around in a day. The most important writing tip is that the author should try to use the present tense. Never use 'was' followed by a verb ending with 'ed': not "the operating unit results *were* finalized for the quarter", but instead "the operating unit finalized its quarterly results".

Always put the important words at the beginning of a sentence: "Increasing productivity by 13% and capacity by 22% over the next quarter. That's our target". Instead of the alternative "Over the next quarter our goal is to increase productivity by 13% and capacity by 22%".

A study of 1,684 executives published by *Harvard Business Review* suggests that three quarters of CEOs are characterized by four distinct styles: the follower (36%), the skeptic (19%), the thinker (11%) and the controller (9%). Three key attributes of these four styles are worthwhile to keep in mind when writing for an investor audience:

1. You need as much credibility as you can garner to persuade a skeptic.

2. Thinkers think best when they know the risks up front and when you appeal to their intelligence.

3. No one shows their cards unless it is a helpful means to get what they want.

Tone of Voice

Effective investor presentations are those that are delivered credibly. In most circumstances, this means a speech that is not terribly animated or lively but leans heavily to the dry side. The transactions of excited executives don't fare well, typically.

It is critical to avoid the use of superlatives or other language that might come across as promotional or "salesy". One of the most difficult slides to deliver is the first: investment highlights.

In 2011, the CEO of Financial Engines wasted no time when explaining the considerable opportunities his firm was exploiting because of recent changes to America's retirement market. In the first two minutes, Jeff Maggioncalda explained how his firm was uniquely positioned to exploit a new and large opportunity and why they were uniquely positioned to execute.

Not surprisingly, Financial Engines was the first transaction to price above the range in five months. Mr. Maggioncalda's opening salvo is a good template for those undertaking an equity offering. By providing some basic education about the business and clearly dimensioning the opportunity, he allowed the story to take root and register with the audience who was working it out for themselves.

The Story Template

Highlight 1 / story kernel 1: Size of the market & opportunity

Highlight 2 / story kernel 2: Competitive strengths & uniqueness

Highlight 3 / story kernel 3: Growth strategies & tactics

Highlight 4 / story kernel 4: Notable financial performance or trend

Table 7: The Story Template

Description	# slides
Cover slide	1
Safe harbor/legal disclaimer	1
CEO 's name slide	1
Investment highlights	1
Kernel 1: size of market opportunity	4
Kernel 2: advantages and strengths	5
Kernel 3: growth strategies	4
CFO 's name slide	1
Kernel 4: financial	5
Investment highlights	1
Total	**24**

Chapter Fifteen

The Roadshow Meetings

Management should expect to encounter several different styles of investor. Depending on geography and meeting type, some investors will exert a disproportionately high degree of influence while others will be boutiques with no influence. On the first day of the Roadshow, the firm will meet with institutional investors that manage billions of dollars in assets for a 401(k) directed mutual fund (T-Rowe Price in Baltimore). At the tail end of the Roadshow, the schedule includes relatively small institutions that manage portfolios on behalf of wealthy clients.

The Roadshow schedule of a large IPO ($500+ million) features a two week schedule of meetings. There are five to eight sixty-minute meeting slots every weekday. There are no meetings held on weekends or bank holidays. Early morning conference calls (6:30 am) and evening update calls (6:30 pm) will populate the schedule if the market warms to the transaction.

A meeting is either a 'one-on-one' or 'group' meeting. It cannot be both.

The audience size and audiovisual (A/V) requirements of each is distinct. Group meetings require technical equipment; a one-on-one does not.

Meeting Overview

Time slots designated as "1x1" on the Roadshow schedule represent the overwhelming majority of meetings. These small, face-to-face meetings are personal, as there are few investors in attendance and they are in close physical proximity. Group meetings occur much less frequently, but are nonetheless equally important to contributing to the success of a transaction.

Figure 16: Typical Large Group Meeting in New York

Table 8: Meeting Frequency and Type

Type	#	Description/notes
Salesforce Meeting	1	1st meeting before Roadshow launch (a "one-off")
		Check and test A/V prior to meeting
		Often recorded live for *RetailRoadshow. com*
Analyst Teach-In	1	Final meeting before Roadshow launch (a "one-off")
		Test A/V prior to meeting
One-on-One	50	At investor's offices - flip books required
Small Group Meeting	10	Held at a hotel - some A/V required
Large Group Meeting	3	Held in large hotel ballroom
		Extensive A/V required

As seen in the table above, two important "one-off" meetings occur before the Roadshow officially kicks off: the "salesforce" meeting and "analyst teach-in". Investors do not attend these meetings. The function of these two special pre-marketing meetings is to educate the institutional salespeople, retail brokers and traders in the IPO syndicate of investment banks.

Both the salesforce meeting and analyst teach-in occur immediately before the first scheduled investor meeting. The analyst teach-in precedes the salesforce meeting(s). If there is more than one large co-lead (which is typical for large transactions), there will likely be multiple salesforce meetings held in a conference room located in the offices of each lead investment bank. The salesforce meeting is often videotaped. The footage is then edited together with the slides from the actual printed color flip books and posted on the internet for anyone to access.[1]

If a CEO conveys that he is cautious about presenting to investors for the first time, bankers may downplay the importance of these two pre-Roadshow meetings. There is no point in heightening existing anxiety. Bankers know that most teams find their rhythm during the first couple of days; the best teams have it from the first minute of the salesforce presentation.

The two pre-Roadshow meetings are important because of their ability to establish legitimate credibility with the banking syndicate's sales and research teams. Management will not be able to fake they know what they are doing or that they have a good story to tell.

Since the audience consists of people who have seen scores of transactions and management teams, if an IPO doesn't look especially appealing they may not be compelled to recommend it -- especially in a busy market. For this reason, the Roadshow team must prepare diligently to make a good impression at both the salesforce and analyst meetings.

One-on-Ones

Apart from these two one-off group meetings, the actual Roadshow itinerary is dominated by "one-on-ones" (approx. fifty meetings). There are also several small group presentations (5-10) and a handful of large group presentations (2-3) to fill out the rest of the two week calendar.

The vast majority of meetings are one-on-ones (90%+). These meeting take place in the offices of the investor, in one of four regions around the country in as many countries in the world. One to four individual investors from each institutional account may attend, although eight or more is possible. In cities such as Baltimore, there may be more than twenty people seated at round tables to hear management's one-on-one presentation. It is impossible to know ahead of time how many people will be attending, so it is prudent to be ready for any number. Bring enough prospectuses and flip books for fifty people. Be certain to collect the presentation booklets back after the presentation.

Although it is extremely difficult for management to be 100% focused in every single meeting, one-on-ones are the source of the largest orders. Many executives are surprised to learn who subscribed -- and at what levels -- when they review the order book in the hours following the end of the Roadshow.

The Salesforce Meeting

The salesforce meeting is a source of great angst for some speaker teams. This is because this meeting seems to "pop up out of nowhere", before the team feels they are completely ready. This meeting qualifies as a large group presentation (without the frills) to a group of sombre-faced bankers, brokers and banking analysts who are responsible for selling the new issue.[3] Often, this meeting is video-taped and its success -- or failure -- can set the tone for the first two days of the Roadshow.

Multiple salesforce meetings are required with multiple co-leads, which is often the case with larger or riskier deals[2]. The salesforce meeting is the first official "look" at the management team and the IPO story, so it is considered to be of the utmost importance.

This salesforce meeting marks the launch of the IPO, even though it is not attended by a single investor. It is closely approximates a large group meeting in San Francisco, where anywhere from 10-25 people attend.

Figure 17: Salesforce Meeting

The firm's banking team may initially characterize the salesforce meeting as "friendly", but this is not quite accurate. Unless your friends try to poke holes in everything you say.

The salesforce meeting is the last chance to fix any major problems, so the various bankers make judgments about management and the IPO story. This can be quite valuable because the feedback is from observers who have not heard the story before. Similar to the investor meetings, some members of the audience will possess solid knowledge of the firm's business, its peers, and the challenges that confront the new issue. The salesforce meeting provides a good venue for some individuals to ask difficult questions in an attempt to display their superior intelligence.

After all questions have been fielded and the meeting concludes, the senior members of each bank will gather together and whisper among themselves. They will then approach the Roadshow team to give each member constructive feedback from the collective. Many executives choose to ignore much of the last minute advice offered by people they have never before met, but do act on the working group's collective feedback.

Figure 18: Analyst Teach-In

To be fair, some bankers will approach this post-game analysis with the goal of being encouraging. But many will not be encouraging, even though the first "real" investor meeting may be less than a few hours away. Some managers may feel victorious after getting through this meeting and conquering the first group presentation in front of a live audience, but after hearing some of the comments from the banking team, the sensation that sets in may feel anything but victorious.

There are likely to be some irksome comments, such as "don't look down at your script so much", "don't scratch your nose", "stand still", "look at the audience" and "punch that slide harder". But these observations are only annoying because they are subjective and relate to personal presentation skills.

One potential problem can occur if the banking team agrees the presentation requires a major re-write or re-order due to some exterior calamity or competitive announcement timed to disrupt the IPO. This can be very unnerving, since the revisions ripple through the presentation and associated scripts. Regardless of the fast turnaround, a new version must be ready for the first investor meeting.

RetailRoadshow and NetRoadshow

Many investors will have already seen management's IPO presentation prior to a scheduled Roadshow meeting. The SEC allows one company the rights to video-record and host Roadshow presentations over the internet. Aptly named *RetailRoadshow*, the bank-owned video company usually videotapes the talking head of each executive at the salesforce meeting. This internet-based presentation site is an excellent and reliable source for institutional and retail investors to contemplate the most recent batch of IPOs. Video of the presentation streams as the slide slides change automatically, closely approximating what one would see during a group presentation. The user has the ability to view the slides full screen and switch to audio only mode.

In late 2010, General Motors introduced a modified version of the standard internet Roadshow format by posting an 11 minute video of GM's vice-chairman and CFO speaking to the slides from inside a car showroom[3]. This marked the beginning of a new era of unmistakably pre-produced and professionally edited Roadshow presentations.

Facebook Inc. took its NetRoadshow presentation to the next level by recording a thirty minute all video presentation featuring the Roadshow team speaking under several layers of slickly produced graphics. Morgan Stanley led both GM and Facebook.

Figure 19: Still frame of General Motors' IPO from RetailRoadshow.com

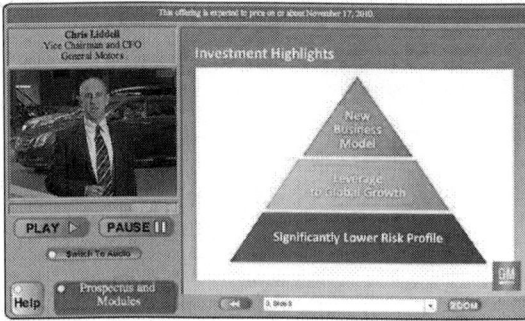

Some internet Roadshows that appear "staged" send the wrong signal to investors. Facebook and GM had good reason to produce a special version of their Roadshow for internet playback. The size of their transactions and profile of their management teams prohibited them from physically meeting with every investor that wanted a meeting. This is not the case with most transactions, so those that choose to record their Roadshow presentations from the privacy of their own boardrooms are taking on risk by deviating from the live recording, which is the norm and for good reason. Like reliability, authenticity as a trait is a credible signal.

Institutional investors have access to most IPOs being marketed via the subscriber-only internet site, *NetRoadshow*. Some will scour the slides or at least take a quick look before meeting management face-to-face. If sentiment in the market or towards the firm turns negative, some investors will simply cancel the one-on-one meeting after learning that the internet version is too long or is sub-par compared to other deals in the market.

Beware of Blue Drape

A dead giveaway that a salesforce meeting has not been recorded live is the presence of a blue velvet drape. This telltale drape hangs in the background behind the presenter on certain *RetailRoadshow.com* IPO videos. There are other signs that management's presentation has been professionally edited: there are nice fades and unmistakable cuts. The rough edges of the live recording have been polished off which can convey to investors that management doesn't feel comfortable with recording their presentation in front of a live audience. In other words, they're not ready for the Roadshow.

For a firm raising capital, this is not a good signal to send. The recording on *RetailRoadshow.com* lives on for the duration of the Roadshow, so be prepared to record it live.

Some IPOs choose not to make their presentation available over the internet. This limits the audience of potential investors and reduces the ability of investors to study the story or the management team. Refusing to make your presentation available also raises questions about what you might be hiding -- and why. Such speculation is not helpful in building trust but may be well worth the trade off. Some lawyers advise against posting the Roadshow online because certain forward-looking statements or other information contained in the presentation could come back to haunt the company.

If the investor has already seen the presentation on the internet, they may want to spend the entire meeting on Q&A. In this circumstance they should still be amenable to reviewing a select few slides. Take them through four or five slides that include the investment highlights, growth strategies and financial highlights.

The Analyst Teach-In

Another one-time meeting is the "Analyst Teach-In". Much like the salesforce meeting, this is a large group meeting that features management delivering a formal speech in front of ten to thirty research analysts. Unlike the salesforce meeting, however, the analyst teach-in can run several hours. Research analysts sit at desks or tables, interrupting to ask questions about every aspect of the firm's business throughout the entire presentation.

The investment banks participating in the underwriting syndicate employ research analysts who may have been included in the syndicate for the sole reason that they will cover the company once it is public.[7] Covering is a term that refers to writing and publishing research on the firm at regular intervals.

Questions from analysts run the gamut. Firms should expect to have detailed discussion about drivers of demand, growth prospects, run-rate multiples and any other input related to performance and valuation. Analysts also seek to understand historical trends and how they are reflected in the crystal ball of forward-looking financial and operating data.

Analysts will probe management to determine proprietary multiples -- the numbers management bases its internal forecasts on -- in an effort to discover insights that will help establish targets baked into forthcoming research reports. These research reports are issued after the bank announces it is "initiating coverage" on the firm soon after the quiet period has ended (usually the night before the stock starts to trade).

It is best to prepare a separate presentation for the analyst meeting to incorporate detailed information that may not necessarily appear in the IPO presentation. Management can use any data, charts, or research sourced from the prospectus to create the presentation. Analysts are hungry for segmented data and other information that drills down into product categories, markets, geographies or any other "bucket" they can think up.[8]

It is somewhat of an art to ascertain the effect that certain scenarios will have on a firm's business and ultimately its share price. Yet this is what research analysts attempt. They are ranked by predictive ability and compensated accordingly. The competition between analysts is intense, so they seek to use as much data as possible to program highly secretive models, ranging from macro-economic data to exotic proprietary ratios. The teach-in may last from ninety minutes to four hours, depending on the scope and detail contained in the firm's presentation and number of questions asked.

It has been shown that IPOs have better stock price performance when analysts ascribe low growth potential rather than when they ascribe high growth potential.[4]

One-On-One Meetings

The majority of meetings in a Roadshow schedule are "one-on-one" meetings. This is a highly-valued format because of the qualitative information it provides. For an hour, investors have face-to-face contact with management.

The term "one-on-one" is a little misleading because it infers there will be a single individual attending the meeting when, in fact, there may be as many as ten. The "one" refers to one investor account. Similarly, a "two-on-one" would mean that two institutional investor accounts are attending the same meeting. If the deal becomes popular, one-on-ones turn into two-on-ones as investors are forced to occupy the same time slots because the schedule is already full. The other alternative is that conference calls start to populate the schedule after 5:30 pm. Flight times and mobile phone connections while in transit to the airport can make investor calls after 5:00 pm challenging.

Large institutional investors will not usually travel to another location to meet with management. Instead, the Roadshow team will fly or drive to where the investor is located, whether that be Denver, Frankfurt, New York or some other city around the world. On a billion dollar plus transaction, Roadshow teams typically "split" to cover the United Arab Emirates, Asia, North America and Europe over a two week period.

Figure 20: One-on-One Meeting

Flip books are used at one-on-one meetings because the audience is seated at a boardroom table and attendance is limited to less than twelve people. In many of the meetings only one or two investors will be present.

It is difficult to know exactly how many investors will attend a given one-on-one meeting, so bring enough color books for a worst case scenario. Professional Roadshow coordinators generally leave a box of 50 flip books and prospectuses in one of the hired vehicles designated to transport management from meeting to meeting throughout the day. A spare supply prevents investors from sharing a color book.

Securities laws prohibit management or its bankers from leaving behind a color book with anyone at any meeting. For this reason, it is a good idea to let investors know that the color books will be collected back when the meeting is over. Some banks affix a unique number on the cover with a warning sticker to facilitate their eventual return. The condition of the books is also monitored, as some investors tend to make notes on the slides. Books that have been marked up must be replaced.

One-on-one meetings always involve printed color flip-books. These coil bound, landscape-oriented presentation booklets are the defacto standard and have been for decades. At a future time, perhaps *iPads* or *SmartBoards* will replace the printed page, but for now it is not at all recommended to use anything else but a printed color book. Although a decidedly "low tech" approach, there are no batteries, cables, wireless passwords, security concerns or adjustments required. Either you have the flip books or you do not.

Expect little or no access to the meeting room in advance as one-on-ones occur in boardrooms and facilities controlled by the investors. It is not advisable to disturb or pester the investor regarding technical equipment required for the meeting unless it is absolutely necessary. Investors are already taking the time to meet with management and do not want to be bothered about a hundred foot power cord or their in-house projection system. These requests will only be met with frustration and will only worsen when the IT manager shows up five minutes into the meeting to sort things out.

The IPO for DreamWorks Animation SKG used both color books and two very large plasma displays for their more than fifty one-on-one meetings around the world. To display the firm's upcoming slate of films, 72" displays and a surround sound audio system was installed prior to each meeting. This enormous undertaking was only possible through advanced logistical planning and technical arrangements. The cachet of the Dreamworks brand and the fact that a luminary in the entertainment business (Jeffrey Katzenberg) was presenting to the small audience aided the process of scheduling load-in times and other technical arrangements.

IPOs that do not enjoy the status afforded by a household name are severely limited to advance access to the investor's boardroom. For this reason, it is impractical to set up equipment beyond what one or two people can plug in and test within three to five minutes. For this reason, management usually brings only one box that contains color books, prospectuses, table tents and name tags. The reality is that logistical snags (security, finding the boardroom) tend to eliminate any disposable free time, so equipment is strictly out of the question.

Figure 21: A Table Tent

Table tents and name tags are a nice touch and greatly enhance the investor's ability to identify each speaker by title and name. The table tents are two sided (in case one side becomes scuffed or damaged) and sit in front of each member of the speaker team so the investor can clearly identify who is the CEO and who is the CFO. Investors ask better questions when they know who is who.

Small Group Meetings

Small and large group presentations usually occur in a hotel conference room as neutral ground is required when several accounts are in the same room. Unlike one-on-ones, small group meetings require audiovisual equipment such as a flat screen or projector to display the presentation on screen. An audio kit is also necessary so that an audience of twelve to thirty people can hear each presenter clearly. Some meeting rooms have tall ceilings that absorb sound, making it difficult on the audience if the speaker is not amplified.

As each executive speaks, the slides change automatically. The investor's attention is split between the presenter and the on-screen content. No flips books are distributed to any one attending a small group meeting.

Small group meetings are generally held in a hotel conference room. This location provides a neutral, easily accessible location with banquet facilities. Small group meetings always involve breakfast, lunch, dinner or cocktails served outside the meeting room or at a refreshment bar that closes five minutes to start time.

With larger IPOs, as many as fifteen small group meetings will be on the schedule. It is common for audience sizes to increase or decrease without notification, so it is best to make arrangements based on the highest number so that adequate seating and audiovisual support is available -- just in case the number of attendees increases. So-called "hot" deals attract large crowds with many showing up at the last minute. The opposite situation occurs with weak IPOs.

Access to the meeting room to set up equipment is generally not a major issue, but it is a critical consideration when booking the meeting space. Usually an extra fee is all it takes to reserve the room the previous night so audiovisual equipment and branding components can be installed in advance. Transactions that involve well-known brands or products should consider taking advantage of the opportunity to add additional elements that make the meeting more of an "experience".

Depending on the audiovisual equipment required for the meeting, up to twelve hours may be required to install and test the necessary sound and display devices. Many hotels employ union labor, so any non-standard equipment must be hired through an external supplier which can cause problems if not booked far enough in advance. For example, a specialized system that allows the meeting producer to communicate with technicians backstage is often not stocked locally. Be prepared for cancellation fees and other penalties if the dates of the Roadshow shift, which is common.

Figure 22: Small Group Meeting

Large Group Luncheons

The hallmark of every large Roadshow is the "New York lunch". On a large transaction, the New York lunch represents one of the three or four large group luncheons that are on the schedule. Firms allocate a significant portion of their Roadshow marketing budget to these lunch events because hundreds of investors attend to witness the presentation first-hand. Some transactions resemble spectacles that look more like *Cirque de Soleil* than an investor meeting.

Large group meetings are an accurate barometer of retail demand. As Jim Cramer says in his entertaining book *Confessions of a Street Addict*, large audiences send a reliable 'buy' signal to many investors. Typically, three large group meetings occur in the US: New York, Boston and San Francisco. Chicago is another city where a large lunch might occur.

In these meetings, investors are served a formal plated lunch while seated at 'crescent rounds' (only half of the seats at the round table are occupied so everyone faces the stage at the front of the room). These meetings almost always happen in a large, five star hotel ballroom that can accommodate a hundred or more people.

In Manhattan, where the largest of these meetings take place, as many as three hundred or more guests will show up to witness the latest billion dollar IPO. As all of the guests must be invited and no media is allowed, check-in can be a complex procedure involving layers of security and registration. Although these meetings are scheduled for 12:30 pm. they usually start later, depending on the mood of the markets and the size of the audience.

Figure 23: Technical Equipment Backstage

Despite the aura that surrounds these large meetings, they adhere to the same format of other investor meetings in the Roadshow schedule except that the lead banker will introduce management and say a few words about the transaction before the CEO takes the podium.

When the banker introduces management and the transaction, she generally includes brief biographical highlights of the top management team followed by a summary of the offering. After the ninety second introduction, the CEO then takes the podium and commences the presentation.

Figure 24: Lectern "Comfort" Monitor

Brand encounters occur more frequently and last longer than many realize. For savvy marketers, there are excellent opportunities to increase the range of touch points and extend the depth of the experience. The benefit of instilling an authentic sense of confidence and memorable impression of the brand's power will produce favorable returns at the time of the IPO and beyond.

Chapter Sixteen
Creative Production

Investors expect large IPOs to pull out all the stops in an effort to impress. The detail and quality of technical production required to execute a flawless large group luncheon for a high-profile IPO involves a level of planning comparable to an exotic destination wedding.

Every detail must be orchestrated to create the perfect environment for investors: scenery, staging equipment, security, lighting, audio, registration technology, experiential "trigger" zones, contingency plans, audiovisual displays, chair coverings, custom branded elements, technical crew scheduling, catering requirements, and even staff uniforms. The task of the meeting planner is significant and important because the meeting must be calibrated for an investor audience.

Marketers have the motivation to create a unique experience that capitalizes on the anticipation and excitement a large IPO brings. The reaction from an audience of retail and smaller institutional investors can influence the buying decisions of larger investors. If sentiment investors (retail) like what they see, this creates the perception that the deal is "hot" and is likely to perform well once the shares trade. The opposite is also true: should a large group meeting fail to attract enough people to fill the room, the result is lower levels of demand and a suboptimal mix of shareholders.

Figure 25: Make the Most of Branding Opportunities

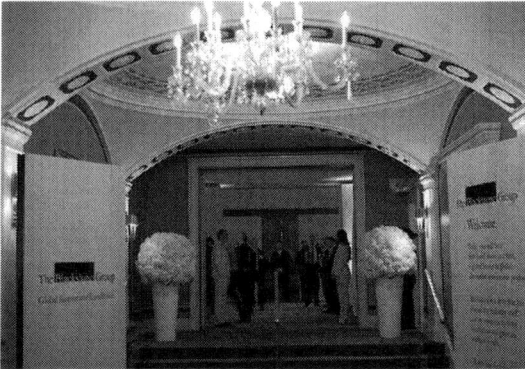

It makes all the difference if a meeting environment exudes positive energy. Prestige, atmosphere and environment reinforce expectations and perceptions. As Dan Ariely points out in his excellent book *Predictably Irrational*:

"Ambiance and expectations add a great deal to our enjoyment. You would expect less in a two-star environment, and as a consequence the identical foie

gras au torchon served at a truck stop would not taste as good as it would in a five-star restaurant. Expectations can triumph over experience. In the right environment, even a mediocre performer receives wild applause. "[1]

Not every large group meeting is a highly produced spectacle. But even moderately attended, non-marquee transactions require considerable attention to detail as there are aspects that must not be overlooked.

For example, the location of the meeting space must be secured well in advance. The room may have restrictions that limit the installation of certain components such as over-sized stages, sets or environmental "scenery". Under the right conditions, the mere presence of just one of these elements can differentiate an IPO from all others, producing a valuable advantage.

Even if a prime venue is secured weeks in advance, it still pays to exercise caution and book one or two backup locations. This is because Roadshow dates remain preliminary until the prospectus is declared effective, and a few factors can stall any transaction for an unknown amount of time.

Figure 26: Branded Table Setting

Stock market conditions, investor availability and other deals in the market can shift or delay a planned Roadshow instantly, rendering all previous bookings and other arrangements useless. From a creative production standpoint, an ever-changing schedule impacts the budget and the allocation of resources. As the largest expenditure -- and risk -- is concentrated on the large group luncheons, it is prudent to make decisions about production details early and stick to the plan if possible.

One such detail is the decision to ensure that investors can read the footnotes on a slide from all vantage points in the room. This requires large screens, high definition projectors, and a version of the presentation that is set in a larger typeface than the one used in the color books. Color books are not provided at group meetings, so it is important to ensure that near-sighted members of the audience can read the slides. For this reason, it is advantageous to have more equipment than necessary and remove or conceal it rather than find yourself needing to source extra displays or audio equipment at the last minute.

Roadshows with large group meetings scheduled in Canada, Europe or Asia require significant budgets. Each large event can cost upwards of $75,000 to produce. But this is a necessary expenditure, as investors who attend these meetings will not only generate large orders but important "buzz" during the IPO marketing period which can extend into the critical first week of trading.

Some institutional investors that have already had one-on-one meetings with management will turn up at a large group lunch to gauge the atmosphere, audience reaction and attendance. They are also interested to watch management perform in front of a large audience.

Professionally produced scenic components and other branded elements maximize the effectiveness of large meetings. Scenery pertains to visual elements that are not hotel property. This includes custom built walls, fixtures or coverings that complement or conceal existing infrastructure. It also includes floral arrangements, carpeting and almost anything an event producer can think up to elevate the prestige of the brand -- and management team -- in the mind of the investor.

A great looking event will be wasted if the logistics aren't handled properly. Security, the registration process, directional signage, and all aspects related to the audiovisual production must be well managed and ready by the time the first investor arrives.

Figure 27: Registration Waiting Area

Production Elements

There are a variety of standard components that can be used to create the perception that the management team is high quality. A painted hardwall backdrop behind a raised stage with a matching head table and lectern looks very polished when lit and branded appropriately.

Other elements include registration desks, directional signage, name tags for investors, table settings, table tents, and uniforms for service staff. There is no shortage of custom-branded components that can be rented or created for the firm that believes the value of their brand is correlated with the value of the company.

Figure 28: Check-in and Name Tag Distribution

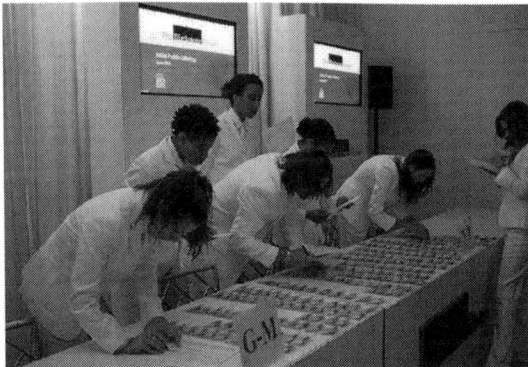

The overall meeting experience must be carefully considered, however, as it can be a big mistake to appear to "overdo" things. Adding elements that look unnecessarily expensive sends the wrong message and might erode management's credibility rather than fortify it. This happens when it is common knowledge that there will be mediocre demand for a deal that is also mediocre.

Big Deals Look Big

Billion dollar IPOs are often elaborate productions featuring strategic branding executions. The well-known private company that strives to become a well-known public company also seeks to build a prominent investor brand. The large group meeting is an important ritual in the private to public rite of passage.

To do this, marketers must consider no more than two of the firm's most salient features. In the context of its peer group, determine the firm's strongest and sustainable advantage. Is it global reach, a strong management team, low operating costs, technology leadership or position in profitable or high growth markets? Look to the investment highlights for answers.

Figure 29: Group Meeting (Chicago)

Figure 30: Group Meeting (Toronto)

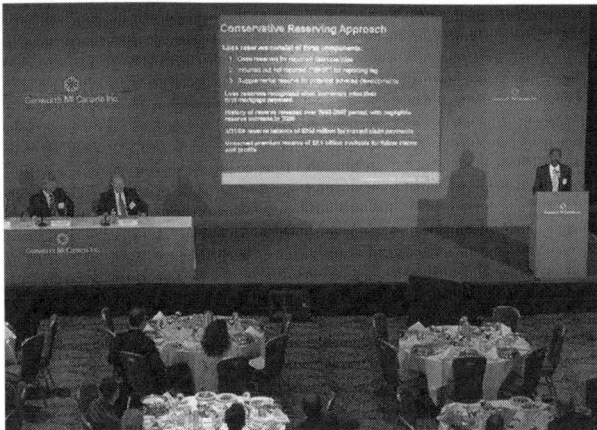

These advantages can then be translated to themes that are adopted for use in a meeting environment. Through the use of creative production techniques, a combination of graphics, video, audio and physical structures can be installed so the key advantages that drive the investment thesis are communicated within the context of the meeting environment.

It is the salience of stimuli, its prominence or tendency to 'stand out' through a high degree of contrast with other stimuli in the environment that provides the means to create a positive environment for positive stimuli. This is an important consideration towards establishing an optimal first impression with investors and forming a link to connect the firm's value as an investment consideration through a pleasurable experience with sophisticated messaging in a meeting space environment.

By putting investors "in a good mood", the marketer influences the audience by making them much more receptive to the firm's ideas and stimulates interest in the transaction itself. The goal is to make the problems at the office melt away, and to ensure every guest enjoys the experience of attending an investor presentation as much as possible. This is more difficult than it sounds, as humans are much more sensitive to negative stimuli than positive stimuli. It takes only one negative experience (no kosher food or toilet paper) to destroy a carefully constructed environment of positive energy.

To think of this behavioral tendency another way, only a few things would make me feel better, but there are dozens of things that would make me feel worse.

The Influence of Branding

Branding positively influences skeptical audiences. When it works, it is because it changes an ordinary experience into something new, better and unexpected. An investor may have attended a hundred meetings in a particular room, but if one meeting stands out because it is remarkably good for whatever reason, it makes an impression. And to truly understand something, it must be experienced.

First impressions are essential as they are encoded deep in memory. Known as "tags", these impressions are subsequently recalled and updated as more information relevant to the tag is learned. Stronger tags are associated with positive impressions and are more difficult to downgrade than weaker ones, which may be neutral or incomplete. If your large group meeting earns the top tag, congratulations. It won't be long before the orders flow in.

To form overwhelmingly positive impressions, the entire meeting space must be viewed as an "investor experience zone" where the firm's brand and messages invite interest.

Walls, windows, nooks and extra floor space provide locations for clever marketers to imprint the firm's best features and attributes before people sit down. Instead of looking like the same hotel ballroom as last week, fake walls provide areas and opportunities that transform the meeting into a targeted, highly useful space that investors actually enjoy because they are intrigued by various aspects of the experience. One aspect all investors appreciate is good and attentive service. This means offering free coat check, friendly service staff, and a wide variety of beverages and conveniences.

Investors covet exclusivity. When they attend a group presentation that stands out (and they have attended plenty) they are more likely to subscribe to the offering because they know other people in the audience feel the same way and are likely to subscribe also.

They don't want to be left out when the IPO jumps fifteen or twenty percent in the first few days of trading because it is perceived to be a "hot" deal. Large gains like these are difficult to make grinding it out day after day on the trading floor.

Figure 31: Rendering of Meeting Environment

The Importance of Branding

It has been shown that vivid information exerts a disproportionate impact on people's judgments.[2] Other literature on brand equity has argued that associations people have with a brand underlie its equity.[3] Both associations appear to contribute to brand equity in two different ways.

First, brand associations related to product attributes create a component of brand equity that is based on the differences between qualities that people judge for themselves versus what they know the market judges of the same qualities. In other words, brand building activities can bias an individual consumer's perception of an attribute away from its objective level. Second, brand associations form a non-product-based component of brand equity, which is another part that determines the preferences for one brand over another.

For example, the masculine image conveyed by the *Marlboro Man* has nothing to do with product attributes (taste or cost), yet it has been shown to be a significant factor in a consumer's preference for that particular brand of cigarette.[4]

As a signal, the credibility of a consumer brand (e.g. *Dial* soap or *Trident* gum) is defined as the believability of the product positioning of the brand, which is dependent on consumer perceptions and the willingness and ability of that brand to deliver what it promises. The higher perceived value and lower perceived risk associated with higher-credibility brands create the expectation of increased benefits.[5]

In the context of a credible investor brand, investors have an expectation that the publicly-traded equity security will perform better than others. Even if it costs a little more, it is worth it. For many, it is simply a matter of "better safe than sorry".

Brand equity is created through three sources: (i) increased brand awareness, (ii) incremental preference due to increases in the quality of certain attributes and (iii) incremental non-attribute preference (such as someone "relating" or having a much stronger preference for one logo over another).[6]

Elements of an Effective Group Meeting

From the moment a guest walks into the venue where the meeting is taking place, the marketer's intention must be to transport the investor to another place; a place where awareness of the brand is increased and attributes of the brand are enhanced.

Research suggests that the venue through which a message is received -- in combination with the characteristics of the message and messenger -- can affect the perceived credibility of that message.[7]

There are dozens of elements that can be branded to reflect the firm's most compelling attributes and identity. When these elements are combined with other sensation-based experiences, the effect can be powerful enough to accomplish the difficult objective of forming a positive impression.

There are several possible investor "touch points" where the investor makes contact with the firm's brand.

Signage. One of the first areas to consider is the experience that guests have when trying to find their way to the meeting room. At the very least, high quality directional signage is a good idea. But why stop there? Personal attendants can be hired to escort guests and instill a positive experience along the way.

Figure 32: Directional Signage

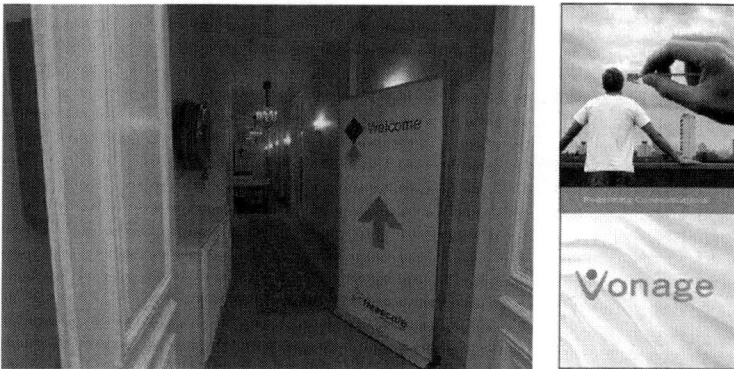

Consider producing branded directional signage that points the way to the meeting room. This signage is easily enhanced with the addition of strategic messages or pictures of management. The design and fabrication of the sign itself is another aspect to consider is polished steel featuring extruded two inch die-cut foam letters better than a classic high density gatorboard with the type knocked out of PMS 288?[8]

Many hotel venues have several floors of meeting facilities, so there are plenty of good branding and messaging opportunities. Directional signage will be required for the lobby, elevators and hallways leading up to the room. It is never a good idea to lead people down a path and then run out of signage with the meeting room still nowhere in sight. This creates a somewhat uncomfortable sensation because the person feels they have somehow been misled and now need help finding the room; not the first impression a marketer wants to create.

There are many types and sizes of signage available, from the standard 24"x36" laminated foam-core that is printed at short notice at Fedex/Kinko's to "pop up" or "pelican" displays that are heavier to transport and require at least a week to produce but look much more professional. Free-standing signage is the most popular because of the flexibility it affords (arrows or numbers can be attached by Velcro and easily oriented to the proper direction) but an easel is required, so be sure to have an adequate supply.

Many hotels will not allow certain types of signage in the lobby and other areas, so contact the venue directly before producing any materials appearing in public spaces.

Professional event coordinators are ready for anything and usually travel with a large portfolio case that includes signage, Velcro, a portable printer, a few collapsible easels and -- just in case -- an iron (to remove the wrinkle from the branded tablecloths that just arrived at the hotel).

Figure 33: Rendering of Group Meeting Check-in

The intent with signage and other branded elements is to communicate the firm's high quality while demonstrating a sincere desire to be helpful and pleasant to guests. The firm that is successful at differentiating itself through mundane details is a firm that is well positioned to execute a successful transaction.

Registration desk branding. A desk is usually set up outside the small group meeting room where someone designated by the bank collects business cards from every investor attending the meeting. The standard desk offers six feet of space on its front plus additional space on each side for those interested in wrapping it with a pre-fabricated shell that features branding or messaging. The other alternative is to cover it with a tablecloth and secure it with clips. The area behind the desk also provides real estate for a branded wall that can be installed on site. Areas to the left and right of the desk are other appropriate locations for signage. On many Roadshows, branded name tags are produced with each investor's name, providing a nice personal touch and an extra layer of security.

Interior branding. Inside the meeting room there are several potential locations the marketer can exploit. Typical executions in small group meeting environments include:

A hard wall set standing between 10' to 16' tall. A hard wall set is the professional choice as it can be covered with custom graphics and painted any color. The set is by far the largest element of scenery as it dominates the room.

Branding the podium -- either by wrapping it entirely -- or affixing a pre-printed sign to its front surface (covering any existing hotel branding);

Branding the plasma stands (tripods) by bolting together three panels of pre-printed graphics that wrap around each stand; and

Branding the front surface area of the head table at which management is seated and the registration desk outside the meeting room.

Setting each table with a floral arrangement that reflects the company's primary color with matching tablecloths and napkins. As these meetings often occur at breakfast or lunch when food is served, color can be an inexpensive and tasteful way to make a favorable impression. Use table tents and name-tags at all group meetings, regardless of the meeting size.

Figure 34: Branding at a Salesforce Meeting

Content displayed on plasmas. Since small group meetings utilize plasma or LCD monitors to display management's presentation, there are opportunities beyond what a paper-based presentation offers. Animated content, motion graphics or video can be produced so that it plays in a continuous loop until the presentation begins. An audio track is not recommended because the loop will play for up to an hour. No one wants to hear the same audio message or effects over and over before breakfast at 7:00 am.

An unobtrusive series of key messages with important bar graphs, pictures of management and facts about the company are appropriate as long as the treatment is understated and lengthy enough so that it does not induce irritation after seeing it ten times. If handled properly, this is actually a good way to frame an audience's expectations.

Figure 35: Technical Sketch

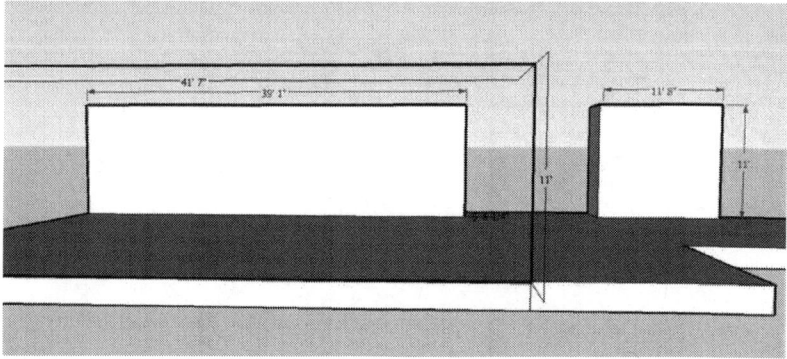

Audiovisual Equipment

New York, Boston, London and Hong Kong represent the world's major financial centers. These cities also draw the largest audiences when a high-profile Roadshow makes a stop. Upwards of 200 people must be processed through registration while they are simultaneously primed for the experience of a great story. Once registered and cleared through security, guests must be greeted, seated and fed. The process must be pleasant and efficient while maintaining tight control over possible risks such as a heckler or other unwanted guest (a journalist or activist) sneaking in.

Figure 36: Hard Wall Set

Figure 37: Concept for a Group Meeting Environment

Just as a theater consists of empty seats and a bare stage on one day and resembles *Les Misérables* the next, the ballroom of *The Pierre* Hotel can be transformed so that it, too, is unrecognizable. All it takes is equipment, and lots of it: lighting, cabling, stands, computers, staging equipment, specialized video and audio switchers, headsets, powerful projectors and other types of displays.

A considerable amount of technical equipment is required to produce a high quality group meeting:

- Install two microphones on the podium so that a fully functional backup with a separate cable run to the mixing board exists.

- Affix one small preview monitor (screen) for the lectern;

- A powerful multi-channel audio system for a large (30+) audience;

- Microphones in front of each chair at the head table for Q&A;

- Both a main and backup computer to play the PowerPoint presentation;

- Two or more "roving" wireless microphones for audience during Q&A;

- Two to four large plasmas so every member of the audience can read every word of the presentation from any vantage point, or a projector capable of displaying the presentation on a screen large enough for all to see;

- A "Clicker" or other device that allows the presenter to advance the slides;

- A CD player with appropriate music to play during "walk-in" (before the presentation starts) and "walk-out" (to form a good last impression);

- Lighting stands and equipment.

Figure 38: Technical Equipment at a Salesforce Meeting

All equipment must be tested and have fully operational "hot" backups in place, including the computer that feeds the presentation to the plasmas or projector. Should a waiter or guest trip over a cable or cause the "show" computer go down for any reason, the results can be disastrous. For this reason, most venues require insurance. To mitigate the risk that the presentation will be disrupted, a separate second cable run is necessary that is linked to a backup computer and the projection system. This way, the slides are clicked simultaneously on two systems; one of them is a ghost that comes alive only if the primary system fails.

Audience members at group meetings are not provided color books.

Never Use a Teleprompter

Presidential campaigns, political debates and annual meetings often make use of a specialized video apparatus known as a *Teleprompter*. This equipment projects the text of a speech in front of the presenter's line of sight, allowing the speaker to look at the audience instead of looking down at a piece of paper on the podium. This is accomplished by tilting two pieces of glass that flank the podium to the left and right, and the light of the text bounces from the left to right glass, scrolling the speech invisibly to the audience.

Do not consider using a teleprompter. It is not appropriate and is never used during an IPO Roadshow. Investors expect management to know the presentation cold and to deliver it without the aid of a teleprompter.

Figure 39: View from the Lectern

Instead, rely on a "comfort" or "confidence" monitor to accomplish the same thing as a teleprompter, but out of sight from the audience. A comfort monitor is simply a large television (52"-72") that sits on the floor and is tilted slightly up so that it faces a presenter standing at the podium. This presenter-facing screen displays whatever the speaker wants to see, whether that is the current slide, speech, or speaker's notes. It requires an operator to click along so that the screen changes in time to the speech. Few in the audience will be aware of its presence and no one is distracted by it. It prevents the presenter from having to look behind him to see what the current slide is.

A much more compact version (8-10") of the comfort monitor is a podium monitor. This is a small, custom-built display that sits on the podium. It allows the presenter to see the same slide that the audience is seeing because it uses the same source signal as the projector. A lectern monitor provides a necessary level of comfort to most presenters who want to know they are synchronized with the slides.

The Priming Effect

Much has been written about the effects of "priming". This is the act of preparing someone for a future experience: a film, novel or Roadshow presentation.

Priming involves communicating words, phrases or images so they have an impact on the participant's physiological response in a way that varies from the individual's normal or unaided response. Priming can involve any of the four senses, from sounds to images to smells or even tastes.

It is well documented that priming works. It is the power of suggestion applied to an audience, and works as well in a laboratory as it does in an investor meeting. One of the world's best known behavioral researchers,

Daniel Kahneman, describes the effects of priming in his book *Thinking Fast and Slow*:

"One group that were shown the words wrinkle, Florida, retirement and other words associated with the sunshine state actually walked out of the laboratory substantially slower than others not primed by words relating to old age."

Venue and Floor Plans

Floor plans are necessary for planning seating arrangements, scenic elements and technical production. They are available for free download on most hotel websites or by contacting the in-house event coordinator. Floor plans are "to scale" and generally depict the meeting space with the most common seating diagrams already provided. Classroom style, rounds, crescent rounds and cocktail seating are all references to seating and meeting formats. Each designation refers to the specific use of a table, chair or configuration.

To ensure there is enough real estate for technical equipment it is necessary to determine the approximate number of investors in attendance and the location of where the rounds or crescent rounds will be set in the room.

Figure 40: Room Diagram for a Large Group Meeting

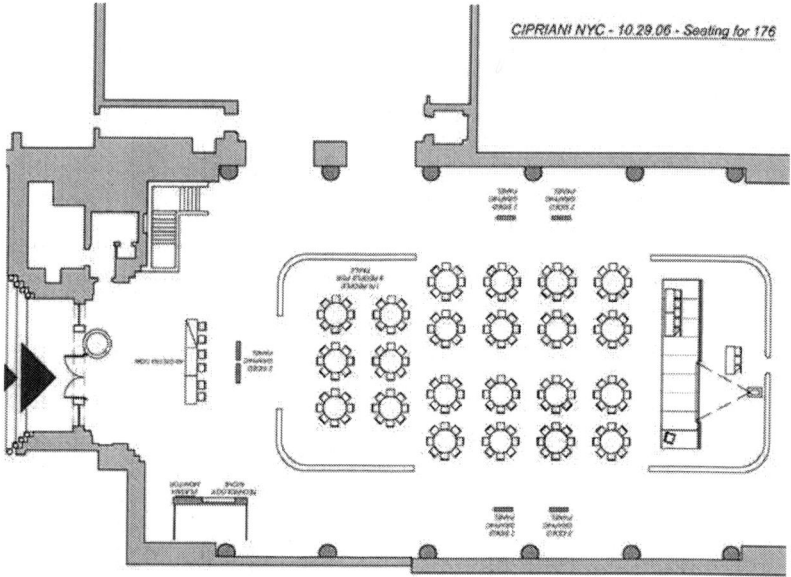

Chapter Seventeen
Execution and Logistics

A Roadshow is an intense fusion of voices, drama, motion and scenery. Every schedule is unique and the quality of execution varies from bank to bank.

Some Roadshows seem as if they will never end. These are the ones that get a lukewarm reaction from the market from the outset. The feeling is there are better deals out there and in fact there probably is.

Other Roadshows function like a well-oiled machine, gathering orders of interest as the team moves smoothly from meeting to meeting, city to city. It the advanced logistics planning that means the difference between a Roadshow feeling like a prestigious corporate retreat or a concert tour for an unsigned band. Delays caused by weather or malfunctioning equipment are a fact of life for every transaction marketed; it is how the delays are dealt with that are the key indicator of execution skill.

Being on Time

Menial logistical snags ravage punctuality. Delays caused by traffic, weather, building security, restroom breaks, and a host of other nuisances sap precious time at every opportunity.

It is always interesting to note how much time and effort goes into preparing the presentation and preparing the speaker team only to realize the execution of the Roadshow itself is an afterthought. With some transactions, it's as if the arrangements are supposed to magically book themselves.

Ground transportation must be available to all Roadshow team members starting the morning the Roadshow begins. Running late for one meeting can make it impossible to be on time for the remaining meetings. Food must also be available throughout the day so that the Roadshow team eats regularly. There is too much constant travel to sit down for a proper lunch.

There are literally hundreds of details relating to transportation, accommodation, technical/audiovisual production and logistics. This is why a perfectly executed Roadshow does not happen without a professional Roadshow manager traveling with the speaker team. It takes experience to anticipate and solve a range of problems in a foreign city. What rock band would go on a world tour without a tour manager? Not a very successful one, likely.

Roadshow desks do a terrific, unheralded job. But there is no substitute for having a person on the ground actively coordinating the cars, moving the luggage, attending to the technical arrangements and making sure the Roadshow team is eating.

Being on time is more than an expectation. It conveys the trait of reliability which is a formative mechanism because it sends the signal that the party can be trusted and is not likely to cause surprises or disrupt the schedules of others.[1] Those that are late to meetings beg the question: if the managers can't make a meeting on time how can they cope with the demands of running a public company?[2] It is a fair question that gets asked.

Being on time every time is not as easy as it might sound. Once the Roadshow begins, everyone realizes the "transfer" times allotted to travel from meeting to meeting are too short. Due to security, it usually takes longer than fifteen minutes to get from one meeting to the next. There is also often a shortage of available cars because bankers show up out of nowhere, wanting to ride with management to the next meeting to brief them on the way. The bankers are also interested in gaining feedback about prior meetings and any personal comments between speaker team members.

For this reason it is advisable to allow twenty-five minutes between meetings in the same city. Even if two locations are next door to one another (as is often the case in Boston, New York and Toronto) the additional time can be used to eat, drink a smoothie or discuss the next meeting with the institutional salesperson.

The Roadshow can be arduous. Traveling from city to city without a break can take a toll. Teams that do not have the luxury of a full-time coordinator must carry their luggage around for two weeks, entering and exiting doors on planes, cars, buildings and meeting rooms thirty to forty times a day. The experience can drive some to drink, which is not uncommon after a long day of ten hours of meetings in two cities.

Information Security

The information shared between bankers, the IPO firm and consultants often traverses insecure security zones such as FTP sites, DropBox, YouSendit, HTTP and other unencrypted connections. Even a USB stick that contains a late stage PowerPoint file of the IPO presentation represents a serious security risk. Should interested parties gain access to restricted or private content that has yet to be released or disclosed, the advantage gained could represent many millions of dollars in profits.

A baseline level of security should be established for all members of the working group, especially design firms and production companies that represent much easier penetration targets than the global investment bank. At the very least, all email communications must be encrypted end to end using certified SSL certificates, and any uploads or file transfers should either be by physical media by way of courier or HTTPS transfer which utilizes an extra secure layer of security beyond the standard HTTP internet transfer protocol.

Javascript presents an especially vulnerable attack vector for corporate espionage, so executives are warned to turn their javascript off unless absolutely necessary and to ensure that Data Execution Prevention (DEP) is turned on for all programs that are internet facing. There are many other precautions to take so that privacy of transaction details and other content is ensured, but the most common mistake to avoid is sending presentations and legal documents over the internet using a free service. There are secure methods to transferring files from point A to B, so it only these secure methods that must be used. This policy must be strictly enforced.

The Smoothie Factor

Relying on one team dinner at the hotel in the evening is not enough nourishment for a full day of travel and meetings the next day. The problem is, there never seems enough time to eat a full meal. The solution is to drink a fresh fruit smoothie two or three times a day. Extra healthy additives – protein, spirulina and vitamins -- will further reduce stress and fatigue. Research shows that strenuous thinking and presenting burns a high number of calories. Much like physical exercise, the mental activity required to ensure an investor meeting is successful expends considerable energy. Although smoothies are a good, practical solution to ongoing dietary requirements, the challenge is that someone has to seek them out in whatever city the team is in and deliver them to a continually moving group of people.

The Roadshow Desk

Most investment banks have a travel and logistics team known as the Roadshow desk. Working between ECM (Equity Capital Markets), the syndicate desk and investment banking, the Roadshow desk is responsible for ensuring the necessary travel and accommodation arrangements are in place: a jet to transport the CEO from his house in the Carolinas, a car to pick up the CFO at his house and drive him to the airport where he will board a business class flight to New York; a meeting room with a plasma and audio for the third presentation on the first day, a venue for dinner in the city the team will overnight in, a hotel available executive suites for everyone to stay on. And on it goes, ad nauseum, change after change to the schedule. There are always numerous changes.

For example, the first city of day two gets swapped with day three. One change like this ripples across the range of bookings and arrangements. Every hotel, car company, jet provider and A/V supplier must shift calendars and associated assets. Availability can be a serious concern at hotels and meeting venues in busy markets.

The fact is, one person behind a desk working with a schedule that is constantly being updated and revised is often lucky to keep up. On a large ($1+ billion) Roadshow, it takes four full-time people to wrestle the Roadshow. One person travels with the team, another travels ahead. One spotter bounces around between the traveling team and advance team to perform hotel check-ins and generally put out fires for two weeks, day after day. The fourth person mans the Roadshow desk, making changes to the schedule and disseminating versions of it to the working group distribution list.

The cost of hiring a third party to assist with the execution of your Roadshow can be well worth it, and is often far less than other, lower value vendors.

Roadshow Expenses

In a survey of 543 IPOs in 1999, four stood out due to their large printing costs.[3] This suggests that the Roadshow expenses were categorized under printing, which is perfectly acceptable under GAAP accounting. Normal printing costs range from $200k to $750k. The printing costs associated with these particular transactions led by Morgan Stanley and Goldman Sachs ranged from $2 million (UPS Courier: $5.4 billion IPO) to $8.8 million (Charter Communications: $3.2 Billion). Goldman Sachs' own IPO reflects $3.6 million in printing expenses. Goldman hired an external Roadshow coordinator to assist with the execution of their own IPO.

IPO	Size	Acct.	Legal	Printing
Charter Communications	$3.2B	$8M	$10M	$8.8M
Goldman Sachs	$3.6B	$1.6M	$0.9M	$3.6M
UPS	$5.4B	$0.5M	$2M	$2M
Delphi	$1.7B	$2M	$1.6M	$3M

Expenses related to Roadshow execution pertain to travel, accommodation and staging costs. Most Roadshows involving international travel are at least $1.2 million and can climb higher than $5 million if there are multiple teams traveling simultaneously to different regions around the world (Europe, Middle East, Asia, and North America).

Typical 3rd Party Costs Associated with an IPO Roadshow (one team)

Group Meetings with Institutions --

Room Rental and Catering	$ 156,800
Transportation – Air	$ 72,670
Transportation – Ground	$ 31,264
Hotel Accommodation	$ 61,407

Presentation Consulting	$ 18,000
Creative Design	$ 26,500
Graphics for Presentation Sets and Meetings Rooms	$ 62,000
Audio Visual and Technical Crews (USA only)	$ 134,400
Presentation Operators	$ 18,200
Color Books and Presentation Materials	$ 3,100
Speaker Coaching	$ 14,250
Miscellaneous Consumables	$ 34,600
SUBTOTAL - EXPENSES	$ 633,191

Logistics Questions

Ahead of a Roadshow, it is worthwhile to understand the answers to these questions:

1) Ground transportation: what kind of cars will be used? How many will be available throughout the day and for how long? Black cars or sedans are best because they are the most comfortable and are soundproof for

conference calls. They are also much more private than minivans or buses. The downside is cost, although in the context of a large transaction the expense is not material ($100k). It's a good idea to have at least one black car available for the CEO, even if a minibus is used to transport the broader party.

2) Air transportation: will private jets be used for the duration of the roadshow? Will executives be able to return home on the weekend and use the jet to return? If necessary, will there be more than one jet available if there is a mechanical failure? What's the response time if a jet 'goes mechanical'? Will helicopters be used whenever possible, such as flying from New York to Princeton, Baltimore or Boston?

3) Audiovisual: when meeting with ten or more investors, will flat screens or projectors be used? Will a microphone and podium be in every group meeting? Will a technician be on-site to ensure the presentation and audio system is working and ready? In terms of the large group meetings involving thirty or more attendees, will there be any branding such as a logo on the lectern or head table? Will all audiovisual systems be thoroughly tested and operational by the time management arrives? Will there be name tags printed

for each investor? Will the name and title of each presenter be displayed on the head table so that the audience can read them from a distance? Will there be directional signage at every hotel to direct investors to the right place? Who is responsible for setting up the signage? Will someone greet investors in the lobby and personally direct them to the room?

4) Investor materials: who will guarantee there will be enough color books and prospectuses at each and every meeting? Is there a backup plan in case these items are mislaid, even if temporarily? Will someone review the presentation on screen prior to every group meeting to ensure it is the correct version? Will someone have an extra copy of each speaker's script on hand at every group meeting?

5) Food: will there be adequate food provided in the vehicles so that management can eat between meetings? Will someone be available to provide fruit smoothies or protein shakes prior to important meetings? Will a private room be available to eat in prior to the large group presentations so management doesn't have to eat at the head table, in front of investors?

6) Security: what steps will be taken to ensure management's personal security is not compromised or that the equipment necessary to operate the

presentation is not tampered with? Some CEOs demand "bug sweeps" in their hotel rooms prior to checking in.

Details that Require Attention

There are a handful of very helpful items that will benefit every Roadshow. For example, a supply of spare mobile phones, extra chargers and batteries always proves useful. The backup cellular phones can be a lifesaver when a manager's phone dies midway through a conference call during a long car ride.

"The Power List" is a useful contact list to add to the phones of the traveling team. This list contains the names and direct numbers of the people who genuinely matter when it comes time to execute the Roadshow. Consisting primarily of confidential phone numbers, the Power List includes the mobile numbers of private jet pilots, the color book printer in New York, the concierge at the Four Seasons, the entire Roadshow team's personal cellular phones and personal emails, a secret travel agent who jumps in when there's an emergency, and the lead drivers in New York, Boston and San Francisco.

The Roadshow team must always be accessible through a phone call, text message, personal assistant or email. All smart phones must maintain an adequate charge at all times, so purchasing all necessary extra batteries and car chargers before they are urgently required is a good idea.

Dial-out codes from various countries are also useful if the Roadshow goes to Europe, Asia or the United Arab Emirates, as dialing prefixes vary from country to country. For example, what are the actual digits that are punched into a mobile phone versus the local hotel phone if you want to call Frankfurt while you're in the UK? What if you're not using the UK hotel phone but your own US mobile phone? This is good information to have handy.

Email or text/SMS the detailed daily schedule for the following day's meetings directly to the team's phones at the exact same time every night. The details should include what time the team is meeting in the hotel lobby, what time they are expected to get in the cars to leave to the first meeting and what the transfer times are for all meetings and all flights throughout the day, including all ground transportation details.

It is also a good idea to courier the prospectuses to various cities and hotels ahead of schedule. This prevents the team from traveling with ten boxes of paper everywhere it goes. Some shipments will still get lost or not delivered (plan on it), but at least most of them will arrive on-site. Affix a very distinctive sticker on the box so a bellman can find it quickly without opening the box.

Reconnaissance -- or 'recces' (pronounced reck-eez) -- are a must for group meeting venues. Be sure to visit each room and the facility itself ahead of time. Meet with the banquet manager and bring the catering and A/V equipment order list. Confirm room dimensions, service entrances, room layouts, audiovisual requirements, the signage policy, and directions to the meeting room.

The Five Immutable Laws of Roadshows

1. The simple tasks are disproportionately difficult to complete.

2. The first ten seconds are key to a good meeting.

3. If you don't care, don't expect anyone else to.

4. Don't say anything that's not in the prospectus.

5. Know where the presentation flip books are at all times.

Chapter Eighteen

Investors You Will Meet

Over the course of two weeks of Roadshow marketing, management will make contact with several distinct types of investors. Some seem like stone cold strangers, constantly judging you, while others are downright neighborly. Whether the investor qualifies as a legend ("Fidelity") or a famous boutique ("Green Light Capital"), each occupies a niche in the IPO market. Strategic investors may be smaller accounts that may understand the firm's business extremely well, while other investors may seem to know less than the security guard.

Large investors are generally institutional investors that have tens or hundreds of billions of dollars under management. They manage complex portfolios with dozens of companies (assets) in various stages of maturation. These are institutions such as T. Rowe Price in Baltimore and Fidelity in Boston. It is important that the firm have good meetings with these accounts because, sooner or later, they will likely be stockowners and in the near term, their opinion matters. The impression a firm leaves with these large investors can ripple through the market.

These large investors are usually pension funds, mutual funds, and money managers. The purpose of these corporations is to invest large sums of capital on behalf of other companies, on a perpetual basis through payroll deductions, dividends or equity appreciation through other investments.

Smaller investors are those that have less than one billion under management. The size and orientation of each investor is identified on the "investor profile" that is distributed by the lead bank's Roadshow desk.

Figure 41: A Typical Day in a Roadshow Schedule

LOCAL	ACTIVITY/MEETINGS	LOGISTICS					
		CAR	AIR	XFER TIME	PAX	COMMENTS	
8:00am	**PRIMECAP MANAGEMENT CO** 225 S Lake Ave STE 400 Pasadena, CA 91101-3010 CONTACT: Joel Fried TEL: 1(626) 304 9222 MS Sales Host: Seyonne Kang TEL: (510) 407 8301						
10:30am	**TRANSAMERICA INVESTMENT MANAGEMENT** 11111 Santa Monica Blvd / STE 820 Los Angeles, CA 90025 CONTACT: John Huber TEL: 1 (310) 996 3219 MS Sales Host: Seyonne Kang (510)407 8301						
12:00pm	**GROUP MEETING** HYATT REGENCY CENTURY PLAZA HOTEL 2025 AVENUE OF THE STAR/Regents Boardroom Los Angeles, CA 90067 CONTACT: Scott Phillips TEL: (310) 407 8301 FAX: (310) 551 3355 MS Sales Host: Seyonne Kang (510)407 8301					Attendees: Employean Capital Partners - Sheila Corriston,Amos Meron **Glovine Capital Group -** Karthik Srinivasan	
2:00pm	**TRUST COMPANY OF THE WEST** 865 S Figueroa Street Los Angeles, CA 90017-2543 TEL: 1 (213) 244 0470 MS Sales Host: Seyonne Kang (510)407 8301						
3:30pm	**CAPITAL GUARDIAN 1:1** 333 South Hope St/ 49th Floor Los Angeles, CA 90071-1406 CONTACT: Andrew Barth TEL: (1 213) 486 9491 MS Sales Host: Seyonne Kang (510)407 8301						

Investor Profiles

An investor profile is like a "rap sheet" on an investor. It outlines the size and composition of the account's investments, current holdings, industry of specialty and philosophy.

Sometimes there is also specific information on the investor's opinion on key issues and their particular sensitivities as demonstrated through investments in publicly-traded peers. If the team is not receiving these investor profiles, demand they do. It is important to anticipate the investor's likely area of interest and address it.

Most underwriters provide management with a detailed synopsis about the investors they will meet. This gives management an opportunity to tailor their individual presentations to suit the investment style of each meeting. The reality is, however, that teams rarely have the experience to incorporate the information and prioritize messages from one meeting to the next.

Experienced CEOs typically ask for a detailed investor briefing the evening before instead of the same day. This enables them to learn what they can about the various hot buttons of each investor. At the very least, it is important to know what meetings are critically important and what topics are sensitive to the large funds with objectives that are aligned with the firm. The knowledge of whether the investor has a position in a peer or is focused on other aspects of the IPO -- such as whether it is valued relatively inexpensively (value-oriented) or has an ability to generate consistent and increasing levels of future cash flows -- is also helpful information.

Figure 42: An Investor Profile

DEUTSCHE ASSET MANAGEMENT AMERICAS

Style	Orientation	Turnover
Index	Passive	High

345 Park Avenue New York, NY 10154-0004 Tel:(212) 336-9260 Fax:(212) 751-0754	Founded: 1903. Deutsche Asset Mgmt Americas, formerly Bankers Trust Co., changed its name following the acquisition of Bankers Trust by Deutsche Bank in 1999. An affiliate of Deutsche Banc Alex. Brown, they manage the Deutsche funds, as well as various Fidelity index funds. On April 8, 2002, Deutsche Bank acquired Zurich Scudder Investments.

Equity Assets		95,029 ↑
Annual Portfolio Turnover		92%
Number of Stocks Held		5,317 ↑
Investor Type		Bank & Tru

KEY CONTACTS

Name	Title	Phone
Joanne A. Smith	Security Analyst	(212) 336-9260

PORTFOLIO COMPOSITION
% Assets Above/Below S & P 500

INVESTMENT APPROACH

Deutsche Asset Management Americas' team-based approach to management offers skill in geographic markets, industry sectors, asset classes, and investment styles. This skill is leveraged through portfolio construction processes emphasizing thorough independent research and strict quantitative attribution and risk control. The goal of their quantitative team is to offer portfolios highly associated with a targeted benchmark, while offering higher returns. The active equity approach consists of products managed through stock selection and proprietary portfolio construction. Their approach relies on strong fundamental research and technical analysis of a specific investment universe. The candidates are then subjected to detailed fundamental analysis. Outstanding prospects display superior competitive characteristics including innovative and forward-looking management, strong balance sheets, as well as improving trends in operating results. From these candidates, the team then selects stocks with the strongest combination of fundamental and technical characteristics in order to construct a portfolio consistent with the product's stated objectives and risk limits. The Quan-

titative Equity approach diversifies the firm's active equity product line-up by providing an array of quantitatively managed strategies. They limit themselves solely to holdings securities contained within a fund's benchmark. The Private Equity Funds Group seeks to identify and provide access to some of the best private equity opportunities and fund managers in the world, including buyouts, expansion capital, restructuring and distress, as well as mezzanine and venture capital.

Decision Making Process:
The investment team provides widespread knowledge in a variety of approaches to quantitative management, as well as the intense technical potential required to employ these strategies effectively.

PEER OWNERSHIP

	03/04 (SMM)	12/03 (SMM)	09/03 (SMM)	06/03 (SMM)
MET	150	150	151	132
PRU	93	93	97	84
TMK	14	14	13	24
NFS	8	8	8	3
MTG	15	15	24	37
PMI	6	6	6	21
RDN	9	9	5	22
JP	60	60	52	58
LNC	62	62	57	61
PFG	50	50	47	73
Total	**467**	**467**	**467**	**515**
%Port	**0.49**	**0.50**	**0.50**	**0.57**

INDUSTRY WEIGHTINGS

Largest Industry Holdings

Industry	S&P	% Port	$ Chg.
Non-Bank Financial	(0.8)	9.5	-1,653.0
High Tech - Hardware	(0.9)	9.1	-1,127.5
Banks & Thrifts	(1.1)	8.9	124.0
Autos/Auto Parts	(9.2)	7.7	-323.0
Multi-Industry	(1.3)	7.3	308.4
Energy	(0.9)	5.1	-1,465.5
Health Care	(0.8)	5.1	-645.4
Drugs/Pharmaceuticals	(0.7)	4.5	-934.0
Food & Beverages	(1.0)	4.5	722.5
Retail	(0.6)	3.8	-756.6

( ) = Relative to S&P 500

Largest Industry Buys

Industry	S&P	% Port	$ Port
Cellular/Wireless	(4.0)	2.2	1,285.7
REIT	(5.1)	1.6	789.1
Food & Beverages	(1.0)	4.5	722.5
Electric Utilities	(1.2)	3.5	324.8
Real Estate	(9.1)	0.6	498.6

Largest Industry Sells

Industry	S&P	% Port	$ Chg.
Non-Bank Financial	(0.8)	9.5	-1,653.0
Chemicals	(1.0)	1.4	-1,492.3
Energy	(0.9)	5.1	-1,465.3
High Tech - Hardware	(0.9)	9.1	-1,127.5
Drugs/Pharmaceuticals	(0.7)	4.5	-934.0

PORTFOLIO DISTRIBUTION
by Market Capitalization

Mid: 9.00%   Small: 4.00%
Large: 87.00%

NON-BANK FINANCIAL HOLDINGS

Rank	Company	$ Mkt Val	$ Chg.	% Port
1	Citigroup Inc	1,317.3	-349.2	1.4
2	American International Group Inc	809.6	-344.6	0.9
3	Fannie Mae	414.0	-143.4	0.4
4	Amsouth BanCorp	384.9	-276.4	0.4
5	SLM Corp	375.8	-32.6	0.4
6	Morgan Stanley & Co	353.1	-37.7	0.4
7	St. Paul Travelers Companies Inc	346.7	307.0	0.4
8	American Express Co	283.0	-29.1	0.3
9	SPDR - Europe	245.2	-291.3	0.3
10	Goldman Sachs Group Inc	210.3	30.6	0.2
11	Merrill Lynch & Co Inc	178.5	-15.8	0.2
12	Nasdaq 100 Trust	168.9	93.6	0.2
13	AFLAC Inc	163.5	-34.0	0.2
14	Freddie Mac	152.3	-124.0	0.2
15	Lehman Brothers Holdings Inc	151.0	-74.0	0.2
16	Metlife Inc	150.1	-31.5	0.2
17	Allstate Corp	142.6	-86.4	0.2
18	XL Capital Ltd	123.7	-17.5	0.1
19	State Street Corp	113.4	-4.8	0.1
20	MBNA Corp	103.1	-86.9	0.1
	Total	6,192.8	-951.3	6.5

PORTFOLIO CHARACTERISTICS

	P/E	Yield	Est.EPS	Price/ 5 yr EPS Gr. Proj.	ROE	Debt/ Equity	P/B	Beta
S&P 500	24.2	1.7	20.9	12.4	18.0	61.2	4.0	1.0
Institution	24.0	1.8	21.9	12.2	17.1	51.6	3.7	0.9
Non-Bank Finan-	16.9	1.8	15.1	12.3	14.3	57.1	2.8	1.0

NON-BANK FINANCIAL ADJUSTMENTS

Top Buys	$ Mkt/Val	$ Chg.	Top Sells	$ Mkt/Val	$ Chg.
St. Paul Travelers Com-	346.7	307.0	Citigroup Inc	1,317.3	-349.2
Amsouth BanCorp	384.9	276.4	American International	809.6	-344.6
Nasdaq 100 Trust	168.9	93.6	SPDR - Europe	245.2	-291.3
Unitrin Inc	84.9	82.9	Fannie Mae	414.0	-143.4
Commerce Group Inc	49.7	49.4	Freddie Mac	152.3	-124.0
State Street Corp	38.6	38.0	MBNA Corp	103.1	-86.9
Willis Group Holdings	37.2	33.1	Allstate Corp	142.6	-86.4
Charter Municipal Mort-	31.8	31.6	SLM Corp	375.8	-82.6
Goldman Sachs Group	210.3	30.6	Lehman Brothers Hold-	151.0	-74.0
MFA Mortgage Invest-	39.8	28.7	Countrywide Financial	56.4	-62.7
Total	**1,392.3**	**971.2**	**Total**	**3,767.1**	**-1,555.1**

MorganStanley

Goldman Sachs

Absent a briefing hours before the meeting, the institutional sales manager generally meets management in the investor's lobby just moments before the meeting and rides with them in the elevator to introduce them to the account. While checking through building security (the largest waste of time over the course of a Roadshow) there is generally five minutes of free time that CEOs use to learn about the account.

The Two Primary Types of Investors

Price discovery and valuation are fundamental to investing in an IPO. The methods used by an institutional investor may vary widely from that of the retail investor.

Institutions appreciate the disparity between long-term corporate cash flow trends and investors' short-term cash flow expectations, as reflected in current share price, and exploit this as a source of alpha (return on investment). It then follows that in order for institutions to consistently generate positive alpha, they must develop superior forecasts of changes in others' expectations -- the 'other' referring to the reactionary retail investor.

Institutional investors are sophisticated professionals with access to a wealth of expensive information. They also dominate the schedule of one-on-one meetings, which are typically not attended by retail investors.

Professional investors fall into two or more of the following categories:

Role/Title
Portfolio Manager (PM)
Asset Manager
Investment Manager

Type of Institution
Hedge Fund
Private Equity
Mutual Fund
Plan Sponsors
Insurance Company
Retirement Fund
Endowment Fund
Pension Fund
Sovereign Wealth Fund

Style
Value Investor
Growth Investor
Momentum Investor
Short & Long

The Retail Investor

The "retail" investor is the second broad investor type. This group is known to purchase stock based on second-hand information (one-on-one meetings provide first-hand information). Comprised of individual investors, they have far less access to capital and credit and are considered to be much less sophisticated than their institutional counterparts. Retail investors do not have access to the wealth of proprietary historical data and financial models that institutions are known to possess. Still, retail investors are an important piece of the investment pie because they ultimately end up buying and owning stock sold by institutions.

Retail investors are known to be prone to episodes of optimistic or pessimistic "sentiment" about the stock market, especially IPOs. Sentiment is a reference to beliefs about the fundamental value of an asset that arise from treating noise as relevant information.[1] At different times in the investing cycle, their beliefs may change even though the noise remains the same.

The average retail investor holds a four-stock portfolio with an average size of $35k. 47% of U.S. households own equities.[2] Fewer than 10% of retail investors have portfolios over $100k and fewer than 5% hold more than ten stocks. A typical investor executes nine trades a year with an average trade size of $8,800. More importantly, individual investors are more likely to hold stock in highly visible companies and are far less likely to purchase treasury securities or corporate bonds.[3]

According to a March 2013 research report published by Goldman Sachs, households own 38% of the US equity market directly, but, that figure is actually closer to 80% when ownership through pension funds, mutual funds and life insurance policy holdings are factored in.[4]

At 80% effective household ownership, the retail investor is an essential component to a healthy shareholder mix. They are buyers when institutions are sellers. They are also sellers when institutions see a buying opportunity. Although institutions account for 48% of US equities ownership, retail investors include the largest money managers, hedge funds, mutual funds, and private equity funds that invest capital sourced from individuals, either through a 401(k), pension fund or other fund.[5] This creates an *IPO eco-system* based on the belief that when the Average Joe buys stocks, confidence improves. When Joe sells, confidence erodes.

The Institutional Investor

Two studies document that institutions sell almost 25% of their IPO allocation within the first two days of trading. These institutions hold their remaining shares for only 9.7 months before selling.[6] This indicates that although institutional investors are considered to be more impervious to factors involving sentiment, they are still focused on a quick exit, if profitable. In a depressed market when the retail investor is busying liquidating his *E-Trade* account, the institutional investor is on the other side of the trade, purchasing the shares with the full intent of selling them later to the same retail buyer.

A quick sketch of the average institutional investor might reveal several of the following traits:

1. Highly adept at processing information and the rapid comparison of existing prototypes.

2. Employs a valuation methodology when analyzing material others would consider subjective.

3. Discounts information as a by-product of inherent skepticism.

4. Judges immediately unless there is an explicit reason not to do so.

5. Relies on management to provide and implement sufficient signals and then interpret the feedback in response to management's signals.

6. Places a high value on precision.

Portfolios

Investors manage portfolios based on multiple factors: risk and volatility (beta), expected return (alpha), and rate of growth -- to name just a few. Dozens or even hundreds of individual equity securities are bundled together with the goal of achieving the fund's objective. By combining criteria based on an array of detailed financial performance metrics (e.g. inventories, accounts receivables, gross margins, selling expenses, capital expenditures, effective tax rates, and labor force sales productivity), the portfolio manager creates a synthetic organism that reduces net exposure to any single security.

If institutional investors believe that retail investors "like" or "buy" an IPO story, institutions will be much more inclined to buy more of the offering. Clues regarding sentiment are gathered privately in conversations and captured publicly through media coverage. Because portfolio managers rely on stock-screen software and portfolio construction tools that allow them to leverage their qualitative stock-selection skills, many fundamental stock-pickers have become quants.[7]

There are three basic approaches when investing in a new company: short, long, or both short and long. Investors that go "long" use various techniques to maximize gains and limit potential losses, but the strategies are predicated on the share price increasing over a given period. Traditionally, retail investors almost always go long. This is based not only on technical limitations but the psychological belief that long shots are preferred because low probabilities of winning are greatly overweighted.

Short Sellers

The number of short-sellers has grown in recent years because statistically it is easier to make money when a stock price falls. Short sellers are extremely well-informed and easily identify what IPOs are likely to perform poorly not only because of market timing or undesirable qualities related to the target's business, but also by looking at the company's capital structure or lack of management team experience. Short volume accounted for approximately 24% of trading volume on the NYSE and more than 30% on NASDAQ in 2005.[8]

Short sellers generate positive abnormal returns by targeting companies (small stocks tend to have more short sales) that are overpriced based on fundamental ratios such as P/E and market-to-book.[9] In the last case, changes in shorting demand are inferred from successive monthly short interest snapshots rather than observed directly in transaction data.[10] This data applies only to companies that are already public, but the over-allotment clause can provide some evidence about future levels of short interest.

Stocks that have been heavily shorted continue to under-perform 95% of the time. In Jim Cramer's book *Confessions of a Street Addict*, he talks about his bubble-era "dot com" IPO (*TheStreet.com*) that priced at $19 per share after the range had been upped twice from the original $9-11 range. Cramer describes what happened on May 11, the day after the IPO priced and opened for its first day of trading:

"At 11:43 the stock opened at $63, with almost the entire buy side coming from a bunch of e-tail market orders all batched together by Knight [Capital Group], which had totally hijacked our deal. Within minutes the stock was at $70...I sat there dumbfounded. Knight/ Trimark had just collected a giant bunch of retail sell orders and taken the other side of the trade -- shorted the stock -- leaving them totally in charge of the game.

At the moment of truth, Knight, not Goldman Sachs, controlled both sides of the operation. What a miserable misallocation of our fees. What a strange process that allowed Knight to turn market orders from an oblivious public to their own personal advantage. They knew where all of the demand was and they totally abused the IPO. They could have opened the stock much lower. But controlling both sides, they wanted it to open as high as possible, and then with their own capital, take the other side of the trade, short the opening, and then watch it go down and profit from each point of decline. The higher the opening, the more [we] would fall, the better for Knight. What a killing they must have made -- they don't break out how much money they make per deal but I bet this was one of their biggest moneymakers of the year, if not their whole corporate existence. They were the only winners on the 11th of May. Goldman, TheStreet.com's shareholders, and TSCM were the losers."

The lesson here is that firms are better positioned when explicitly stating their primary objective is not to leave money on the table. If "leaving money on the table" is a concern for the issuer, the IPO will not "pop" as it would otherwise. On an equal-weighted basis, the average first day return for IPOs in 2013 was 21%. In 1999 it was 70.9%. That translates to $7.42 billion versus almost $37 billion of money left on the table in 2013 versus 1999.[11]

Current Holdings

When reviewing the investor profiles ahead of a meeting, look at the investor's current holdings. Does it include companies in your sector? If not, perhaps they are more interested in financial performance such as earnings or revenue growth or some other financial metric. Maybe they are long-term investors who see value in investing in businesses that are losing money now but won't in a year.

Ask your investment banker these questions to learn the answers so that you are prepared to highlight certain content in your presentation or provide specific answer to likely questions. Components of many portfolios turn over in a twelve month period which provides an opportunity for IPOs with suitable characteristics.

Hedge Funds

Hedge funds are distinguished by three prevalent strategies: "long/short equity", "quantitative equity market-neutral" and "statistical arbitrage".

The long/short equity strategies category is the broadest category, including any equity portfolios that engage in short selling, that may or may not be market-neutral (many long/short equity funds are long-biased), that may or may not be quantitative (fundamental stock-pickers sometimes engage in short positions to hedge their market exposure as well as to bet on poor-performing stocks), and where technology need not play an important role. In most hedge-fund databases, this is by far the single largest category, both in terms of assets and the number of funds.

The second category is more general, involving broader types of quantitative models, some with lower turnover, fewer securities, and inputs other than past prices such as accounting variables, earnings forecasts, and economic indicators.

The third category is highly technical and involves large numbers of securities (hundreds to thousands, depending on the amount of risk capital), very short holding periods (measured in days to seconds), and substantial computational, trading, and IT infrastructure.

More recently, a fourth category has emerged, the "130/30" or "active extension" strategies, in which a fund or, more commonly, a managed account of, say $100 million, maintains $130 million of long positions in one set of securities and $30 million of short positions in another set of securities. Such a strategy is a natural extension of a long-only fund where the long-only constraint is relaxed to a limited extent. It is currently one of the fastest-growing areas in the institutional money management business, and because the portfolio construction process is rather technical by design, the managers of such products are primarily quantitative.[12]

IPO Participation

A wealth of IPO data exists related to the timing, size, pricing and performance of initial public offerings. An analysis of this historical data suggests that more than twice as many investors participate in a subsequent offering if they first experience a hot offering rather than a cold offering. The effect continues to be strong for subsequent offerings as well. By the tenth offering, 65% of investors in the hot IPO group will have subscribed to another IPO, compared to only 39% in the cold IPO group.[13] This supports the belief that loss has about two and a half times the impact of a gain of the same magnitude, which is one of many well known behavioral traits displayed by some investors.[14]

Chapter Nineteen

Pricing and Valuation

Theoretically, a firm's stock price reflects the value of its growth opportunities.[1] There are several methodologies available for calculating the present and future value of a firm and the corresponding value of its newly issued equity shares.

A "pricing range" is established for the sale of IPO equity shares. This range states the lowest and highest asking price set by the underwriters for the initial public offering. The average of these two numbers is called "the midpoint of the range." The midpoint reflects the expected price given a reasonable level of demand for the IPO.

Approximately 39% of IPOs price above the midpoint of the original price range and 48% price below.[2]

The range may change at any time to reflect higher or lower levels of demand. The vast majority of issuers do not divulge the offering price range in the S-1 (the "filed range") until shortly before the Roadshow. The announcement that "terms have been set" signals that the Roadshow is imminent.

The IPO price and number of shares constitute the "terms" of an offering.

IPOs that price below the original range have the smallest initial returns (2.59%) compared to firms within (14.4%) and above (44.5%) the original file range. The SEC mandates that the final price be within 20% of the filed range, meaning no more than 20% above the high end and no more than 20% below the low end.[3] Price changes beyond this threshold necessitate an amendment to the S-1 (resulting in an "S-1/a" filing with the SEC).

IPOs that price above the range experience two times the underpricing of those that price within the range.[4] Studies show that more than any other factor, buyers care about *relative* prices.[5] This explains why the multiples of comparable firms are critical to gaining to understanding the value of one firm relative to another, and the standard method for conjuring up a concrete number that depicts future value.[6]

This was clearly the case in early 2008 when some of the largest companies lost 90% or more of their value. This detonation of wealth was not caused by a sudden 90% implosion in fundamentals. It was caused by an acute aversion to loss. The traditional methods used to calculate value went out the window as investors focused on relative prices based on what companies were more likely to survive. Firms with tangible cash, less risky assets and positive news became heavily favored.

On the final hour of the Roadshow, management participates in what is known as the "pricing call". This is a conference call to discuss how much demand exists for the issue, what investors will get preferred allocations, and what the final agreed price is for the total number of shares offered. After the pricing call, one last amendment is filed with the SEC and the transaction is considered closed. No further changes are allowed. The Roadshow -- and the IPO is complete. The firm is now public.

But even though the IPO is finished, the firm is still not allowed to say anything to the media until the SEC declares the final amendment "effective". Fortunately, many IPOs are declared effective as soon as they price, not 25 or 40 days after the first day of trading which is a widely-held belief but not the truth. Even though the stock may be trading, sometimes it takes more than a month for the SEC to give the green light necessary for an issuer to communicate normally again.

Once the prospectus is deemed "effective", the firm enters the third and final phase of the IPO communications life cycle.

Pricing Mechanics

Pricing a transaction is a game of supply and demand. Large orders inherently have more influence. The bank earns more if the offering prices at the top of the range, resulting in more capital raised.

If a large order is not placed in the first two or three days of the Roadshow, investors know they have leverage. In this situation, they are more likely to express interest at the midpoint or below.

Throughout the Roadshow, the lead bank compiles orders and expressions of interest from investors into something known as "The Book". This is why the lead manager of an IPO is often called the "bookrunner", a direct reference to the process of identifying orders and potential demand. The book consists of a list of potential buyers and how much stock they might be interested in buying at various price levels. It is only during the last few hours of the Roadshow that the "book" is revealed. Many management teams are surprised when they see who invested and who did not.

Many large investors keep their real intentions confidential until the final day of the Roadshow when the IPO price is negotiated. Many investors will increase their orders if they learn of high levels of interest from other investors. In contrast, if demand for the issue is tepid, downward pressure will be exerted on the final price.

Leaving Money on The Table

To understand why some IPOs perform like rockets while other flat-line, it is useful to examine how the original price range is established.

Although there are numerous components to valuing assets or future cash flows, the argument about what something is "really worth" usually boils down to one or two deciding factors. Because the S-1 is available months before the Roadshow, the key characteristics often emerge before the final investor presentation is complete. The most influential and interested investors will read and analyze the S-1 and form opinions based on their knowledge of peers and other pertinent characteristics (capital structure, industry trends, growth strategies, and competitive dynamics). The perspective of these early informed investors are collected by the lead bankers of the IPO and conveyed to the company.

Some academics suggest that the difference between an IPO that spikes and one that trades within a range is attributable to the market's adjustment based on new or clarified information received during the Roadshow.

Since the IPO firm receives second-hand information about investors desiring to buy shares at the lowest possible price from investment banks with an incentive to generate additional fees by allocating stock at levels well above the price at which they agreed to underwrite the transaction, it is plausible that setting a lower range would be an efficient and legal means to earn substantially higher fees.

Shares sold above the offering price are not received by the issuer, which raises the important question of why so many IPOs voluntarily "leave money on the table".[7]

Comparables and Valuation

Investors are highly focused on valuation -- what the firm is worth, per share -- and will seek a comparable frame of reference. Management should provide these comparisons and be convincing about their legitimacy. One proven method is to identify similarities and differences between certain peers using concrete examples and analogies as evidence. Another way is to draw parallels between the firm with others using specific information from the S-1 or credible third-party sources.

A firm's SIC (standard industrial classification) is an effective criterion for selecting comparable firms.[8] This code relates to a category comprised of a subset of correlated risks that vary by sector and industry. This code is a starting point in determining relative valuation. Narrower industries have a three or four digit code while a one or two digit code signifies a broader, less defined business.

Valuation errors go down when the peer group is based on an industry affiliation. Because industrial sectors are defined more narrowly -- that is, when moving to the three digit Standard Industrial Classification (SIC) code level from one or two digit level, valuation accuracy -- and the process of valuation -- improves.

Growth Stocks

Companies with earnings that are expected to grow at an above-average rate are known as "growth stocks". On average, these stocks respond very negatively to subsequent earnings announcements for several years. Growth stocks have a stable record of past growth, sound ROE and predictable P/E.

Value Stocks

Undervalued companies are "value stocks". These stocks trade at a lower price than their fundamentals would suggest. Value stocks have low P/E, low P/B, less than 1 PEG (defined as the PE ratio divided by growth rate) and the firm's debt does not exceed its equity. The firm's liabilities are typically no higher than half of its assets, and its stock price or pre-IPO valuation is less or equal to tangible book. These characteristics provide value stocks with a tangible margin of safety because they are relatively inexpensive.

Financial Models

These tale-of-the-tape comparisons (or "comps") are useful to evaluating how a firm measures up against its peers. Comps are an essential ingredient in the financial models created by investors and analysts. These models form a basis for predicting the firm's future value through benchmarks and components of similar stocks. Models are programmed to send signals to buy, hold or sell once certain events are triggered.

A typical financial model includes dozens of inputs: revenue, cash flow, capital expenditures, GDP forecasts, interest rates and so on. These models are usually proprietary and are closely guarded. They are updated automatically and are refined to reflect changing conditions in a sector or the broader market.

Many investors employ valuation methodologies that fall into one of three main categories: fundamental ratio analysis, accruals analysis, and fundamental value analysis.[9]

Calculating Multiples

Valuations rely on the use of multiples, where x is the number multiplied by some other metric such as sales. Facebook's IPO, for example, priced at "26 times sales" or 26x sales, which is the same as saying the transaction priced at a multiple of 26 times the gross annual revenue Facebook generates in a year. Looking at another metric, Facebook priced its IPO at 107 times trailing 12-month earnings which is the same as saying "at $38 per share, the IPO price implies an earnings multiple of 107 times what Facebook earns in a 12 month period."[10]

When using multiples, investment banks rely mostly on future earnings and cash flows. Multiples based on post-IPO forecasted earnings and cash flows have been shown to result in more accurate valuations. When forecasted earnings are used, the accuracy of the valuation improves substantially.

In contrast to cash flow calculations, multiple valuation does not require the tough work of adequately forecasting cash flows and appropriate discount rates. Price to earnings and Price to Cash Flow are the most popular multiple approaches.

Valuation Models

Understanding valuation models is necessary to identify the information investors will find helpful when making such calculations. Several valuation methods are used, but Discounted Free Cash Flow (DFCF) is the most popular with IPOs. Equity analysts most often base target prices on P/E ratios and forecasted long-term earnings growth rates, or a combination of these two constructs (the PEG ratio). Almost all analysts use earnings multiples in their reports.[11]

The quality of the following key factors determine the appropriate valuation scheme:

1) Earnings

2) Sales

3) Assets

4) Liabilities

P/E

The ratio of "price to earnings" (P/E) or "earnings per share" (EPS) is a pervasive benchmark used for valuation purposes to compare a firm's stock price relative to its earnings. A firm with negative earnings will result in negative ratios. One highly-visible research company specializing in IPOs calculates the EPS for new offerings over three periods: the last 12 months, the current fiscal year's forecast, and next year's forecast.[12] The same calculations for two similar firms are also included so that investors can make an easy comparison without looking up the data themselves. Research suggests that a pure focus on earnings leads to systematic errors, as it neglects the incremental information contained in cash flow value-added.

Valuation multiples based on forecasted earnings lead to higher valuation accuracy than multiples using trailing earnings. This is not unexpected, as other studies suggest that earnings forecasts capture information on value that is not reflected by historical earnings.[13] One study shows that in a setting of unobserved information, forward earnings are better valuation attributes than trailing earnings.[14]

Cash Flow Models

The offer price of most IPOs are mainly valued by determining future free cash flows, to which a discount is applied. Discounted Future Cash Flow (DFCF) is designed to produce a relatively unbiased estimate of value.

Calculating cumulative free cash flows contain some incremental information about the firm's prospects that are not included in cumulative earnings. Only current cash flows are significantly and positively associated with future cash flows.

The formula for DFCF inputs include the following: Latest Cash Flow, Discount Rate, Cash Flow Growth Rate and the duration of the period expected to generate cash flow.

Based on revenue growth over the period, the growth rate is either slow (single digits) or high (10+%). An example would be 25% growth in the first year, 20% the next, 15%, then 10% and 5%. What's the best case versus a realistic case over a five year period?

Based on current cash flows, $100 million in revenue would produce $125 million in year one, $120 million in year two, $115 million in year three, $110 million in year four, and $105 million in year five.

Free Cash flow (FCF) deducts operating costs, taxes, net investment and working capital. Depreciation and amortization are not included as they are non-cash charges. Cash flow = cash earnings + changes in (Δ) working capital + (sale of assets less capex) + (financing proceeds less (-) dividends - share repurchases - debt repayments).

Asset Pricing Models

Specific asset pricing models include the CAPM, Fama-French multi-factor model, Black-Scholes option pricing model and the stochastic discount factor (SDF).[15] The ability of Net Operating Assets (NOA = Operating Assets - Operating Liabilities) to predict returns goes beyond the ability of new equity issues to predict returns, also known as the new issues puzzle.[16] A basic accounting corollary states that a firm's net operating assets are equal to the cumulation over time of the difference between net operating income and free cash flow.

Research suggests investors weight NOA much too positively in forecasting future earnings.[17] A high level of net operating assets, scaled to control for firm size, indicates a lack of sustainability in recent earnings performance, and investors do not fully discount for this fact. Cumulative free cash flow (used in NOA calculation) is incrementally informative beyond cumulative earnings about future prospects. First, since accruals and cash flows have different persistence (DeChow, 1994), information about the separate pieces provides better forecasting power than knowing earnings alone.[18]

The book *High-Stakes Dealmaking* advises to monitor the following areas when evaluating assets:[19]

- receivable quality and likelihood of collection;

- inventory quality and aging;

- LIFO/FIFO issues (current value of inventory);

- market value versus historical costs of fixed assets;

- depreciation, amortization, and allocation systems;

- investments in illiquid corporate securities;

- lease values;

- natural resource asset values;

- related-party loans;

- patents, trademarks, and the like;

- goodwill (it is really "good?")

Price to Book, Book to Market

Book value (total assets minus total liabilities minus intangible assets) is the metric most often cited as whether an equity transaction is priced fairly or not relative to others. The price-to-book ratio (PB) is the company's book value per share.

Book-to-market is a standard inverse proxy for a firm's growth opportunities. IPOs seeking to raise capital in difficult markets at a higher book-to-market value than recognized peers should justify the valuation or demonstrate why another method is a better basis for comparison.

The inverse of book-to-market (market-to-book) is more important for assessing information than for assessing risk or returns.[20] Analysts state that the market-to-book ratio is the most important of the factors in assessing misvaluation, as they believe firms with high market-to-book ratios have lower future returns. Such firms are overpriced relative to their peers. This is because a high market-to-book ratio signals higher, rather than lower, risk.

Some researchers argue that the market-to-book ratio is a proxy for the financial distress risk not captured by beta. Market-to-book and size may affect expected returns, because they serve as a proxy for higher-order factors that result from a more dynamic equilibrium.[21] Therefore, because of risk, investors should expect low market-to-book firms (and small firms) to generate higher returns than high market-to-book (and large size) firms.

Some analysts prefer Tobin's Q to market-to-book.[22] Tobin's Q postulates that the equilibrium market value of an asset set composing a firm is equal to the replacement value of its assets. A 'Q value' of 1.0 is interpreted to mean that the market value of a firm is equal to the replacement cost of its tangible assets, and nothing more.

Non-Financial Valuation Inputs

Some believe the importance of financial information (e.g., earnings, cash flows, and book values) in determining equity values has decreased steadily over the past two decades.[23] The decreasing relevance of financial information has motivated a stream of research that indicates the increasing importance of non-financial information in determining equity valuations.[24]

For good reason, brand strength is one such non-financial metric that is often cited in the S-1 as an important competitive strength. Brands increase the perceived value of similar products and influence choice. Perhaps the most powerful and recognized intangible asset of any company, the IPO marketing campaign must exploit ways for investors to experience the brand for themselves. Since the vast majority of new listings are not household names, retail investors will have an easier time understanding the value of LinkedIn than Bucyrus or Orbcomm, even though they are all leaders in their respective industries.

To establish and gain acceptance of a 'brand leadership multiple,' marketers must achieve immediate brand impact. Demonstrate to investors why the brand creates value. A Roadshow featuring an unfamiliar brand affords the opportunity to imprint and shape a valuable long-term impression.[25]

Cyclical Considerations

Every industry has cyclical characteristics as measured by the return of assets, expansion of margins and opportunities for growth. A company in the bottom of a cycle usually generates historically low revenues or is only able to sell assets at or below book value. Those in the high point of the cycle can attract buyers that will pay a premium for their assets, because they are able to generate revenue or returns above what was previously possible.

In a 1990 survey, 75% of investors surveyed said they did *not* perform any kind of fundamental analysis to derive a valuation. The survey concluded that the key to maximizing the offer price is getting investors to truthfully reveal their private value to the underwriters.[26]

Accruals

The amount of liabilities and non cash-based assets that accrue over time on a balance sheet is an important metric. One study showed that firms with extensive discretionary accounting accruals perform poorly in the aftermarket.[27] Discretionary accruals are negatively associated with future cash flows only when the impact of a more independent audit committee is taken into account. The number of independent members on the audit committee has been shown to correlate negatively with discretionary accruals.[28]

Discretionary accruals used to meet earnings forecasts are more valued by investors, suggesting they are not able to see through accruals management to meet voluntary earnings forecasts. Larger audit committees are generally viewed as less effective. Discretionary accruals are positively associated with future cash flows, with a more independent audit committee improving the quality of the signal. Some research suggests that there is information in operating accruals that makes earnings more highly correlated than cash flow with contemporaneous stock returns.[29]

Current period accruals are more or less determined in a systematic manner by its current performance (delta sales), the level of its property, plant and equipment, lagged cash flow from operations and whether it reports net income or a loss. Change in sales is a proxy for firm performance. The other factors are non-discretionary. Apparently the predictive value of discretionary accruals does not differ between forecasting and non- forecasting firms.

Accounting Methodology

There is evidence that investors make some adjustments for accounting methods when evaluating reported earnings. For example, for apparently equal risk firms, price/earnings ratios are on average higher for firms that use accelerated depreciation than those that use straight-line depreciation. The difference in price/earnings ratios essentially disappears when researchers notionally restate earnings to match the methods.[30] The market values R&D

expenditures as generating an asset even though they are reported as an expense.[31]

Risk-Related Variables

Variables often interpreted as risk factors are book/market, firm size, market dividend yield, the term premium, and the default premium. Analysts believe that beta and size are more important for assessing risk than for assessing returns. Senior analysts indicate a strong belief that the firm with the higher beta will also have a higher stock return. As predicted by the CAPM, high values of beta lead investors to expect higher returns, apparently because they reflect higher risk, not because they believe high beta indicates underpricing. A classic result in asset pricing theory is that risk premium to any asset can be expressed as the product of the asset's beta with respect to any risky market volatility (MV) portfolio and the risk premium of the MV portfolio.[32]

Chapter Twenty

Post-IPO

Once the Roadshow ends, a new era of communications and marketing arrives. Like clockwork -- quarter after quarter, year after year -- a relatively inexperienced firm is expected to skillfully communicate with investors.

Now that the firm has achieved its goal of achieving public ownership, its shares trade among thousands of others. Attracting new investors that were aroused by media reports about the IPO is a liquidity opportunity. To thrive, the firm must maintain a high profile because any investor can sell (or buy) the stock with the click of a mouse.

Lead underwriters typically attempt to prop up the prices of weak offerings until about a month after the company starts trading and then the support stops.[1] Investors may see this as an opportunity to short the stock as the price has been artificially supported.

The initial shareholder base is fragile. Management's first few moves following an IPO often dictate the short-term fate of the stock. Investors that passed on the IPO might become buyers if the stock performs as they expected. Still others may sell if media coverage wanes because management has failed to create interest.

High trading volumes will attract professional traders looking to capitalize on familiar patterns they see with new stocks. Low volumes prevent traders from making an exit because demand from buyers does not exist at all price levels (or "depths").

Announcing Guidance

With the quiet period finally over, the firm is free to say anything it wants at any time. But what exactly will the firm say to investors and when? What style and tone will emerge from its initial series of press releases? Will it opt for a defensive approach or be more aggressive? Will it announce something unexpected or update investors on a recent development related to a growth initiative? Will it announce its intention to issue guidance or simply provide the date and time of its first earnings call with investors? Will results be released before its peers or will the firm wait until others have reported?

Over what period will the firm issue guidance? For the full year, updated every quarter? Or quarterly? Will it confirm or update guidance prior to reporting results? What metrics will it provide guidance for?

How soon after the quiet period will the firm announce details relating to its first conference call with investors? Will it issue a press release after the markets close and host a call at the same time or will it delay the call so that analysts have time to digest the results? For many teams, preparations for the next quarter begin the day after the current quarterly call ends.

These questions are best answered during the Roadshow, well before the firm is forced to make a decision.

The Opening Trade

During the first day of IPO trading, various institutions will begin trading at different times of the day. This "staged" trading allows traders to hold off on entering trades until more information is available about the day's trading levels, allowing some to be better positioned to profit from those that have no information, such as those that entered trades before the market open. See Chapter 18 for Jim Cramer's personal account of his own IPO's first day of trading.

Once a stock officially starts trading, a firm can and should release "regularly released factual business information and forward-looking information about its business". The firm should not comment on the outcome of its IPO or discuss anything that might differ materially from what was communicated during the IPO.2

Every new public company has a duty to report quarterly financial results soon after it lists. A myriad of logistics and decisions related to press releases, conference calls scripts, Q&A, and its own website are necessary elements that require a week or more to complete.

Securing a conference call provider and website manager ahead of time eliminates two tedious tasks. Drafting scripts and planning the announcement dates and call times ahead of time will drastically reduce the pressure experienced by new managers.

After going public, it is critical that firms establish and build liquidity quickly. A month-long post-IPO public relations and media campaign supported through a program of news releases is a common planning approach but may prove more difficult to execute as the firm may feel as if it is completely out of newsworthy material. Nevertheless, management must ensure interest in the newly-listed stock remains high. The company's earnings guidance, earnings results, and "lock-up" period provide at least three mandatory opportunities for newly-listed companies to exploit.

The Share Listing Announcement

The very first press release issued immediately after the SEC declares the firm's registration effective is the "IPO Prices" announcement. Because quiet period regulations are still likely to be in place during the announcement, the firm's first official release is often issued by the lead investment bank on behalf of the issuer. The announcement details the number of shares sold and at what price, and may include other supplementary data such as the total gross proceeds raised, market capitalization, use of proceeds, number of shares outstanding, banking participants, and information related to strategic partners that purchased shares in the IPO. Certain disclaimers must also exist. Journalists may include other information about the offering or the company.

The example below is from E2Open, an IPO that priced on July 26, 2012, two weeks after announcing its terms:

E2open Announces Pricing of Initial Public Offering

Shares to Trade on NASDAQ under Ticker Symbol "EOPN"

FOSTER CITY, Calif. (BUSINESS WIRE) - E2open, Inc., a leading provider of strategic, cloud-based solutions for collaborative execution across global trading networks, today announced the pricing of its initial public offering of 4,687,500 shares of its common stock, including 3,750,000 shares from the company and 937,500 shares from the selling stockholders, at a price to the public of $15 per share. The shares are expected to begin trading on the NASDAQ Global Market on July 26, 2012, under the symbol "EOPN." In *addition, certain selling stockholders have granted the underwriters a 30 day option to purchase up to 703,125 additional shares of common stock.*

BofA Merrill Lynch is acting as sole bookrunning manager for the offering and William Blair & Company, L.L.C., Pacific Crest Securities, Canaccord Genuity Inc. and Needham & Company, LLC are acting as co-managers for the offering. A registration statement relating to these securities has been filed with, and declared effective by, the Securities and Exchange Commission. This press release shall not constitute an offer to sell or the solicitation of an offer to buy, nor shall there be any sale of these securities in any state or jurisdiction in which such offer, solicitation or sale would be unlawful prior to registration or qualification under the securities laws of any such state or jurisdiction.

The offering will be made only by means of a prospectus. Copies of the prospectus related to the offering may be obtained, when available, from BofA Merrill Lynch, 222 Broadway, 7th Floor, New York, NY 10038, Attn: Prospectus Department or by emailing dg.prospectus_requests@baml.com.

The Earnings Announcement

Absent any new material information that requires to be released after the company's shares are listed (securities laws stipulate material changes be disclosed within 24 hours), all newly public firms must contend with a press release announcing the date and time of their first earnings call.

The degree to which gray hairs start sprouting on the heads of senior management depends on the expectations that were set with investors during the Roadshow.

Those who gave themselves ample wiggle room to accommodate for unforeseen changes in demand shifts (or any number of other factors contributing to missed forecasts) have justified their bonus. Other firms find themselves crossing the finish line wishing they had run a little slower.

Announcing that the firm will miss forecasts or fail to meet expectations on the first conference call should not happen. But it does. For this reason it is critical to think about guidance while the Roadshow presentation is being authored so that a conservative posture can be legitimately established, which then ripples naturally through the Roadshow meetings and into the first month or two until it comes time to announce actual results.

Q1: First Quarter

Firms that are set to report Q1 numbers will be expected to issue guidance, but are in an optimal position because the prior quarter's results are known and have been recently subsumed by investors. In short, investors will be interested to understand the percentage growth rates for the metrics covered under guidance relative to the firm's previously reported annual numbers. These firms can take advantage of stepping up guidance as the year progresses. By using ultra-conservative annual guidance before the actual Q1 earnings are reported, the firm can then provide an improved outlook around future reporting periods.

Regardless of what quarter is being reported, all firms may elect to give guidance -- quarterly, annually or bi-annually -- and to re-affirm or adjust guidance as the earning period nears.

Firms may also want to build in, if possible, news that can be announced around the IPO lockup expiration date (usually 180 days). This is when all the outstanding shares are released for trading. Insiders and selling shareholders are prevented from selling within the first 180 days, on average. Lockup lengths that are shorter than the median (the length and amount is specified in the prospectus) have been shown to have a much higher likelihood of conducting a subsequent equity offering (31% vs. 18%).[3]

Q2/Q3

Firms set to report Q2 or Q3 numbers have a relatively easier task with guidance because of the higher level of visibility into the numbers; they are not required to look as far ahead as those reporting full year Q4 financials.

Firms reporting Q2 and Q3 performance tend to announce full year guidance ahead of the conference call after the details of the call time and date have been announced. This provides the maximum number of new events: announcement of the earnings date and call-in details; the announcement that guidance is forthcoming at a date not too far in the future; the guidance release and reminder of the upcoming conference call; and finally the earnings release followed by the call itself discussing the results which features senior management from the Roadshow discussing the actual results.

Q4

Whether or not guidance is issued separately or not at all depends on what fiscal quarter the firm will be reporting on its inaugural conference call with investors.

Firms reporting Q4 results are stating annual results as well as those for the fourth quarter, relative to the comparable period of the prior year. Q4 firms generally elect to issue guidance for the next full year as the final item on the conference call agenda. But, as a newly reporting issuer, some firms prefer to delay guidance and instead schedule it for a future date. The decision to delay guidance is most often based on the actual performance and subsequent reaction by the investment community. If Q4 outperformed expectations, the guidance release becomes another event that helps accelerate the stock's momentum as it sets the expectation that more good news is likely to come, compelling shareholders to increase holdings.

On the other hand, those that fail to meet expectations during Q4 may choose to delay next year's guidance with the goal of minimizing the impact of bad news. The company that misses its numbers on its first call will likely see a substantial outflow of investors and an immediate erosion of credibility, so waiting to announce guidance may make sense if timed to coincide with other good news.

Analyst Coverage

Research shows that switching analyst coverage from prestigious underwriters improves liquidity. The switched-from IPO lead underwriter provided a mere 1.27 research reports in the six months prior to the seasoned equity offering (SEO), compared to 3.11 reports available for non-switching firms. Following the SEO, the new SEO lead underwriter provided an average of 5.00 research reports for the firms that switched, a number insignificantly different from the 4.62 reports provided for the non-switching firms by their lead underwriter. Still, firms are more likely to switch when research coverage is minimal or untimely.[4]

The research department is responsibie for publishing 'coverage' or information about a firm on a regular basis (usually quarterly) once it is publicly traded. Research analysts have ongoing contact after the investment bankers disappear. The world has access to the financial models and published forecasts of certain analysts.

By law, research analysts are required to act independently of the bank that employs them. The regulation strictly requires that investment banking and research be separate and that information between these two groups not be shared.

Analysts provide a crucial source for independent opinion and analysis. The financial models and assumptions they publish may result in recommendations that can be vitally influential or perhaps disastrous. For this reason it is extremely important that you meet or exceed the expectations of the core group of analysts that follow your stock from the firm's first quarter reporting as a new public company.

Even though firms may initially have only one or two analysts, more may initiate coverage if the firm demonstrates an ability to attract retail interest, achieve financial objectives, and manage expectations better than established peers.

The Consensus Number

The universe of analysts -- whether they are known or unknown to the firm and whether they are friendly or not -- derive data points and form opinions related to key metrics. The average (and weighted average) of these opinions will yield one number for each guidance metric. This number is known as the consensus number.

Websites such as *trefis.com* publish a wealth of freely available information on consensus numbers and highlight the companies that fail to live up to expectations.

You will quickly learn that your stock price thrives or dies by how well you perform against the consensus number, even if the data used to calculate it is, in your mind, inaccurately derived. Therefore, you must work to set expectations with the analyst community to ensure they fully understand your own expectations relating to financial and operating performance, so that their views are in-line with your own. You should start managing expectations with the analyst community while you are preparing your IPO so that there is some sort of a relationship in place in case the firm needs a friend at some point down the road. Most companies, if not all, need a sympathetic ear of a key analyst at one time or another.

Pre-Announcing Bad News

Bad news happens all the time. What action will the firm take if it becomes apparent that it will be unable to meet its stated forecasts? Or if a key customer or opportunity is lost unexpectedly, resulting in negative implications for future results? When it inevitably does happen, know that analysts believe that management's communications have greater integrity, is more competent, and causes less of a surprise when 100% of the total news is included in the preannouncement.[5]

Firms have "levers" at their disposal that can be used to adjust financial results in an entirely appropriate and legally acceptable manner. It is wise to identify what those levers are and what impact they have on certain results. Some will influence net income, others revenue or operating cash flow. The classification of certain expenses and investments are popular levers, as are the arbitrary value of mark-to-market assets. When times are good, some managers quietly decrease the value of impaired assets so that they can increase them later. Adjusting marketing expenses are another way to adjust earnings.

There is also the widely used "one time charge" or "adjusted EBITDA/EPS" to finesse square results into an all-important round hole. This will fool some of the people some of the time, but don't make a habit of it. Investors will see it for what it (often) truly is and begin to liquidate their positions. Read Jeff Matthews' excellent blog for his take on firms -- like Target Corporation -- who fiddle around with adjusted EPS and other non-GAAP treatments.[6]

Investor Day

After the IPO, a solid and proven method of attracting and retaining interest in a new equity security is to schedule an annual Investor Day. This important event is most effective if regular contact is maintained with investors who were on the Roadshow schedule. The lead banks may also be able to contribute investor lists for further outreach. The key is to stay on the radar of investors in the months and weeks leading up to the event and then to email and phone them to confirm attendance. Creating an investor event registration website is a helpful approach. By maximizing the time spent with accounts during the Roadshow, this task is much less daunting -- and expensive -- when fresh capital and interest in the security becomes a necessity.

Chapter Twenty-One

Summary

Very little information exists on how a new equity issue -- or IPO (initial public offering) -- is sold to investors. This is perplexing considering that last year 864 deals closed globally, raising $163 billion in capital. Much of the academic research fixates on a subject known as "underpricing", a reference to the widely-held belief that many IPOs are sold to investors at a price below what the new shares are really worth. In an underpricing scenario, as soon as the stock starts to trade, instant profits are created.

But price alone does not determine whether investors decide to buy stock in a newly-formed company. If only things were that simple.

In reality, the price of an IPO often changes while it is being marketed to investors. Changes in perceived demand dramatically influence the amount of capital that is ultimately raised. Good securities marketing practices strive to create positive changes in demand; changes that may translate into many millions of extra dollars. Well-timed, cleverly marketed "new equity issues" fetch prices that would have been impossible the previous year.

The process of preparing a successful Roadshow is largely secretive. Too often, management teams realize what they are up against only after they have announced their intent to go public. By then, most "pre-marketing" opportunities are lost. Strict laws prohibit investor-oriented communication once the initial registration statement has been filed with stock market regulators (SEC). Similarly, methods available to prepare management may only become a priority once the IPO presentation is nearly complete which is too late to administer the level of comprehensive coaching required by must-do deals. Preparation makes a big difference in a commoditized environment like the capital markets.

When the market is receptive to IPOs, do you know what experienced investment bankers will do to ensure a high-profile transaction is launched successfully? The answer: anything. As long as it is legal.

An oversimplified formula captures the essence of 'anything legal':

Well Prepared Executives + Decent Story + Media Coverage = Enduring Demand.

Every company that seeks a new listing by raising equity capital through an initial public offering must do a Roadshow -- there is no way around it. This affords investors the opportunity to compare apples to oranges, because companies of all sizes in all industries adhere to the same formulaic structure when presenting their stories. Although the issuer may believe its main objective is to raise as much capital as possible, some realize after it is too late that the *real* fundamental objective is to establish a strong base of shareholders while attracting new long-term shareholders.

Executives involved with an IPO need to think about liquidity before the Roadshow, because the first six months after a stock starts to trade is likely to be difficult. The Roadshow is simply a preview of the demands of life as a public company; managers must use the time leading up to the Roadshow to reduce the range of aggravating factors waiting to surface once the stock begins to trade.

Just ask Facebook. After the firm went public, shares of the massively hyped social media giant stayed submerged for five *quarters* until it finally clawed its way back up to the IPO price of $38. Was that a rough fifteen months for the world's largest social media stock? Of course it was.

Once Facebook shares finally represented a profitable trade, some insiders took the opportunity to cash in. COO Sheryl Sandberg sold enough shares to net $91 million.[1] It is not surprising that many other investors also took profits. One study determined that institutions sell 70.2% of their allocations within the first year.[2] If a new stock fails to meet expectations early, there is a risk that a destructive vacuum will be created through the high volume of fleeing investors.

After a firm completes an IPO, management quickly realizes that the expectations of investors must be managed to protect the credibility of the firm and the value of its shares. But successfully charting a course through the depths of the capital markets requires experience gained from hands-on practice. Mistakes that could have been prevented are often made, altering the course of the firm.

The IPO marketing period provides an appropriate opportunity for a management team to start acting like the public company they will soon be, before the realization sets in that they *are* a public company. There is no rewind button. Executives pursuing an IPO must use the limited time they have to prepare thoroughly for the Roadshow and beyond.

The introduction of the 2011 US JOBS Act ("Jumpstart Our Business

Startups") created a new category of equity issuer, the Emerging Growth Company (EGC). This legislation re-defined the rules of how communications around an offering can take place, with the most notable change being the ability to pre-market an offer and engage investors prior to filing an S-1 with the SEC. But regardless of the firm's still-private company status, investors expect the information to be consistent with other publicly-traded firms in the peer group. In what some have called an unintended consequence, firms that pre-market their IPOs under the JOBS Act must satisfy a significant communications benchmark compared to the period before the legislation was introduced.[3]

Firms that consciously attempt to establish recognizable signals also try to convey aspects of their value and quality. This process occurs throughout the Roadshow and its marketing campaign. Time will soon tell if there are enough valid signals that investors deem authentic and acceptable. As the chapters in this book show, there is enormous emphasis on face-to-face communication and sophisticated disclosure. In an asymmetrical information-rich environment that defines the Roadshow marketing period, investors are presented with ample evidence to determine what management teams are likely to thrive in the combative arena of the capital markets.

To be sure, most transactions are green lit but only a select few are deemed truly ready for the massive popularity stock stardom brings. If your firm is destined for greatness, get your communications team ready. You will need them.

Many new companies underestimate the importance of meeting expectations and pay a steep price for over-optimism. Both overconfidence and a lack of confidence can lead to temptations that are hard to resist (e.g. aggressive forecasts, lengthy presentations). But influential investors have a good idea about what management's real degree of confidence is.

This is because investors count on an ability to interpret answers to any question they want to ask during a Roadshow meeting.

Selling an equity story requires that every pertinent aspect of a firm's strategy, advantages, differentiation and valuation are conveyed through a PowerPoint presentation. Management then delivers this "IPO story" to investors across the country or around the world. A Roadshow can resemble an epic undertaking or impressive mission, but it is a task that is critical to get right. There are no second chances.

In the world of IPOs where companies like Twitter and Facebook raise unprecedented sums, psychology plays a huge role in the marketing of the underlying transaction. If marketers seek to maximize the success of a given transaction, they must be aware of the many opportunities that define the process of planning and executing the Roadshow.

Every IPO consists of new information delivered by a team of managers who are probably not familiar to investors or, more importantly, familiar *with* investors. Confidence is an important factor in determining how enthusiastically any Roadshow is received. But it is not just confidence in the CEO or the company's balance sheet, but also the *perception* of confidence that investors have of *other* investors' confidence, not only in the transaction itself, but also in the management team and overall market.

So the decision to buy, pass or wait on an IPO is largely based on the fickle concept of confidence. Not only does marketing shape confidence, but it manufactures it. It is especially important during periods of stock market turbulence when the threat of losses or declines force investors to focus on limiting downside risk. But, even in solid markets it is impossible to know how a new stock will perform once it starts to trade, so it is imperative that managers convince investors of their conviction.

Fortunately, the Roadshow provides a perfect arena to do just that. It also serves as a proven testing ground that investors use to divine future fortunes. The number of IPOs that have successfully priced or are "in the pipeline" preparing for a Roadshow is an accurate barometer of stock market health and investor sentiment: if relatively large numbers of IPOs are pricing, the market is in good shape. Since 2000, an average of 102 initial public offerings gained a new listing each year. This includes the busiest period of the last decade (2004-2007) when no fewer than 160 IPOs priced. But this is still a far cry from 1996 when 676 companies went public in a single year.[4] Now, far fewer companies raise more money.

During periods when IPOs are being routinely canceled or postponed, investor sentiment is poor. What has become apparent over the last few years is that the wild variability in stock price changes can often make it difficult to find a two week period when conditions are stable enough to conduct a Roadshow; it is only recently that conditions have improved materially.[5]

It is an awfully discouraging experience to start marketing only to be blindsided by an external event that turns investors off all IPOs. Marketers must prepare for this challenge by using a combination of media relations (PR) and specialized coaching techniques to ensure the Roadshow team is adequately prepared. Well-timed media executions saved the Tesla Motors IPO while other transactions also in the market-- some not adequately prepared -- were killed off.[6]

An obviously high quality management team running a transparent, solid and growing business is enough to pique the interest of many investors. But it is the unequivocal communication of future financial performance that every effective IPO marketing campaign must deliver. By highlighting the firm's most attractive qualities and depicting how each generates growth, marketers compel investors to subscribe to the transaction at the IPO price rather than after some future benchmark has been achieved.

The IPO firm that differentiates itself from peers usually combines two or three qualities in a story that provides legitimate comparisons to other through contrast and similarity to others. Constructing a believable narrative is a process that involves more science than art, but the art comes into play when management demonstrates its ability to move investors off the fence by convincing them to subscribe to the offering.

Groupon's high-profile IPO was almost canceled after the CEO sent a confidential memo that was quickly leaked to the media. This infraction prompted the SEC (the regulator of the stock market) to remind the internet firm to abide by "quiet period" rules. Groupon then decided to cancel its IPO but then reconsidered. The internet coupon marketer ended up slashing its deal size by 60% shortly before the Roadshow.

Even Facebook had troubles with the SEC that remained a secret until several quarters after the IPO was completed. Documents released by the SEC showed that it had troubling concerns about how Facebook characterized growth in its mobile advertising segment. Some investors were outraged after the comments were made public, saying such disclosure should have delayed the offering.

The financial crisis of 2008 has had lasting effects. This means that IPOs can no longer score simply by shooting through the goalposts of growth and upside. New equity issuers must also make investors feel comfortable that considerable risks and uncertainties are worth it in stock markets where anything can happen.[7] The infamous and still unexplained "Flash Crash" of 2009 is but one bizarre example.

Investor Behavior

An amazing fact is that *half of the returns in the stock market over the last fifty years have occurred over just ten days*. This is true. The flip side is that in the last 49.9 years every day has had weak or negative returns.[8] This important data point highlights the importance difference between retail (amateur) and institutional (professional) investors. Are institutional investors are well aware of this startling fact? Many, yes. Retail investors? No. Institutional investors are comfortable grinding out single digit gains, as long as they are gains. Retail investors shoot for the stars, looking for home runs and double digit returns that rarely emerge. Institutional investors rely on this tropism; the behavioral tendency of people to take a $10 winning lottery ticket and purchase another with the proceeds. The IPO market offers all investors with some of the best odds in the capital markets of earning an out-sized, get rich quick return. The house always wins and the issuers that make a determined effort to rise to the occasion can also be big winners.

New research implies that human behavior affects trading activity more than previously thought. Even the trading symbol of an IPO has been shown to have an effect on how the stock performs. One study determined that of the 665 IPOs listed between 1990 and 2004, those with pronounceable stock symbols (e.g. KAR) gained 11% more in the first day of trading than their less-pronounceable counterparts (e.g. RDO).[9] This finding implies that simple, cognitive approaches to modeling human behavior are behind choices not available through traditional or more complex alternatives.[10] Of course, a marketer must be familiar with the psychology to benefit from the techniques, as even the simple choice of selecting a trading symbol has long-term implications.

This concept extends across the IPO marketing cycle. "Framing" or "priming" are very useful tools that reliably achieve desirable results across the range of marketing activities. During a busy period, investors may meet face-to-face with ten different IPO teams in a week, so it is evident quickly what team is prepared and what team is not; what team is the best prepared and what team is the worst. Based on this simple judgment, transactions price and trade accordingly.

Preparing for the Ritual

The Roadshow represents the sum total of the planning, preparation and marketing behind an Initial Public Offering. Every meeting in the schedule should get off to a good start and finish equally well. Even in rare circumstances where the order book maxes out on the first day, the IPO team must press on, ignoring the insurance that assured success brings. All meetings with all investors must be executed as if the firm truly needs (and wants) them as shareholders.

Inevitably, all public companies reach a day when new capital from new investors is required to keep the stock price buoyant. Investors that did not subscribe to the IPO but were impressed by management are a reliable source of future liquidity.

Executives must take the task of Roadshow preparation seriously. Other IPO hopefuls, equally determined, are likely to be marketing at the same time, competing for the same capital. Investors can easily compare one Roadshow to another -- all it requires is a few clicks -- but it is the teams who are perceived as being better prepared that are also perceived as less risky. This is a key feature when selecting between various choices.

A great act is tough to follow (unless you surely have a better act), so managers must aggressively attempt to set the highest bar possible from the outset.

In choppy markets, the launch date of an IPO may move several times -- in either direction. It is common for deals to launch ahead of the planned date, at short notice. This occurs when negative sentiment suddenly turns positive, stimulating a desire for investors to take advantage of the environment and engage seemingly assured gains. Recent positive performance of the broader stock market eliminates the most serious external threat posed by the equity capital markets, and one that is impossible to control. Certain conditions will compel underwriters to decide to start marketing as soon as possible (tomorrow) on the evening just before the proposed start date.

This is why IPO teams must be fully prepared several days or even a week in advance of the anticipated launch date. It is very unpleasant to disappoint investors who expect to be fully engaged but are not.

The Privilege of Information Asymmetry

A unique aspect of every IPO is something known as "information asymmetry". Asymmetry exists because investors view the IPO firm as a new company while the CEO regards it as a long-standing operation. The CEO has deep knowledge about the firm: its history, operations, inner workings, risks and expected performance. The investor has no such knowledge. It is this imbalance of information that creates the asymmetry between investors and management.

To gain a trading advantage, the institutional investor introduced to the company for the first time will try to exploit any information advantage. There are less information privileged IPO investors. Period. The concept of profiting from an information advantage is nothing new; in the era of Thomas Edison traders of gold and oil stocks relied on faster telegram technology to deliver profits.[11] More recently, the postponed March 2014 IPO of Virtu showed in its S-1 filing that over thousands of trading days, the firm lost money on only one day; a truly remarkable advantage gained through information disclosure infrastructure.

This imbalance creates a self-reinforcing "reflexive" system that inherently reduces information asymmetry and allows some investors to gain an essential advantage by reducing *ex ante* uncertainty through the establishment of a *prima facie* acceptable range of *ex-post* valuation accuracy. Say what?

In other words, during a Roadshow, investors are triggered by specific signals that reveal insights about the IPO's future performance. The investor that actively seeks evidence of signals and knows how to interpret them will use them as a profitable and reliable proxy for a firm's future performance. The investor that does not or cannot incorporate the information encoded in well-known, legitimate signals is at a disadvantage. The advantage one investor has over another translates to a significant trading opportunity. It is the marketer's responsibility to know what signals exist, and how to create and disperse them.

The Power of Signals

The online retailer *Amazon.com* developed a media strategy designed to emit strategic signals by continuously releasing information about a variety of actions, rather than pursuing "big bang" announcements.[12] Research suggests this approach recognizes the positive correlation between continuous information disclosure and media attention.[13] This makes sense: the more often a firm releases information, the more likely it is to attract coverage. Successful IPOs use the media to their advantage to gain exposure and establish credibility and reduce uncertainty.

Investors that meet one-on-one with management early in the Roadshow also gain a valuable advantage relative to other investors that are relegated to hearing the story later in the schedule or in a less intimate setting -- such as at a large group meeting. The most disadvantaged are those that read about the transaction in the newspaper at some future point in time. They are often the same ones that buy shares from other investors that managed to make a clean and profitable exit.

Investors will attempt to maximize the advantage afforded by face-to-face meetings. For example, some will try to extract as much information as possible regarding topics that are not exhaustively discussed in management's PowerPoint presentation or the prospectus (S-1).

For this reason, the transactions of highly credible and prepared executives result in stronger public companies than those who are not, balance sheets being equal. Newly-minted companies require experienced leadership and knowledge to overcome the considerable challenges inherent to creating shareholder value, and the Roadshow is a convenient preview of what's to come.

If the goal of every CEO is to achieve ever-higher levels of operating performance and reward investors with increases in share price gains, it may be surprising to learn that the relationship between first day and three-year returns is not correlated.

The best marketed IPOs create anticipation among prospective investors. Anticipation arouses interest in the transaction and sways the decision to own newly issued shares. Should a Roadshow succeed in stirring excitement, the perceived demand for the new listing is broadcast to the financial community, creating "information cascades". These cascades increase the likelihood of attracting more attention. The ability to create a palpable sense of anticipation is a proven method for increasing demand for the transaction because investor confidence increases due to the belief that *other* investors will want to own the stock at future price levels above the IPO price. Many less informed investors predictably follow the crowd, imitating the recent actions of those presumed to be better informed.[14]

Table 9: IPO Returns by Year and Holding Period [15]

Average Returns for IPOs between 1999-2011

First Day Closing Price vs. Three Year Closing Price

(The larger the negative delta, the steeper the 3 year decline)

Year	1st Day Return (%)	3 year Return (%)	3 year change (%)
2011	13.3	-11.1	-24.4
2010	9.2	3.1	-6.1
2009	9.8	37.0	27.2
2008	6.4	11.4	5.0
2007	13.9	-16.3	-30.2
2006	12.1	-28.8	-40.9
2005	10.2	14.2	4.0
2004	12.3	51.2	38.9
2003	12.1	36.1	24.0
2002	9.2	68.6	59.4
2001	14.2	17.8	3.6
2000	56.3	-60.2	-116.5
1999	70.9	-47.8	-118.7

The experience required to stir up anticipation in a new equity offering is predicated on the ability to craft a succinct story derived from material facts. This is the role of the investment bank and communications team. Once the Roadshow begins, it is left to the Roadshow traveling team to convey the story through a ritualistic performance that is judged by influential participants in the equity capital markets over two weeks of investor meetings and events.

The thing is, many forget that after the IPO prices and the stock starts to trade that the firm is now established with a base of shareholders who are most likely looking to exit. Who will replace them?

This is why the firm that sets out to make the transition from private to public ownership must ask itself: how can we best prepare? And then it must get to it.

Index

Important Definitions

Buy-Side: Investors that evaluate and purchase IPO stocks for their own portfolios. The buy-side is much more skeptical about the future prospects of a given IPO than the dealer who is earning a fee from selling the stock (see "sell-side"). Usage: *We have some really important meetings with the buy-side today so watch out for that question on the retirement rates of underperforming run-off assets in that European mortgage portfolio.*

Common Shares: a class of equity security that is most commonly sold to investors. Also known as "A" shares. Other types of equities may also be offered as part of an IPO or equity transaction, such as convertibles or "series B" preferred shares.

Comp Table: a grid that compares various metrics of the IPO firm to selected peers using valuation and financial performance data.

Green Sheet: (Canadian). A four to eight page summary of the prospectus. It includes a complete description of the investment highlights, risk factors, management biographies and summary financials.

Guidance: The firm or management's official forecast or formal estimate or expectation of some aspect related to future financial performance, such as earnings or revenue growth.

Institutional Investor: institution, the buy-side, professional investor, pro investor, hedge fund, money manager, fund manager, portfolio manager, asset manager, wealth manager, value investor, growth investor, endowment fund, sovereign wealth fund, life insurance company.

IPO: Initial Public Offering. Also known as the deal, transaction, IPO, new issue, new equity issue, or new offering of common shares. Requires the IPO applicant to perform a rigorous rite of passage ceremony known as the IPO Roadshow.

IPO Presentation: a sixty minute meeting that involves one or more managers at the IPO firm speaking to a carefully prepared set of slides and then answering questions. Also known as the investor presentation, the slides, the PowerPoint presentation, the flip book, the color book, the deck.

Issuer: The firm or company responsible for issuing the equity securities. Also known as the firm going public, the IPO firm, the IPO company, the corporate issuer, the firm, the new company, newco, pubco, unseasoned issuer.

JOBS Act: Acronym for Jumpstart Our Business Startups. Introduced in 2011, this securities legislation allows companies with revenues under $1 billion to file confidentially with the SEC. The laws relax many restrictions related to marketing and disclosure that are traditionally required when a firm announces its intention to go public.

Liquidity: trading volume, number of shares traded, depth level, net buyers or sellers of stock, demand.

Listing Day: The date on which a stock starts trading for the first time on a stock exchange or bourse such as The New York Stock Exchange, NASDAQ, Toronto Stock Exchange, London, Hang Seng or any number of the 20 or so major exchanges around the world.

Offering: Also known as share offering, equity offering, IPO, Initial Public Offering, securities offering, the deal, the transaction, offering of common shares, offering of "A" shares, pubic offering of common equity.

Pricing: the final conference call that concludes The Roadshow during which the final price of the IPO and number of shares issued (sold) is determined.

The Range: the highest and lowest price the underwriters are expecting to sell the IPO on a per share basis (also known as the indicative range). Usage: *the indicative range for the offering was $16-$20 per share; investors must have loved that IPO because it priced above the range at $22.* 'Below the range' or 'within the range' are other variations.

Retail Investor: An average or "household" investor. Also known as a broker, brokerage house, non-professional or small investor. Retail investors include private wealth managers and private equity funds.

Roadshow: A schedule of back-to-back meetings with investors that often takes place in dozens of cities across a broad geography that may include two or more continents. The Roadshow schedule spans approximately two weeks, followed immediately by the official listing on a stock exchange. This may or may not include the ringing of a ceremonial bell to open or close the market. A well-received IPO -- one that investors expect will be attractively under-priced in decent markets -- will almost always open with the expectation of seeing some astronomical gain within the first few hours of trading. The Roadshow can be a very difficult fortnight because of the hardcore travel involved. Even the most seasoned executive will exhibit distinct signs of withering after a full week on the road. Fatigue and stress arise from the combination of delivering the same pitch six times a day across two or more cities in the same period.

Roadshow Team: The people who travel with the Roadshow. Also called management, company executives, speaker team, top management team (TMT), senior executives, or managers.

S-1: The prospectus, the initial registration statement, the filing, the SEC filing, the preliminary prospectus, red herring, the reds, the F-1 (for non-US companies).

Secondary: also known as a secondary offering, this refers to an equity transaction that follows an initial public offering, usually at least a year after. Usage: *There's not much appetite for a secondary at this point because the IPO didn't go over so well.*

Secondary Market: Where the stock gets traded after the investment dealers (a.k.a. investment banks) sell the primary shares offered as part of the Initial Public Offering. Also known as the stock market, the market, post-IPO trading, trading, aftermarket, NYSE, Nasdaq, TSX.

Sell-Side: Investment banks and other dealers that earn fees from recommending or effecting a transaction in a certain security they are affiliated with. Usage: *I wouldn't put much credence in that sell-side analyst report.*

Speaker Team: The two or three executives that present to investors over the duration of the Roadshow schedule. Also called the Roadshow team. This core team is responsible for the success or failure of the transaction, as they are entirely responsible for communicating the corporate story and engaging with investors during the Roadshow.

Ticker: The trading symbol or trading designation. Usually a three or four letter designation associated with the equity security listed on a stock exchange. (NYSE allows up to 3 letters; Nasdaq up to four). The ticker is used, quoted or entered when buying or selling stock (e.g. F relates to Ford Motor Company common equity shares on NYSE, GOOG relates to Google, Inc.'s common shares on Nasdaq).

Tranche: A geographic or other class of securities offering in a transaction. Usage: *Only the European tranche of the IPO features convertibles because the Germans really eat them up.*

Underpricing: a condition that occurs when the IPO price is below the firm's initial trade which causes the trade to become immediately profitable as it can be sold for more than it was purchased.

Underwriter: investment bank, lead manager, the lead, the banker, the sell-side, bookrunner, bank on the far left. (Usage: Morgan Stanley is Groupon's underwriter -- not Goldman -- because Morgan is on the far left of the prospectus cover. Related: investment bank, co-manager, co-lead, co-bookrunner, syndicate, other banks on the deal, other bankers, i-banker.

Valuation: an exercise that involves ascribing worth to assets owned by the firm or the firm itself. There are many approaches, some of which require that certain intangible aspects (qualitative components) be factored into the calculation.

Notes

Introduction

1. Akerlof, G. and Shiller, R.J. (2009). *Animal Spirits: How Human Psychology Drives the Economy, and Why it Matters for Global Capitalism.* Princeton University Press, Princeton and Oxford. p.144

2. Stinchcombe, A. L. (1965). "Social Structure and Organizations," in J. G. March (Ed.), *Handbook of Organizations*, Chicago: Rand McNally and Company, pp. 142-193.

3. Zuckerman, E. W. (1999). "The Categorical Imperative: Securities Analysts and the Illegitimacy Discount". *American Journal of Sociology.* Vol. 104, 1398–1438.

4. Rao, S. M., and A. Mayer & D. Harrington, (2001). "The Evolution of Brain Activation During Temporal Processing". *Nature Neuroscience.* Vol. 4, No. 3. (March 1), pp. 317-323, doi:10.1038/85191

5. Peterson, R. L. (2007). *Inside the Investor's Brain: the Power of Mind Over Money.* Hoboken, New Jersey: Wiley & Sons p. 180

6. Posner, Kenneth A. (2010). *Stalking The Black Swan: Research And Decision Making In A World Of Extreme Volatility.* Columbia University Press.

7. Kahneman, Daniel; Slovic, Paul & Tversky, Amos (eds.) (1982). *Judgment Under Uncertainty: Heuristics and Biases.* Cambridge University Press.

8. Hobson, J. L. and S. J. Kachelmeier, (March 2003). "Strategic Disclosure of Risky Prospects: A Laboratory Experiment". Available at SSRN: http://ssrn.com/abstract=390701 or http://dx.doi.org/10.2139/ssrn.390701

Chapter One

1. Ritter, J. R. (2013), "Initial Public Offerings: Updated Statistics" (September 25) http://bear.warrington.ufl.edu/ritter/IPOs2012Statistics.pdf

2. Ritter, J. (2013). "Initial Public Offerings: Updated Statistics". (September). Data extracted from Table 1. Available at http://bear.warrington.ufl.edu/ritter

3. Kuhn, R. L. (1990). Investment Banking: The Art and Science of High-Stakes Dealmaking. Harper and Row, New York, NY.

4. LinkedIn (LNKD:NYSE), an online professional network, opened for trading up 84 from its IPO price. Qihoo360 (QIHU:NYSE), a China-based company returned an even more astonishing 135 on its first day.

5. China Shengda Packaging Group (CPGI:NYSE) declined 83 from Jan. to Sep. in 2011 and Kips Bay Medical (KIPS:NYSE) declined 86 from Feb. to Oct. in 2011.

6. Taleb, N. (2007). *The Black Swan: The Impact of The Highly Improbable*. New York: Random House. p.221

7. Bradley, D., and B. Jordan. (2002). "Partial Adjustment to Public Information and

IPO Underpricing". (December) *Journal of Financial and Quantitative Analysis.* 37(4). Cambridge University Press.

8. Verrecchia, R., (June 2001) "Essays on Disclosure". *JAE Rochester Conference* April 2000. Available at SSRN: http://ssrn.com/abstract=276699 or http://dx.doi.org/10.2139/ssrn.276699

9. Booth, James R. and Chua, Lena, (1996), "Ownership dispersion, costly information, and IPO underpricing." *Journal of Financial Economics*, 41, issue 2, p. 291-310, http://EconPapers.repec.org/RePEc:eee:jfinec:v:41:y:1996:i:2:p:291-310.

10. According to Sherwin Rosen, an economist from the University of Chicago. Quoted from three decades ago in (2007) *The Black Swan*, by N. Taleb. p. 21.

11. Asch, Solomon E. (1955). "Opinions and Social Pressure". (November) *Scientific American*. Vol. 193, No. 5. pp 31-35.

12. Womack, Brian. 2013. , "Twitter Learns from Facebook Stumble as it Prepares for Much-Awaited IPO." Vancouver Sun, September 13. Accessed September 14, 2013 at http://www.vancouversun.com/technology/internet/Twitter+learns+from+Facebook+stumble+prepares+much+awaited/8912831/story.html and "How Twitter flew from obscurity to IPO Feeding Frenzy." The Associated Press. (2013). Metro News, Vancouver, September 16. Accessible at http://metronews.ca/news/world/795696/how-and-why-twitter-flew-from-obscurity-

to-the-height-of-popularity/

13. Camerer, C., and G. Loewestein, and D. Prelec., (2005). "Neuroeconomics: How Neuroscience Can Inform Economics" *Journal of Economic Literature*. (March) Vol. XLII. p.52.

14. Srull, T., and R. Wyer, Jr. (1989), "Person Memory and Judgment". *Psychological Review*. Vol. 96, No. 1, p. 59.

15. Hogarth, R. M., and H. Einhorn, (1992) "Order effects in belief updating: The belief-adjustment model". *Cognitive Psychology*, 24: 1-55.

16. Akerlof, G. and R. Kranton, (2010). *Identity Economics: How Our Identities Shape Our Work, Wages, and Well-Being*. Princeton University Press. p. 87.

17. Schroeder, A. (2008). The Snowball: Warren Buffett and the Business of Life. Bantam Books.

18. Rogers, P. (1999). "CEO presentations in conjunction with earnings announcements: extending the construct of organizational genre through competing values and user-needs analysis". (July 22). Working paper. no. 99-015. Available at http://deepblue.lib.umich.edu/bitstream/handle/2027.42/36040/b2014166.0001.001.pdf?sequence=2

19. Gassman, K. (1995). "The Analyst's Secret Mission". (Jan-Feb). *Financial Executive*. Vol. 11, No.1 pp. 48-51.

20. Daniel, K., and S. Titman, (2006). "Market Reactions to Tangible and Intangible

Information." (August 3). *The Journal of Finance*. Vol 61, No. 4. pp. 1605-1643.

21. One researcher determined that Coca Cola's cumulative advertising spend has resulted in some $64 Billion worth of intangible equity. Relative to a similarly-valued peer (Cott), Coca-Cola enjoys higher operating margins, higher returns on capital and higher growth rates relative to a generic beverage maker. Damodaran, A. "The Value of Intangibles". Lecture. *NYU Stern & L2 Innovation 2010 Forum*. (Nov 5, 2010). See http://people.stern.nyu.edu/adamodar/pdfiles/ovhds/dam2ed/intangibles.pdf

22. Mattingly, P. and R. Runningen. (2013). "Blankfein Says Finance CEOs Urge Action on Debt Limit" www.bloomberg.com (Oct. 2). Available at http://www.bloomberg.com/news/2013-10-02/blankfein-says-finance-ceos-urge-action-to-raise-debt-ceiling.html Available at http://www.columbia.edu/~kd2371/papers/published/jf_06.pdf

23. Brenner, L., and D. Koehler, and A. Tversky. (1996). "On the Evaluation of One-sided Evidence". *Journal of Behavioral Decision Making*. Vol. 9, pp. 59-70. Available at http://bear.warrington.ufl.edu/brenner/papers/brenner-jbdm96.pdf

24. Newport, E. and T. Supalla. (2004) "Short Term Memory's Effectiveness Influenced by Sight, Sound" (August 31). Available online at https://rochester.edu/news/show.php?id=1850

25. Mandelbrot, B. and R. Hudson. (2004). The (Mis)Behaviour of Markets: A Fractal View of Risk, Ruin and Reward. Basic Books.

26. On August 13, 2007 Goldman Sachs CFO David Viniar stated "we are seeing things that were 25-standard deviation moves, several days in a row".

27. Tesla priced above the range at $17 and traded as high as $30.42 on its second day of trading, a gain of 78. Six days later it traded for $15.83

28. Refer to 2010 IPO data detail_14 Nov 2010_1_oct.xls

29. Kuhn, R. L. (1990). Investment Banking: The Art and Science of High-Stakes Dealmaking. Harper and Row, New York, NY.

Chapter Two

1. LinkedIn (LNKD:NYSE) sold 7.8 million shares for $45.00 per share on May 18, 2011. Morgan Stanley, BofA Merrill Lynch and J.P. Morgan led the transaction.

2. LNKD:NYSE closing price on July 2012. It was $78.49/share in November 14, 2011.

3. Facebook (FB:NASDAQ) wasn't the largest IPO ever, but it was the third largest. Visa's $17.86 Billion IPO in 2008 and Enel's $16.45 Billion IPO in 1999 ranked ahead of Facebook's IPO.

4. For an interesting opinion on Facebook's involvement with *The Social Network*

ahead of the firm's IPO, see http://bit.ly/gSHZ2t. Full link located at http://www.

stockhouse.com/blogs/a-new-york-nickel-day-one/january-2011/facebook-s-ipo-

insurance

5. Willis, J., and Todorov, A. (2006). "First impressions: making up your mind after a

100-ms exposure to a face." (July) *Psychological Science*. 17(7):592-8.

6. Srull, T., and R. Wyer, Jr. (1989), "Person Memory and Judgment". *Psychological

Review*. Vol. 96, No. 1, p. 59.

7. From http://www.ipolockups.blogspot.com

Chapter Three

1. Based on our research and experience, we believe a 24 minute presentation is

optimal.

2. Kwoh, L. (2013). "Want to be CEO? What's Your BMI?" (Jan. 16). www.wsj.com.

Available online at http://online.wsj.com/news/articles/SB100014241278873245957

04578241573341483946

3. Srull, T., and R. Wyer, Jr. (1989), "Person Memory and Judgment". *Psychological

Review*. Vol. 96, No. 1, p. 59.

4. Hogarth, R. M. and H. J. Einhorn. (1992). "Order Effects in Belief Updating: The

Belief-Adjustment Model." *Journal of Cognitive Psychology*. Vol. 24, no. 1, pp.

1-55.

5. Taleb, N. (2007). *The Black Swan: The Impact of The Highly Improbable*. New York: Random House. p. 307.

6. Shawver, T. and T. Shawver. (2009). "Predicting Management Fraud in IPO Companies." *Management Accounting Quarterly* (Fall): 22-26.

7. Nenkov, G. and J. Inman, and J. Hulland and M. Morrin. (2010), "The Impact of Outcome Elaboration on Susceptibility to Contextual and Presentation Biases." (December 1). *Journal of Marketing Research* Vol. 46, pp. 764-776. Available at SSRN: http://ssrn.com/abstract=1756889

8. SKY | Alphabet is a communications consultancy focused on transaction marketing and the special requirements of new public companies. +1(778) 927-4989.

Chapter Four

1. Aaron Sorkin, writer of "The Social Network" disclosed during an interview with Charlie Rose that Facebook had script approval. (September 27, 2010). Available at *http://www.CharlieRose.com/watch/50088402*

2. Kim, M. and Jay R. Ritter. (1999). "Valuing IPOs". (September) *Journal of Financial Economics*. Vol. 53. No. 3. pp. 409-437.

3. Facebook is the most recent famous example. The social media company went

public at $38 per share and traded for only $19 per share four months later. It took the firm fifteen months to return to its IPO. During that period, much speculation about what went "wrong" with the IPO was covered by the mainstream media.

Chapter Five

1. Packman, Janet and Battig, William F. (1978). "Effects Of Different Kinds Of Semantic Processing On Memory For Words". *Memory & Cognition.* September. Volume 6, Issue 5, pp 502-508

Chapter Six

1. Stinchcombe, A.L. (1965). "Social Structure and Organizations" In: March, J.G. (ed.), *Handbook of Organizations.* Chicago: Rand McNally & Company, 142-193.

2. Ritter, J.R. (2013) "Initial Public Offerings: Updated Statistics: 2013". (September 25). Available at http://bear.warrington.ufl.edu/ritter/IPOs2012Statistics.pdf

3. Bloomberg. September 15, 2013. Twitter filed its S-1 Oct. 3, 2013, two weeks after the article mentioning Twitter's valuation.

4. Peng, Lin and Wei Xiong. (2006) "Investor Attention, Overconfidence And Category Learning" (January 4) *Journal of Financial Economics* vol. 80 p. 580 available at https://www.princeton.edu/~wxiong/papers/attention.pdf

5. Gao, Hongzhi. (2004) "Corporate Strategy Type As A Signal In The NASDAQ IPO Communication Process". (December 16) *Journal of Business Communication.* 2008 45: 3 Available at http://job.sagepub.com/content/45/1/3. DOI: 10.1177/0021943607309349

6. Kahneman, D., & Lovallo, D. (1993). "Timid Choices And Bold Forecasts: A Cognitive Perspective On Risk Taking". *Management Science, 39* , 17-31.

7. De Bondt, Werner F M et al. (2008) "Behavioral Finance: Quo Vadis?." *Journal of Applied Finance* 18(2): 7–22.

8. Sometimes referred to as "Target Operating Model" or "Long-Term Financial Model" on a slide.

9. Brown, A. S., Brown, L. A., & Zoccoli, S. L. (2002). "Repetition-Based Credibility Enhancement Of Unfamiliar Faces" (Summer) *American Journal of Psychology* Vol 115(2), 199-209.

10. Bacon, Frederick T. (1979), "Credibility of Repeated Testimonials: Memory for Trivia" *Journal of Experimental Psychology: Human Learning and Memory*, 5 (3), 241-252

11. Begg, Ian M. and Victoria Armour (1991), "Repetition and the Ring of Truth: Biasing Comments," *Canadian Journal of Behavioral Science*, 23 (2), 195-213

12. Lang, M. H. and Lundholm, R. J. (2000), "Voluntary Disclosure and Equity

Offerings: Reducing Information Asymmetry or Hyping the Stock?" *Contemporary Accounting Research*, 17: 623–662. doi: 10.1506/9N45-F0JX-AXVW-LBWJ

13. Ibid.

14. Fombrun, Charles and Shanley, Mark. (1990) "What's in a Name? Reputation Building and Corporate Strategy" (June). *The Academy of Management Journal*. Vol. 33, No. 2 pp. 233-258 Article Stable URL: http://www.jstor.org/stable/256324

15. Williams, David, Duncan, W. and Ginter, Peter, (2010), "Testing A Model Of Signals In The IPO Offer Process", *Small Business Economics*, 34, issue 4, p. 445-463.

16. Bloomfield, Robert J. and Wilks, T. Jeffrey (2000) "Disclosure Effects In The Laboratory: Liquidity, Depth, And The Cost Of Capital". (January) *Accounting Review*, Vol. 75, No. 1. Available at SSRN: http://ssrn.com/abstract=284966

17. Simon, Hermann and Bernard Ebel & Markus B. Hofer. (2002) "Investor Marketing" (July 16). Working Paper. Available at http://www.docstoc.com/docs/1958261/Investor-Marketing

18. Panasian, C., Prevost, A. K. and Bhabra, H. S. (2008), "Voluntary Listing Requirements and Corporate Performance: The Case of the Dey Report and Canadian Firms". *Financial Review*, 43: 129–157. doi: 10.1111/j.1540-6288.2007.00189.x

19. Lester, R.H., Certo, S.T., Dalton, C.M., Dalton, D.R. & Cannella, Jr. A.A. (2006) "Initial Public Offering Investor Valuations: An Examination Of Top Management Team Prestige And Environmental Uncertainty". *Journal of Small Business Management*, 44: 1–26.

20. Benveniste, Lawrence M., and Walid Y. Busaba. (1997) "Bookbuilding Versus Fixed Price: An Analysis Of Competing Strategies For Marketing IPOs." *Journal of Financial and Quantitative Analysis* 32:4 (1997): 383-403.

21. Bach, Seung B. and William Judge and Thomas Dean,. "A Knowledge-Based View of IPO Success: Superior Knowledge, Isolating Mechanisms, and the Creation of Market Value." *Journal of Managerial Issues.* 2008. HighBeam Research. (October 31, 2013). http://www.highbeam.com/doc/1G1-193141031.html p.509

22. Cohen, B.D., Dean, T.J., (2005) "Information Asymmetry And Investor Valuation Of Ipos: Top Management Team Legitimacy As A Capital Market Signal". *Strategic Management Journal.* 26, 683-690.

23. McConaughy, D. and M. Dhatt. (1995) "Agency Costs, Market Discipline and Market Timing: Evidence from Post-IPO Operating Performance," (Winter) *Entrepreneurship: Theory and Practice*, 20 (2), pp. 43-58.

24. Benveniste, Lawrence M. and Ljungqvist, Alexander and Yu, Xiaoyun and Wilhelm, William J., "Evidence Of Information Spillovers In The Production Of Investment

· Banking Services". Available at SSRN: http://ssrn.com/abstract=282289 or http://dx.doi.org/10.2139/ssrn.282289

25. Sanders, Gerard W.M & Steven Boive. (2004) "Sorting things out: Valuation of new firms in uncertain markets." (February). *Strategic Management Journal.* Volume 25, Issue 2, Pages 167-186.

26. Wu, Congsheng. (2005) "All Initial Public Offerings (IPOs) Are Not Created Equal" (Spring). *Journal of Business & Economic Studies*, Vol. 11, No. 1.

27. Barth, Mary E. and Clement, Michael B. and Foster, George and Kasznik, Ron. (1998). "Brand Values and Capital Market Valuation. *Review of Accounting Studies*, Vol 3, No. 1-2. Available at SSRN: http://ssrn.com/abstract=165849

28. Keller, Kevin Lane and Donald R. Lehmann (2006), "Brands and Branding: Research Findings and Future Priorities" *Marketing Science*, 25 (6), pp. 740-759.

29. Kumar, Alok & Charles Lee. (2004). "Mass Psychology and Stock Returns: The Case of Retail Trades". *University of Notre Dame.* Presentation on Wednesday, March 17, 11:30-1:00, 339 MCOB.

30. Maat, Henk P. (2007). "How Promotional Language in Press Releases Is Dealt With by Journalists: Genre Mixing or Genre Conflict?" (January) *Journal of Business Communication*, Volume 44, Number 1, pp. 59-95. doi: 10.1177/0021943606295780

31. Ibid.

32. Kumar, Alok & Charles Lee. (2004). "Mass Psychology and Stock Returns: The Case of Retail Trades". *University of Notre Dame.* Presentation on Wednesday, March 17, 11:30-1:00, 339 MCOB

33. Francis Gaskins maintains a subscription-based, IPO research website at http://www.IPOdesktop.com

34. Gaskins, F. (2011) "Zynga Is Going To Have A Hard Time Justifying Its $14 Billion Valuation" (Sept 26). *www.SeekingAlpha.com* Available at: http://seekingalpha.com/article/295829-zynga-is-going-to-have-a-hard-time-justifying-its-14-billion-valuation

35. Grocer, Stephen. (2011) "Reason to Worry Before Zynga's IPO" (Sept. 27) *www.Blogs.WSJ.com.* Available at http://blogs.wsj.com/deals/2011/09/27/reason-to-worry-before-zyngas-ipo/

36. Bloch, A. (1979) "White's Chappaquidick Theorem" from *Murphy's Law and Other Reasons Why Things Go Wrong!* Price/Stern/Sloan.

37. Gaskins, Francis. (2011) "All is Not Well with Zynga". *www.SeekingAlpha.com.* (July 13). Available at http://seekingalpha.com/article/279230-all-is-not-well-with-zynga.

38. Data and charts from google.finance.com. ZYNG share price graph with timeline news references available at: http://www.google.com/

finance?q=NASDAQ3AZNGA

Chapter Seven

1. Toys "R" Us filed its first S-1 in May 2010. It remained in the quiet period for

   almost three years until it finally decided to pull its $800 million IPO on March

   30, 2013. Bain Capital, KKR Group, and Vornado Realty Trust took the company

   private on July 1, 2005 through a $6.6 billion buyout.

2. Cook, Douglas O. and Robert Kieschnick and Robert A. Van Ness "On the

   Marketing of IPOs". (March 22). *Journal of Financial Economics* 82 (2006) p. 44.

3. Pollock, T. G., and V. Rindova, and P. Maggitti, (2008). Market Watch: Information

   and Availability Cascades Among the Media and Investors in the U.S. IPO Market.

   Academy of Management Journal, 51(2): 335-358. Pollock, T.G. & Gulati, R. 2007

4. Maat, Henk P. (2007). "How Promotional Language in Press Releases Is Dealt With

   by Journalists: Genre Mixing or Genre Conflict?" (January) *Journal of Business*

   Communication, Volume 44, Number 1, pp. 59-95. doi: 10.1177/0021943606295780

5. Demers, Elizabeth and Lewellen, Katharina. The Marketing Role of IPOs: Evidence

   from Internet Stocks (April 18 2002). *Journal of Financial Economics*, #68 (2003)

   pages 413-437. Doi: 10.1016/S0304-405X(03)00072-2

6. Pollock, T. G., and V. Rindova, and P. Maggitti, (2008). Market Watch: Information

and Availability Cascades Among the Media and Investors in the U.S. IPO Market. *Academy of Management Journal,* 51(2): 335-358. Pollock, T.G. & Gulati, R. 2007

7. Kuran, Timur and Sunstein, Cass. Availability Cascades and Risk Regulation. *Stanford Law Review,* Vol. 51, No. 4, 1999.

8. Based on 2,457 stock picks at March 5, 2014, Mr. Cramer's accuracy is 44.87

    Source: *http://caps.fool.com/player/trackjimcramer.aspx*

Chapter Eight

1. Hirshleifer, David and Lim, Sonya S. and Teoh, Siew Hong (2004): Disclosure to a Credulous Audience: The Role of Limited Attention. (Oct 11). MPRA Paper No. 5198, posted 8. October 2007. Online at http://mpra.ub.uni-muenchen.de/5198/

2. Yanor, Stephen. (2013). "2009-2011 Survey of 107 IPO Presentations". Working Paper. (December).

3. General Motors Company priced its $20.1 Billion IPO on November 17, 2010 (GM:NYSE).

4. The first investment highlight of *Bright Horizons Family Solutions* and *Norweigan Cruise Line Holdings*, respectively. Both IPOs debuted in January 2013 and priced above the range. Bright Horizons listed five investment highlights. Norweigan Cruise Lines listed seven, including 'Highly experienced and Accomplished

Management Team' as its sixth highlight, before Strong Financial Performance with an Industry-leading Margin and Growth Profile. It is unusual to see the management highlight occupy anything but the last position, if seen at all.

5. Tversky, A., Kahneman, D., (1973). "Availability: A Heuristic For Judging Frequency And Probability". *Cognitive Psychology* 5, 207--232.

6. Srull, T., and R. Wyer, Jr. (1989), "Person Memory and Judgment". *Psychological Review.* Vol. 96, No. 1, p. 59.

7. Budescu D. and T. Wallsten (1985). "Consistency In Interpretation Of Probabilistic Phrases". *Organizational Behavior and Human Decision Processes.* Vol. 36:391–405; and Wilkins, Trevor and Zimmer, Ian. (1983). "The Effects of Alternative Methods of Accounting for Leases -- An Experimental Study". (June). *Abacus.* Volume 19, Issue 1, pp. 64–75. Article first published online: 26 JUL 2005 DOI: 10.1111/j.1467-6281.1983.tb00240.x

8. Butt, Jane L. & Campbell, Terry L., (1989). "The Effects Of Information Order And Hypothesis-Testing Strategies On Auditors' Judgments," (October) *Accounting, Organizations and Society*, Elsevier, vol. 14(5-6), pp. 471-479.

9. These highlights were included in the IPOs of Campus Crest Communities and Swift Transportation. Both transactions priced below the range.

10. Mattress Firm Holding Corp. priced at the top of the range despite a lengthy

presentation (38 minutes). "Experienced and invested management" was the final highlight of five. Chatham priced at the midpoint.

11. These investment highlights appeared in the IPO presentation of Financial Engines, Nielsen Holdings, Angie's List and SS&C Technologies, respectively. All priced at the top of the range or above.

12. Chatman, S. C. (1978). *Story and discourse: Narrative structure in Fiction and Film*. Ithaca: Cornell University Press.

13. Begg, Ian M. and Victoria Armour (1991), "Repetition and the Ring of Truth: Biasing Comments," *Canadian Journal of Behavioral Science*, 23 (2), 195-213

14. MaxLinear, Inc. priced its $89.6 million IPO on March 23, 2010. The transaction priced more shares at a higher revised range. The original terms implied a $65 million IPO at the midpoint. Led by Morgan Stanley and Deutsche Bank.

15. China-based Country Style Cooking priced its IPO on September 27, 2010 at $16.50 per ADS -- above the expected range of $14-$16 per ADS.

Chapter Nine

1. Akerlof, G. and Shiller, R.J. (2009). *Animal Spirits: How Human Psychology Drives the Economy, and why it Matters for Global Capitalism*. Princeton University Press, Princeton and Oxford. p.51

2. Findings based on a sample of 107 IPOs (2009-2011)

3. Miller, Carolyn. Genre as Social Action. Quarterly Journal of Speech, 70 (1984) p. 151-157

4. Previts, G., Bricker, R., Robinson, T. & Young, S. (1993) "Financial Analysts Use of Business Information: A Working Summary of Findings (Research Report)". In Improving Business Reporting, A Customer Focus, Meeting the Information Needs of Investors and Creditors: Research Database, *American Institute of Certified Public Accountants* (AICPA). (Comprehensive report of the special committee on financial reporting).

5. Quinn, R. E., Hildebrandt, H. W., Rogers, P. S., & Thompson, M. P. (1991). "A Competing Values Framework For Analyzing Presentational Communication In Management Contexts". *The Journal of Business Communication*, 28(3), 213-232.; and Rogers, Priscilla S., & Hildebrandt, H. W. (1993). "Competing Values Instruments For Analyzing Written And Spoken Management Messages". *Human Resource Management*, 32(1), 121-142

6. Rogers, Priscilla S., (2000). "CEO Presentations in Conjunction with Earnings Announcements: Extending the Construct of Organizational Genre Through Competing Values Profiling and User-Needs Analysis". Working Paper. *Management Communication Quarterly*. Feb 2000, 13(3): 484-545

7. From LinkedIn's IPO Presentation. Slide 36. Filed as an 8K June 29, 2011

8. Akerlof, G. and Shiller, R.J. (2009). Animal Spirits: How Human Psychology Drives the Economy, and why it Matters for Global Capitalism. Princeton University Press, Princeton and Oxford. p.51

9. Taleb, N. (2007). The Black Swan: The Impact of The Highly Improbable. New York: Random House. p. 63

10. Rogers, Priscilla. (2000). "CEO Presentations in Conjunction with Earnings Announcements: Extending the Construct of Organizational Genre Through Competing Values Profiling and User-Needs Analysis" Management Communication Quarterly. Vol. 13. No. 3. Page 5.

11. Ryack, Kenneth & Kida, Thomas. Recall of Financial Information for Investment Decisions: The Impact of Encoding Specificity and Mental Imagery. Journal of Behavioral Finance, 2006, Volume 7, Number 4.

12. Abrahamson, E. Amir, E. "The Information Content of The President's Letter to Shareholders". *Journal of Business Finance and Accounting.* Vol 28, No. 8 (1996) pp. 115-82.

13. There's a big difference between the spoken and written word. What reads well on the page might not read the same aloud. An effective speech has a few imperfections that make it sound natural. Notice how the word "even" appears at the end of the

sentence rather than before "we didn't see". It is more convincing that way.

14. Brenner, Lyle, Koehler, Derek & Tversky, Amos. (1996). "On The Evaluation of One-Sided Evidence". Journal of Behavioral Decision Making. Vol 9, pp. 59-70. Doi: 10.1002/(SICI)1099-0771(199603)9:1<59::AID-BDM216>3.0.CO;2-V

15. Hirshleifer, David and Lim, Sonya S. and Teoh, Siew Hong (2004): "Disclosure to a Credulous Audience: The Role of Limited Attention". (Oct 11). MPRA Paper No. 5198, posted 8. October 2007. Online at http://mpra.ub.uni-muenchen.de/5198/

16. Paul Aaron, formerly of GE, is the person who coined this term, to my knowledge.

17. Recall of financial information for investment decisions: the impact of encoding specificity and mental imagery. Ryack and Kida. P. 214

18. Vera Bradley's IPO Presentation was 29 slides, including the "fluff" slides. Oct 2010.

19. Aylwin Lewis was the former CEO of Sears Holdings Company which operated 3,900 stores through the merger of Kmart and Sears. He took the helm of Potbelly Corporation prior to the neighborhood-style restaurant chain's IPO.

20. The term 'Electric Weiner' was coined by PowerPoint producer Joel Freeman of Toronto.

21. On August 18, 2004, Google's indicative range was $108-135. It priced at $85 and opened Aug 25 at $100.01. Shares offered: 19.6 million. Original offering: 25.7

million. via http://powershow.com/view/3c4a5-ODUSO/Google_IPO_flash_ppt_ presentation.

22. From Google's initial S-1 filed April 29, 2004. Available at *http://sec.gov/Archives/ edgar/data/1288776/000119312504073639/ds1.htm*

23. Verrecchia, Robert E. (April 3, 2001) Essays on disclosure, Journal of Accounting and Economics. Vol. 32. Pp. 97–180

Chapter Ten

1. Lang, M. H. and Lundholm, R. J. (2000), "Voluntary Disclosure and Equity Offerings: Reducing Information Asymmetry or Hyping the Stock?" *Contemporary Accounting Research*, 17: 623–662. doi: 10.1506/9N45-F0JX-AXVW-LBWJ

2. Draho, Jason. *The IPO Decision*. Edward Elgar Publishing (Feb 2006) p. 73

3. Pollock, T. G., and V. Rindova, and P. Maggitti, (2008). "Market Watch: Information and Availability Cascades Among the Media and Investors in the U.S. IPO Market". *Academy of Management Journal,* 51(2): 335-358. Pollock, T.G. & Gulati, R. 2007

4. Cook, Douglas O. and Robert Kieschnick and Robert A. Van Ness "On the Marketing of IPOs". (March 22). *Journal of Financial Economics.* Vol. 82 (2006) p. 44.

5. Pollock, Timothy and Rindova, Violina. "Media Legitimation Effects In the Market

for Initial Public Offerings". *Academy of Management Journal* (2003). Vol 46. No. 5 pp. 631-642

6. Caesares Field, Laura. "Is Institutional Investment in Initial Public Offerings Related to Long-Run Performance of These Firms?" (Jan 1995) *John E. Anderson Graduate School of Management at UCLA.*

7. Akerlof, George. and Kranton, R. (2010). *Identity Economics: How Our Identities Shape Our Work, Wages, and Well-Being.* Princeton University Press. p. 87.

8. Tetlock, P. "Giving Content To Investor Sentiment: The Role Of Media In The Stock Market". *Journal of Finance.* Vol LXII, No. 3, June 2007.

9. Cook, Douglas O., Kieschnick, Robert & Van Ness, Robert A. "On the Marketing of IPOs". (March 22). *Journal of Financial Economics* 82 (2006) p. 44.

10. Henry, Elain. "Are Investors Influenced By How Earnings Releases Are Written?". *Journal of Business Communication.* (November 2006)

11. Hirschleifer, David, Lim, Sonya S. & Teoh, Siew Hong. "Limited Attention and Stock Market Misreactions to Accounting Information". *The Society for Financial Studies.* July 27, 2011.

12. Booth, James R. & Chua, Lena. "Ownership Dispersion, Costly Information, And IPO Underpricing". *Journal of Financial Economics.* Vol. 41 pp. 291-310.

13. Pollock, Timothy, Chen, Guoli, Jackson, Eric &, Hambrick, Donald "Certification

and Substantive Resources: Assessing the Value of Multiple Types of Prestigious

Affiliates for Young Firms" (July 2006).

14. *online.wsj.com/article/BT-CO-20110719-716573.html*

15. *http://business.transworld.net/68872/features/skullcandy-raises-share-prices-to-20-expected-to-begin-trading-today/*

16. Srull, T., and R. Wyer, Jr. (1989), "Person Memory and Judgment". *Psychological Review*. Vol. 96, No. 1, p. 59.

17. Reuters headline "SkullCandy Inc Announces FY 2011 Guidance Below Analysts' Estimates". Aug 16, 2011.

18. Gibbins, Michael, Richardson, Alan J. & Waterhouse, John. "The Management of Financial Disclosure: Theory and Perspective". (1992) *Canadian Certified General Accountants' Research Foundation*. No. 20. p 132.

19. Barber, Brad and Odean, Terrance. "All That Glitters: The Effect of Attention and News on the Buying Behavior of Individual and Institutional Investors" (2008) *Review of Financial Studies*. 21(2): 785-818.

20. Sanders, Gerard and Boive, Steven. "Sorting Things Out: Valuation of New Firms in Uncertain Markets" (2004) . *Strategic Management Journal*. Vol. 25, Issue 2, p. 167-186.

21. Henry, Elain. Are Investors Influenced By How Earnings Releases Are Written?

Journal of Business Communication. (November 2006)

22. Brown, Alan S., Brown, Lori A and Zoccoli, Sandy L. "Repetition-Based Credibility Enhancement of Unfamiliar Faces". *The American Journal of Psychology*. (2002); 115(2): 199-209.

23. DealBook.NYtimes.com

24. *Bloomberg* Radio. Jan 8, 2013.

25. Morton, Linda. "How Newspapers Choose the Releases They Use".

26. Chacksfied, Marc. (Dec 2, 2009) "Facebook: Farmville is Bigger than Twitter". Via http://www.techradar.com/news/internet/facebook-farmville-is-bigger-than-twitter-655373 and

27. Dec 8, 2011. "GSV Capital: Invest in Facebook, Twitter and Other Private Companies". *Helix Investment Research*. Via www.seekingalpha.com/article/312591-gsv-capital-invest-in-facebook-twitter-and-other-private-companies

28. Raymond, Nate and Stempel, Jonathan. "Twitter Hit with $124 million Lawsuit over Private Stock Sale". October 30, 2013. *Reuters*. Available www.news.net/article/606004/Tehnology

29. *www.youtube.com/watch?v=6V2Tv-a3Xg0*

Chapter Eleven

1. Jumpstart Our Business Startups Act from en.wikipedia.com/wiki/Jumpstart_Our_
   Business_Startups_Act

2. www.sec.gov/answers/quiet.htm

3. Khandani Amir E. and Lo, Andrew W. "What Happened To The Quants In August
   2007"? *Journal Of Investment Management*, Vol. 5, No. 4, (2007), pp. 5-54.

Chapter Twelve

1. Disclosure Policy from PGE Corp. *www.pgecorp.com/aboutus/corp_gov/dp.html*

2. A Canadian operating division of Rail World, Montreal, Maine & Atlantic Railway,
   filed for bankruptcy shortly after one of its rail cars destroyed the small town of Lac
   Megantic.

3. The italicized sentence was added by a website that reported on Cisco's guidance. It
   is included to emphasize the investor community's focus on guidance.

4. Data from The National Investor Relations Institute's 2012 Guidance Survey.
   Available at http://niri.org

5. Bloomfield, Robert J. & Wilks, T. Jeffrey. "Disclosure Effects in the Laboratory:
   Liquidity, Depth, and the Cost of Capital" (January 2000). *Accounting Review*. Vol.
   75, No. 1

6. Camerer, Colin, Loewenstein, George & Prelec, Drazen. "Neuroeconomics: How Neuroscience Can Inform Economics" (March 2005). *Journal of Economic Literature*. Vol. XLIII. Pages. 9-64.

7. The audit committee is responsible for reviewing and approving any forecast included in the IPO prospectus (not allowed in the US but is allowed in Canada, the UK, France and Australia).

8. Grover, Ronald. (July 11 2005). "A Scary Picture at Dreamworks". *Bloomberg Business Week*. At *BusinessWeek.com/2005-07-11/a-scary-picture-at-dreamworks*

9. For example, as of January 10, 2010, the SEC has updated guidance principles relating to climate change.

10. Rogers, Priscilla. (2000). "CEO Presentations in Conjunction with Earnings Announcements: Extending the Construct of Organizational Genre Through Competing Values Profiling and User-Needs Analysis". *Management Communication Quarterly*, Volume 13, Issue 3, Pp. 426-485.

11. Kim, M. and Jay R. Ritter. (1999). "Valuing IPOs". (September) *Journal of Financial Economics*. Vol. 53. No. 3.

12. Parish, Anthony. "Some Say Regulation FD Will Have a Chilling Effect on Corporate Communications. Freeze or No Freeze the Word Must Get Out". (Oct

1, 2000) *IR Magazine*. www.irmagazine.com/articles-disclosure-regulation/17243/
breaking-ice

13. Apple beat earnings estimates for thirty straight quarters (2004) until October 18,
2011, two weeks after CEO Steve Jobs passed away.

14. Hirshleifer, David and Teoh, Siew Hong. "Limited Attention, Information
Disclosure, and Financial Reporting". (September 2003). JAE Boston Conference
2002. Available at http://ssrn.com/abstract=334940 or http://dx.doi.org/10.2139/
ssrn.334940

15. Mercer, Molly. "How do Investors Assess the Credibility of Management
Disclosures?" *Accounting Horizons*. (2004), 18(3) p. 185.

16. Baginksi, Stephen, Conrad, Edward. & Hassell, John. "The Effects of Management
Forecast Precision on Equity Pricing and the Assessment of Earnings Uncertainty".
The Accounting Review. (October 1993) Vol. 68, No. 4. Pp. 913-927.

17. Merrill, Sharon. "Hit Or Miss – Transparency is Key" (June 2009). Sharon Merrill
Associates. Available at www.niri.org/findinfo/Guidance/Hit-or-miss--Transparency-
is-Key-service-provider-white-paper.aspx

Chapter Thirteen

1. Akerlof, G. and R. Kranton, (2010). Identity Economics: How Our Identities Shape Our Work, Wages, and Well-Being. Princeton University Press. p. 211

2. McAdams, D. (1992). "The Five-Factor Model In Personality: A Critical Appraisal". Journal of Personality. 60, p. 329-361.

3. Borkenau, Peter and Liebler, Annette. (1992). "Trait Inferences: Sources of Validity at Zero Acquaintance". Journal of Personality and Social Psychology. Vol 62. No. 4, pp. 645-657.

4. Camerer, C., and G. Loewestein, and D. Prelec., (2005). "Neuroeconomics: How Neuroscience Can Inform Economics" Journal of Economic Literature. (March) Vol. XLII. p.52.

5. Peterson, R. L. (2007). Inside the Investor's Brain: the Power of Mind Over Money. Hoboken, New Jersey: Wiley & Sons p. 71.

6. Hirshleifer, David. (2001). "Investor Psychology and Asset Pricing". The Journal of Finance. Citing Gassman (1995), Melcher (1993) and Unseem (1998).

7. Khandani Amir E. and Lo, Andrew W. "What Happened to The Quants in August 2007?" Journal Of Investment Management, Vol. 5, No. 4, (2007), pp. 5-54.

8. Bayar, O., & Chemmanur, T. (2011). "IPOs Versus Acquisition and the Valuation Premium Puzzle: a Theory of Exit Choice by Entrepreneurs and Venture

Capitalists". Journal of Financial and Quantitative Analysis. 46(6); pp. 1755-1793.

9. Scharlemann, Jorn, Eckel, Catherine, Kacelnik, Alex & Wilson, Rick. (2001). "The Value of a Smile: Game Theory with a Human Face". Journal of Economic Psychology. Vol. 22, Issue 5. A well-known application of game theory is the predictive outcome resulting from the choice given to two prisoners who can either cooperate or betray one another. The game demonstrates how a prisoner focuses on his own reward based on the belief that the other will not cooperate. Both go to jail as each rats the other out.

10. Benveniste, Lawrence M. and Spindt, Paul A. (1989) "How Investment Bankers Determine The Offer Price and Allocation of New Issues". Journal of Financial Economics. Vol. 24, No. 2, Pp. 343-362.

11. Brenner, Lyle, Koehler, Derek & Tversky, Amos. (1996). "On The Evaluation of One-Sided Evidence". Journal of Behavioral Decision Making. Vol 9, pp. 59-70. Doi: 10.1002/(SICI)1099-0771(199603)9:1<59::AID-BDM216>3.0.CO;2-V

12. Budescu, David; Weinberg, Shalva; and Wallsten, Thomas. (1998). "Decisions Based on Numerically and Verbally Expressed Uncertainties". Journal of Experimental Psychology. Vol. 14, Issue 2. P. 281

13. Chaiken, S. & A. Eagly (1983). "Communication Modality as a Determinant of Persuasion: the Role of Communicator Salience" Journal of Personality and Social

Psychology. 45(2); pp. 241-256.

14. Griffen, Dale and Tversky, Amos. (1992). "The Weighing Of Evidence and The Determinants of Confidence". Cognitive Psychology. Vol. 24 p.413

15. Hirshleifer, David, Lim, Sonya S. and Teoh, Siew Hong. (2002). "Disclosure to a Credulous Audience: The Role of Limited Attention". Munich Personal RePec Archive. Paper No. 5198, posted 8. October 2007. Online at http://mpra.ub.uni-muenchen.de/5198/

16. Barrett, H. Clark. (2008). "Evolved Cognitive Mechanisms and Human Behavior". In Crawford, C. & Krebs, D. (eds) Foundations of Evolutionary Psychology: Ideas, Issues, Applications and Findings. (2nd Ed.). Mahwah, NJ: Erlbaum Associates.

17. Posner, K.A. (2010). Stalking The Black Swan: Research And Decision Making in a World of Extreme Volatility. Columbia University Press. New York, NY. p.143

18. Wellman, Francis. (1992). The Art of Cross-Examination. NY: Barnes and Noble Books.

19. Porter, S., Woodworth, M., & Birt, A. R. (2000). "Truth, Lies, And Videotape: An Investigation of the Ability of Federal Parole Officers to Detect Deception". Law and Human Behavior, Vol. 24, pp. 643-658.

20. Gladwell, Malcolm. (2005). Blink: The Power of Thinking Without Thinking. New York, NY: Little, Brown and Company. p. 63

21. Porter, S. and ten Brinke, L. (2010). "The Truth About Lies: What Works in Detecting High-Stakes Deception?" Legal and Criminological Psychology. Vol. 15. Pp. 15-75.

22. Simons, Tony. (2002) "Behavioral Integrity: The Perceived Alignment Between Managers' Words and Deeds as a Research Focus". Organizational Science. Vol. 13, No. 1. Pp. 18-85.

23. Deutsch, M. (1958). "Trust and Suspicion". Journal of Conflict Resolution. Vol. 2, Pp. 265-279.

24. Finkelstein, Sydney. (2003). Why Smart Executives Fail. Portfolio, New York, NY.

25. Chang, L.J., Doll, B., Van't Wout, M. Frank, M.J., Sanfey, A.G. (2010) "Seeing is Believing: Trustworthiness as a Dynamic Belief". Cognitive Psychology, 61(2), Pp. 87-105.; and Kahneman, D. (2000) "Evaluation by Moments: Past and Future". In D. Kahneman & A. Tversky (Eds.), Choices, Values and Frames (pp. 693-708). New York: Cambridge University Press and the Russell Sage Foundation.

26. Rogers, Priscilla S., (2000). "CEO Presentations in Conjunction with Earnings Announcements: Extending the Construct of Organizational Genre Through Competing Values Profiling and User-Needs Analysis". Working Paper. Management Communication Quarterly. Feb 2000, 13(3): 484-545

27. Schweitzer, Maurice & Hsee, Christopher. (2002). "Stretching the Truth: Elastic Justification and Motivated Communication of Uncertain Information". Journal of Risk and Uncertainty. Vol 25(2), Pp. 185-201.

28. Lana, Robert E. (1963). "Familiarity and the Order of Presentation of Persuasive Communications". Journal of Abnormal and Social Psychology. Vol. 62: pp. 573-577

29. Transcript available at SeekingAlpha.com. Gogo is a provider of wireless and digital in-flight entertainment to airlines. Gogo shares listed on Nasdaq June 20, 2013. Their first conference call occurred on August 7, 2013.

30. Hirschleifer, David. (2001) "Investor Psychology and Asset Pricing". The Journal of Finance. Vol 56. Pp. 1533-1597.

31. Posner, Kenneth (2010) Stalking The Black Swan: Research And Decision Making In A World Of Extreme Volatility. Columbia University Press. p.162

32. The author acknowledges the work of "Louder than Words", an excellent book on non-verbal communication. The decision to include the micro-gesture gallery was based on the illustrations appearing in the chapter "How the Body Talks".

Chapter Fourteen

1. Jameson, Daphne A. (2000). "Telling The Investment Story: A Narrative Analysis of Shareholder Reports". *Journal of Business Communication*. Vol. 37(1); Pp. 7-38.

2. Thill, John & Boivee, Courtland. (1993). *Excellence in Business Communication*. NJ: Pearson Prentice-Hall. p.124.

3. Fitzherbert, Nick. (2011) *Presentation Magic!* Marshall Cavendish (pub).

4. Chatman, S. C. (1978). Story and discourse: Narrative structure in Fiction and Film. Ithaca: Cornell University Press.

5. Smith, Malcolm & Taffler, Richard J. (2000). "The Chairman's Statement A Content Analysis Of Discretionary Narrative Disclosures". *Accounting Auditing & Accountability Journal*, Vol. 13 No. 5, pp. 624-646.

6. Hyland, Ken (1998). "Exploring Corporate Rhetoric: Metadiscourse in the CEO's Letter". *Journal of Business Communication*. Vol. 35, No. 2. Pp. 224-225.

7. Porter, S. and ten Brinke, L. (2010). "The Truth About Lies: What Works in Detecting High-Stakes Deception?" *Legal and Criminological Psychology*. Vol. 15. Pp. 15-75.

8. Hyland, Ken (1998). "Exploring Corporate Rhetoric: Metadiscourse in the CEO's Letter". *Journal of Business Communication*. Vol. 35, No. 2. Pp. 224-225.

9. Jaeger, T. Florian (2010). "Redundancy and reduction: Speakers Manage Syntactic

Information Density". *Cognitive Psychology*. Vol. 61, No. 1. Pp 23-62.

10. Begg, Ian M. and Victoria Armour (1991), "Repetition and the Ring of Truth:

Biasing Comments," *Canadian Journal of Behavioral Science*, 23 (2), 195-213

Chapter Fifteen

1. Visit www.retailroadshow.com for IPO presentations currently in progress.

2. Riskier from an execution standpoint. No investment bank wants to see a large

transaction fail, so multiple co-leads spread the exposure.

3. Chris Liddell, CFO, was the frontman for General Motors' $20 Billion IPO

November 17. 2010. The transaction priced at $33/share, above the original range of

$26 to $29. The firm's share price dipped to as low as $18.85 before recovering to

its IPO price two years after the IPO.

4. Loughan, T. and Ritter, Jay (2004)."Why has IPO Underpricing Changed Over

Time?" *Financial Management*. Autumn 2004. Pp 5-37.

5. Wall street jargon is legendary. Every wave of fresh deals brings new terminology to

investors.

6. Rajan, Raghuram and Servaes, Henri. (June 1997). "Analyst Following of Initial

Public Offerings" Journal of Finance. Vol. 50, No. 2. Available at SSRN: http://ssrn.

com/abstract=8235

Chapter Sixteen

1. Ariely, Dan. (2010) Predictably Irrational: the Forces that Shape Our Decisions. New York: Harper Perennial. P. 218

2. Chaiken, S. & A. Eagly (1983). "Communication Modality as a Determinant of Persuasion: the Role of Communicator Salience" Journal of Personality and Social Psychology. 45(2); pp. 241-256.

3. Aaker, D.A. (1991). Managing Brand Equity. New York: Free Press; and Keller, K.L. (2003). Strategic Brand Management. 2nd edition. Upper Saddle River, NJ: Prentice Hall.

4. Park, Chan Su and Srinivasan, V. (1994). "A Survey-Based Method for Measuring and Understanding Brand Equity and its Extendability". Journal of Marketing Research. Vol. 31. No. 2 Pp. 271-288.

5. Swait, Joffre and Erdem, Tulin. (October 2007). "Brand Effects on Choice and Choice Set Formation Under Uncertainty". Marketing Science. Vol. 26, No. 5, Pp. 679-697.

6. Srinivasan, V., Park, Chan Su and Chang, Dae Ryan. (2005). "An Approach to the Measurement, Analysis, and Prediction of Brand Equity and Its Sources". Management Science. Vol. 51, No. 9. Pp. 1433-1448.

7. Mercer, Molly. "How do Investors Assess the Credibility of Management Disclosures?" Accounting Horizons. (2004), 18(3)

8. PMS is the acronym for Pantone Matching System, a global standard for specifying and matching colors over a range of materials. Blue is the most prevalent color used by corporations around the world, by far.

Chapter Seventeen

1. Behavioral Integrity: The Perceived Alignment Between Managers' Words and Deeds as a Research Focus. Tony Simons. p. 21

2. Certo S., Daily Catherine., and Dalton Dan. (2001). "Signaling Firm Value Through Board Structure: An Investigation of Initial Public Offerings". *Entrepreneurship Theory and Practice*. Vol. 26, Vo. 2, pp. 33-50.

3. Arkebauer, James and Schultz, Ron. (1998). Going Public: Everything You Need to Know to Take Your Company Public, Including Internet Direct Public Offerings. Dearborn Financial Publications, Chicago.

Chapter Eighteen

1. Ljungvist, Alexander; Nanda, Vikram, and Singh, Rajdeep. (2003) "Hot Markets, Investor Sentiment, and IPO Pricing". Mimeo, Stern School of Business, New York

University.

2. *Securities Industry Fact Book* (2008). New York: Securities Industry Association.

3. Frieder, Laura and Subrahmanyam, Avanidhar. (December 2003). "Brand Perceptions and the Market for Common Stock". Available at SSRN: http://ssrn. com/abstract=299522

4. "US Public Equity Ownership And Flow From The Flow Of Funds Report". (March 11, 2013). *Goldman Sachs Global Economics, Commodities and Strategy Research.*

5. U.S. Census Bureau, Statistical Abstract of the United States: 2012. Data is from 2010. Foreign investors account for 13.7 of US equities ownership.

6. Aggerwal, Reena (2003). "Allocation of Initial Public Offerings and Flipping Activity". *Journal of Financial Economics.* Vol. 68, pp. 111-135; and Chemmanur, Thomas & Hu, G. (2010). "The Role of Institutional Investors in Initial Public Offerings". *Review of Financial Studies.* Vol. 23, Pp. 4496-4540.

7. Khandani, Amir E. and Lo, Andrew W. (2007). "What Happened To The Quants In August 2007?" *Journal Of Investment Management,* Vol. 5, No. 4, pp. 5-54.

8. Dechow, P.M.; Kothari, S.P. and Watts, R.L. (1998) "The Relation Between Earnings and Cash Flows". *Journal of Accounting and Economics.* Vol. 25. Pp. 133-168.

9. Boehmer, Ekkehart; Jones, Charles M. And Zhang, Xiaoyan (2008). "Which Shorts

Are Informed?" *The Journal of Finance*. Vol. 63. Pp. 491-527.

10. Ritter, Jay. (2013). "Mean First-day Returns and Money Left on the Table, 1980-2012 (Nov. 24, 2013 update): Table 1". Available at Bear.warrington.ufl.edu/ritter/IPOs2012Statistics.pdf

11. Khandani, Amir E. and Lo, Andrew W. (2007). "What Happened To The Quants In August 2007"? *Journal Of Investment Management*, Vol. 5, No. 4, Pp. 5-54.

12. Kaustia, Markku and Knupfer, Samuli. (2008). "Do Investors Overweight Personal Experiences? Evidence from IPO Subscriptions". *The Journal of Finance*. Vol. 63. Pp. 2679-2702.

13. Kahneman, Daniel and Lovallo, Dan. (1993). "Timid Choices and Bold Forecasts: A Cognitive Perspective on Risk". *Management Science*. Vol. 39. Pp. 17-31.

Chapter Nineteen

1. Hirshleifer, David; Hou, Kewei; Teoh, Siew and Hong & Zhang, Yinglei. (2004). "Do Investors Overvalue Firms with Bloated Balance Sheets?" *Journal of Accounting and Economics.*Vol. 38 (December). Pp. 297-331. Doi:10.1016/j.jacceco.2004.10.002

2. Edwards, Amy K. and Hanley, Kathleen Weiss. (2008). "Short Selling in Initial Public Offerings". SSRN Working Paper.

3. Bradley, Daniel & Jordan, Bradford. (2002). "Partial Adjustment To Public Information and IPO Underpricing". *Journal Of Financial and Quantitative Analysis*. Vol. 37, No. 4, December.

4. Bruner, Robert; Chaplinsky, Susan and Ramchand, Latha. (2004) "US-Bound IPOs: Issue Costs and Selective Entry" *Financial Management*, Vol. 33 pp. 36-90.

5. Akerlof, G. and Shiller, R.J. (2009). *Animal Spirits: How Human Psychology Drives the Economy, and why it Matters for Global Capitalism*. Princeton University Press, Princeton and Oxford. P. 44

6. Kim, M. and Jay R. Ritter. (1999). "Valuing IPOs". (September) *Journal of Financial Economics*. Vol. 53. No. 3. pp. 409-437.

7. Loughan, T. & Ritter, Jay (2004)."Why has IPO Underpricing Changed Over Time?" *Financial Management*. Autumn 2004. Pp 5-37.

8. Diether, Karl B.; Lee, Kuan-Hui & Werner, Ingrid. (2007) "Can Short-sellers Predict Returns? Daily Evidence". Working Paper. Ohio State University. http://ssrn.com/abstract=1439652

9. Valuing Branded Businesses (2009) Natalie Mizik & Robert Jacobson. p139

10. Investor Psychology in Capital Markets: Evidence and Policy Implications. Kent Daniel, David Hirsshleifer, Siew Hong Teoh

11. May 18, 2012 The IPO price was set at $38, which values the company at $104.2

billion and 26x sales. LinkedIn (LNKD) currently trades at 15.57x sales, Tencent Holdings Ltd (700:HK) at 11.64x sales, Baidu (BIDU) at 15.88x sales, and Google (GOOG) at 5.04x sales. via http://www. distressedvolatility.com/2012/05/facebooks-38-ipo-price-values-company.html

12. DeLoof, Marc; De Maeseneire Wouter, and Inghelbrecht, Koen. (2009). "How Do Investment Banks Value Initial Public Offerings (IPOs)?" *Journal of Business Finance & Accounting*, 36(1) & (2), Pp. 130-160. January/March 2009, 0306-686X. Doi: 10.1111/j.468-5957.2008.02117.x

13. Renaissance Capital is a leading provider of free IPO research. www. renaissancecapital.com

14 Yee, Kenton. (2004) "Forward Versus Trailing Earnings in Equity Valuation", *Review of Accounting Studies*, Vol. 9, Pp. 301-29.

15. DeLoof, Marc; De Maeseneire Wouter, and Inghelbrecht, Koen. (2009). "How Do Investment Banks Value Initial Public Offerings (IPOs)?" *Journal of Business Finance & Accounting*, 36(1) & (2), Pp. 130-160. January/March 2009, 0306-686X. Doi: 10.1111/j.468-5957.2008.02117.x

16. Shefrin, Hersh. (2008) "Risk and Return in Behavioral SDF-Based Asset Pricing Models" *Journal of Investment Research*, Vol. 6, No. 3. Pp. 1-18.

17. Loughan, Tim, and Ritter, Jay. (1995). "The New Issues Puzzle". *The Journal of*

Finance. (March). Vol. 50, Pp. 23-52.

18. Hirshleifer, David; Hou, Kewei; Teoh, Siew and Hong & Zhang, Yinglei. (2004). "Do Investors Overvalue Firms with Bloated Balance Sheets?" *Journal of Accounting and Economics.*Vol. 38 (December). Pp. 297-331. Doi:10.1016/j. jacceco.2004.10.002

19. Ibid.

20. Kuhn, R. L. (1990). Investment Banking: The Art and Science of High-Stakes Dealmaking. Harper and Row, New York, NY.

21. Bloomfield, Robert and Michaely, Roni. (2004) "Risk or Mispricing? From the Mouths of Professionals". *Financial Management*, Vol. 33. Pp. 61-81.

22. Berk, Jonathan; Green, Richard, and Naik, Vasant. (1999). "Optimal Investment, Growth Options and Security Returns". *Journal of Finance*. Vol. 54, Pp. 1153-1607; and Lettau, Martin and Ludvigson, Sydney. (2001). "Resurrecting the (C)CAPM: a Cross-Sectional Test When Risk Premia are Time-Varying". *Journal of Political Economy*. Vol. 109, No. 6.

23. Mizik, N. & Jacobson, R. (2009). "Financial Markets Research in Marketing". *Journal of Marketing Research*, Vol. 46, Pp. 320-324.

24. Lev, Baruch & Zarowin, Paul. (1999). "The Boundaries of Financial Reporting and How to Extend Them". *Journal of Accounting Research*. Vol. 37. Pp. 353-385.

25. Certo, Trevis. (2003) "Influencing Initial Public Offering Investors with Prestige: Signaling With Board Structures". *Academy of Management Review*. Vol. 28. Pp. 432-446. See also Amir, E. & Lev, B. (1996). "Value Relevance of Non-Financial Information: the Wireless Communication Industry". *Journal of Accounting & Economics*. Vol. 22, Pp. 3-30.

26. Mizik, Natalie & Jacobson, Robert. (2008) "Valuing Branded Businesses". *Journal of Marketing*. Vol. 73, No. 6. Pp. 137-153.

27. Draho, Jason. *The IPO Decision*. Edward Elgar Publishing (Feb 2006) p.164

28. Rajan, Raghuram and Servaes, Henri. (June 1997). "Analyst Following of Initial Public Offerings" Journal of Finance. Vol. 50, No. 2. Available at SSRN: http://ssrn.com/abstract=8235

29. Cormier, Denis; Lapointe-Antunes, Pascale & McConomy, Bruce. (Jan 15, 2012) "Forecasts in IPO Prospectuses: The Effect of Corporate Governance on Earnings Management". CAAA Annual Conference 2012. Available at SSRN: http://ssrn.com/abstract=1985762

30. Teoh, Siew Hong; Wong, T.J. and Rao, Gita R. (1998). "Are Accruals During Initial Public Offerings Opportunistic?" *Review of Accounting Studies*. Vol. 3, Issue 1-2. Pp. 175-208; and Dechow, Patricia. (1994). "Accounting Earnings and Cash Flows as Measures of Firm Performance: The Role of Accounting Accruals". *Journal of*

Accounting and Economics. Vol. 18, Issue 1. Pp. 3-42.

31. Beaver, William & Dukes, Roland. (1974). "Delta-Depreciation Methods: Some Analytical Results". *Journal of Accounting Research.* Vol. 12. Pp. 205-215.

32. Daniela, Kent; Hirshleifer, David & Teoh, Siew Hong. (2002). "Investor Psychology In Capital Markets: Evidence And Policy Implications". *Journal of Monetary Economics.* Elsevier, Vol. 49(1), Pp. 139-209. See also: Lev, Baruch & Sougiannis, T. (1996) "The Capitalization, Amortization and Value-Relevance of R&D", *Journal of Accounting and Economics.* Vol. 21, Pp. 107-138; and Aboody, David & Lev, Baruch. (1998). "The Case of Software Capitalization". *Journal of Accounting Research*, Vol. 36. Pp. 161-191.

33. Shefrin, Hersh. (2008) "Risk and Return in Behavioral SDF-Based Asset Pricing Models" *Journal of Investment Research*, Vol. 6, No. 3. Pp. 1-18.

Chapter Twenty

1. Ellis, Katrina; Michaely, Roni & O'Hara, Maureen. (1999) "When the Underwriter is the Market Maker: An Examination of Trading in the IPO Aftermarket". *Journal of Finance.* Vol. 55, Pp. 1039-1074; and Aggarwal, Reena (2000). "Stabilization Activities by Underwriters after Initial Public Offerings". *The Journal of Finance.* Vol. LV, No. 3 (June); and Geczy, Christopher; Musto, David & Reed, Adam.

(2002). "Stocks are Special Too: An Analysis of the Equity lending Market".

Journal of Financial Economics. Vol. 66, No. 2-3, Pp. 241-269

2. For more information on the quiet period, refer to the SEC's website at http://www. sec.gov/answers/quiet.htm

3. Brav, Alon & Gompers, Paul. (2003). "The Role of Lockups in Initial Public Offerings". *The Review of Financial Studies*. Vol. 16, No. 1. Pp. 1-29.

4. Krigman, Laurie; Shaw, Wayne & Womack, Kent. (2001) "Why Do Firms Switch Underwriters?" *Journal of Financial Economics*. Vol. 60. Pp. 245-284

5. Tan, Hun-Tong; Libby, Robert & Hunton James. (2002). "Analysts' Reaction to Earnings Pre-announcement Strategies"

6. Jeff Matthews discusses Target Corporation's earnings call and the CFO's reference to adjusted EPS on his blog *http://jeffmatthewsisnotmakingthisup.blogspot.com* on August 23, 2013: *A Question for Mary Jo: What is Your Definition of Earnings?*

Chapter Twenty-One

1. Rusli, E. M. (2013). "Sandberg Sells $91 Million in Facebook Stock" blogs.wsj. com. (August 9). http://blogs.wsj.com/digits/2013/08/09/sandberg-sells-91-million-in-facebook-stock/

2. Chemmanur, T. J., and G. Hu, (2010). The Role of Institutional Investors in Initial Public Offerings (November 21). *Review of Financial Studies*, Vol. 23, pp. 4496-4540, 2010; WFA 2007 Big Sky Meetings Paper; EFA 2006 Zurich Meetings Paper. Available at SSRN: http://ssrn.com/abstract=959645

3. Minton, P. I. (2012). "4 Unintended Consequences of the JOBS Act for the Startup Community" www.forbes.com May 18. http://www.forbes.com/sites/theyec/2012/05/18/4-unintended-consequences-of-the-jobs-act-for-the-startup-community/

4. Ritter, J. R. (2013), "Initial Public Offerings: Updated Statistics" (September 25) http://bear.warrington.ufl.edu/ritter/IPOs2012Statistics.pdf p.4

5. The IPO of Tesla Motors raised $226 million and surged 41 on its first day of trading, June 19, 2010. On that same day that the Nasdaq lost 3.85 and the Dow fell 2.65, Tesla opened at $17 and closed at $23.89. from http://wired.com/autopia/2010/06/tesla-ipo-raises-226-1-million/ Noboa Renewable Energy, MagnaChip Semiconductor and Resaca Exploration all pulled June 2010 IPOs, citing poor market conditions. A total of 20 companies postponed their IPO in the first 6 months of 2010, while 63 made it to market. Of the 63, only 24 traded above their IPO price. From http://marketwatch.com/story/tesla-primerica-shine-in-dull-2010-ipo-market-2010-06-03

6. The volatility index (VIX) is a benchmark comprised of futures on the Chicago Board Options Exchange (CBOE). Many traders and investors regard rely on the VIX as a primary risk metric. The various implied volatility indexes are located at http://www.cboe.com/micro/volatility/introduction.aspx

7. Tett, G. (2011). "Flash Crash Threatens to Return With a Vengeance" cnbc.com (Dec 30) http://www.cnbc.com/id/45822986

8. Taleb, N. N. (2007). *The Black Swan: The Impact of The Highly Improbable*. New York: Random House. p. 307.

9. Alter, A. A., and D. M. Oppenheimer. (2006). "Predicting Short-Term Stock Fluctuations by Using Processing Fluency." Proceedings of the National Academy of Sciences 103: 9369-9372. (published online before print June 5, 2006, 10.1073/pnas.0601071103).

10. Peterson, R. L. (2007). *Inside the Investor's Brain: the Power of Mind Over Money*. Hoboken, New Jersey: Wiley & Sons p. 270.

11. Damasio, A. R. (1999). The Feeling of What Happens: Body and Emotion in the Making of Consciousness. Harcourt Brace and Co.

12. Stross, R. E., (2007). The Wizard of Menlo Park: How Thomas Alva Edison Invented the Modern World. New York: Crown Publishers.

13. Rindova, V. and K. Suresh, (2000). Building Reputational Stocks Through Strategic

More Books!

i want morebooks!

Buy your books fast and straightforward online - at one of the world's fastest growing online book stores! Environmentally sound due to Print-on-Demand technologies.

Buy your books online at

www.get-morebooks.com

Kaufen Sie Ihre Bücher schnell und unkompliziert online – auf einer der am schnellsten wachsenden Buchhandelsplattformen weltweit!
Dank Print-On-Demand umwelt- und ressourcenschonend produziert.

Bücher schneller online kaufen

www.morebooks.de

OmniScriptum Marketing DEU GmbH
Heinrich-Böcking-Str. 6-8
D - 66121 Saarbrücken
Telefax: +49 681 93 81 567-9

info@omniscriptum.de
www.omniscriptum.de

39991893R00383

Made in the USA
Lexington, KY
19 March 2015